THE FOUR ROADS TO HEAVEN

Also by Edwin Mullins and published by Signal Books

The Pilgrimage to Santiago
In Search of Cluny: God's Lost Empire
Avignon of the Popes
Roman Provence
The Camargue: Portrait of a Wilderness

THE FOUR ROADS TO HEAVEN

France and the Santiago Pilgrimage

Edwin Mullins

SIGNAL BOOKS · Oxford

For Jason

First published in 2017 by Signal Books Limited
36 Minster Road
Oxford
OX4 1LY
www.signalbooks.co.uk

A catalogue record for this book is available from the British Library.

ISBN 978-1-909930-50-6 (paper)

Typesettting, pre-press production and cover design: Baseline Arts Ltd
Cover Images: front and flaps © shutterstock.com; back © Adam Woolfitt
Printed in India

Contents

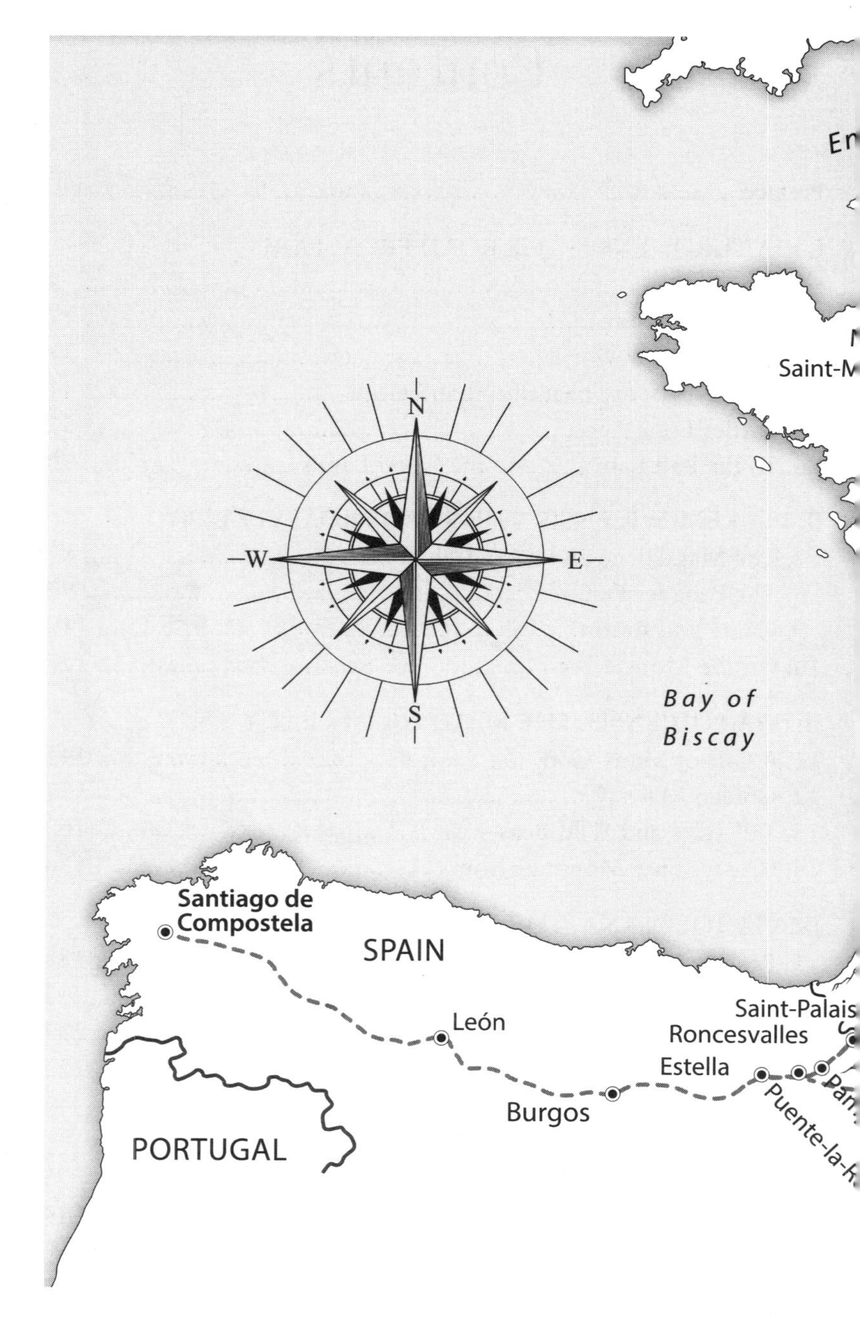
N
W
E
S
Bay of
Biscay
Santiago de
Compostela
SPAIN
León
Burgos
Estella
Roncesvalles
Saint-Palais
PORTUGAL

© S.Ballard (2017)
BELGIUM
GERMANY
FRANCE
ITALY
Seine
Paris
Chartres
Orléans
Saint-Benoît
Tours
Vézelay
Autun
Poitiers
Cluny
Limoges
Massif Central
Périgueux
Le Puy
Rhône
Conques
Toulouse
Saint-Gilles
Arles
Les Saintes-Maries -de-la-Mer
Mediterranean Sea
0
150
km

Preface

'There are four roads leading to Santiago, which converge to form a single road.'

THESE ARE THE OPENING WORDS written almost a thousand years ago in a manuscript which can lay claim to be the world's very first travellers' guide.

The four roads are all in present-day France, and the manuscript (in Latin) was written early in the twelfth century for the benefit of Christian pilgrims preparing to travel to the tomb of the apostle St James at Santiago de Compostela in north-west Spain. The *Liber Sancti Jacobi*, the Book of St James, is generally known as *The Pilgrim's Guide*, and was the work of a Benedictine monk – or possibly several monks – at the instigation of the powerful Burgundian abbey of Cluny. The abbey possessed strong vested interests in promoting the Santiago pilgrimage as a vehicle for expanding the power and influence of the Christian Church in Spain during the turbulent era of the Reconquest.

The Pilgrim's Guide originally existed in a number of copies which were made available in the libraries of major monasteries along the pilgrim routes to Santiago. Today only two copies survive, one in the library of Santiago Cathedral, the other in the monastery of Ripoll in north-east Spain. Only a tiny literate minority who could understand and read Latin were able to take advantage of the *Guide*'s words of wisdom and information about where to stay and where to avoid murderous boatmen and bad wine on their journey. Nonetheless the message was handed down through the social ranks and widely preached from the pulpit. And so popular did the pilgrimage become that by the later Middle Ages as many as half a million travellers are estimated to have undertaken the journey in a year.

Today even greater numbers, pilgrims and tourists alike, make the same trek across France and into Spain. The historical and cultural significance of the four roads to Santiago has meanwhile been recognised by UNESCO, which added this 'serial site' to the World Heritage List in 1993.

The four routes described in *The Pilgrim's Guide* are the principal threads in a huge spider's-web of ancient roads laid across the French landscape. They were distinct from other roads because a high proportion of those using them shared a single objective – the shrine of St James far away in Spain. They were not only pilgrims on foot: wealthy travellers made the journey on horseback, often accompanied by a small retinue. There would also be merchants, traders, craftsmen, masons, musicians and story-tellers, adventurers, fugitives from the law or from their wives, as well as convicted criminals sentenced by magistrates to make the pilgrimage as an alternative to prison or a hefty fine. It would have been a lively mob on the roads to Spain.

These are roads I have traced and have come to know well over the course of many years. In this book I am the invisible traveller on a journey of yesterday and today. I shall be exploring the range of magnificent buildings and works of art which are the legacy of the pilgrimage, as well as trying to capture something of the spirit of hope and endeavour which drove our ancestors to make this same journey all those centuries ago.

*

Many years ago I wrote an account of my first travels along the pilgrim roads in France and Spain. The book was *The Pilgrimage to Santiago*, published in 1974 and reissued by Signal Books in the millennium year 2000. This was a journey of discovery, and the experience of making that journey has remained vivid in my mind ever since. The first impact of the abbey church of Conques or the cathedral of Santiago can never weaken. And since that time I have seized the chance to make numerous shorter journeys in different parts of France, filling in pieces of the jigsaw I had previously missed. I have also scripted and presented two films on the Santiago pilgrimage for British and French television, which reacquainted me with many of my favourite places on the pilgrim roads. Besides, in recent decades much work has been done on the subject, and on areas closely related to it, including my own book on the history of Cluny, the great Burgundian abbey which was responsible to a large extent for making the pilgrimage possible by creating facilities and protection for medieval travellers in a lawless world frequently torn apart by insurrection and war.

This, then, is a fresh look at an old friend. And it has been a special pleasure that the majority of the illustrations in the book are the work of one of our most distinguished photographers, Adam Woolfitt, who travelled with me on long stretches of the pilgrim roads in both France and Spain, and shared my love of the landscape and the rich variety of historic sites that greeted us.

I. Via Turonensis: The Road from Paris

1. Setting Out

PILGRIMAGES ARE JOURNEYS OF THE HEART. More than a thousand years separate the modern traveller and pilgrim from those who first trekked across the length and breadth of France, then southwards over the Pyrenees into Spain. Here they followed the pale arm of the Milky Way to guide them to their goal close to the Atlantic Ocean and – for all they knew in those centuries before Christopher Columbus – the very edge of the world. It was an awesome journey, and not one for the faint-hearted.

The goal they sought was a tomb believed to be that of St James, cousin of Christ and the first of his twelve apostles to be martyred, decapitated by a Roman sword in the year 44 AD. The city that grew up around that tomb became named after him: in Spanish St Iago, hence Santiago or, in full, Santiago de Compostela, meaning St James of the Field of the Star, a star having led to the tomb's discovery, so the legend goes.

Since that time so great has been the cult of the saint that over the succeeding centuries the roads leading to his city were adorned with some of the finest monuments of Christian civilisation – cathedrals and churches, abbeys and castles, masterpieces of sculpture and painting, bridges and shrines, as well as lined with countless silent witnesses to the slog and hardship of foot-travel in medieval Europe – hospices and primitive shelters, stepping-stones across turbulent rivers, stretches of ancient road in the midst of nowhere, a wayside cross marking a death or a thanksgiving, or graffiti of a horseshoe on the wall of an inn scratched by some pilgrim grateful to have made it this far.

For these and so many other reasons, taking the roads across France and into Spain to Santiago can be one of the most uplifting journeys to be undertaken anywhere in the world. It is a journey through surroundings created by some of the most dramatic events of history. The ghosts of past travellers accompany us everywhere we walk, in the places where they worshipped, where they ate and slept, and on the long roads they took. In France it is a journey that can be made along a broad network of pilgrim roads, the *chemins de Saint-Jacques*, all converging into a single principal route across northern Spain known universally as the *camino*, or traditionally as the *camino francés*, the 'French road', so-called because pilgrims wherever they came from in northern Europe inevitably had to cross France to reach Spain.

There were also other reasons for the name. Not only did France provide the greatest number of pilgrims to Santiago, but it was in France where the impetus for the pilgrimage arose and gathered strength. The Church in France, supported by its feudal aristocracy, largely facilitated the pilgrimage movement – by building churches, priories and hospices along the way, and by giving support to the beleaguered Spanish rulers in safeguarding the route across northern Spain against the Saracens who controlled much of the country.

And here lies a powerful reason why the Santiago pilgrimage captured the imagination of Christian Europe. There were other important pilgrimages at the time, notably to Jerusalem, and to Rome as the city of the martyrs St Peter and St Paul. But Jerusalem was far-distant and in the hands of the Saracens. Rome had its obvious appeal, yet to get there involved crossing the Alps: furthermore, it lacked a key element which Santiago possessed – a passionately-held cause. And that cause was the *Reconquista*, the Reconquest of Spain. St James, who had reappeared in Spain's darkest hour, became a symbol of the fight against the Infidel. Christianity had found a champion. And the road to his shrine was like a journey to the Promised Land. Piety and politics went hand in hand.

*

So, where to begin? One monument has the strongest claim to be the starting-point. The city is Paris, and the monument bears the name of the saint himself. This is the Tour Saint-Jacques – the Tower of St James. It stands in the centre of a public garden on the Right Bank, gaunt and lofty, with spiky gargoyles high above craning against the sky. Originally this was the bell-tower of a church called Saint-Jacques-de-la-Boucherie, so named because it stood near the Paris meat-market. The church itself became a victim of anti-clerical passions during the French Revolution. In the orgy of destruction what the mob also obliterated was a milestone which the original architect, a certain Michel de Felins, had placed meaningfully at the base of his tower. The milestone was inscribed – quite simply – 'Zero'.

In other words, for pilgrims this was the point of departure: the beginning of the journey of a lifetime. Santiago de Compostela, in north-west Spain, was more than 700 miles away. A few well-to-do pilgrims would be making the pilgrimage on horseback, perhaps with a retinue of servants. But for the vast majority this was a journey on foot – with the aid of a staff, a broad-brimmed hat against the sun and rain, a flask of some sort for water, the stoutest of boots, a few modest worldly possessions, and bountiful hope that charity and the hand of God would guide them safely there and back again six months later. They would depart in the spring, and return – all being well – before winter set in.

The inscription 'Zero' was as much a memorial as a milestone, because pilgrims had been setting out from here for at least 400 years before the Tour Saint-Jacques was built early in the sixteenth century. The Church of Saint-Jacques-de-la-Boucherie itself, where they assembled for their last mass before departure, was also a replacement for a much earlier pilgrim church. The site had always been of huge strategic importance, being set at the junction of the two oldest roads in Paris. They were the former Roman roads which sliced right through the city from north to south, forming its principal artery which it continued to be right up until the reshaping of Paris by Baron Haussmann in the mid-nineteenth century, and the creation of the broad boulevards of today.

Here, where the Tour Saint-Jacques now stands, was the great gathering-place. Pilgrims from northern France, northern Germany and the Low Countries would make their way to this church or its predecessor, arriving by way of what is now the Rue Saint-Martin, and once here they would join up with travellers from the east and west of the city, all preparing to head south together on the journey to Spain. Before departure, at the climax of the celebratory mass, their pilgrim staffs would be ceremonially blessed by the priest: this would be followed by emotional scenes as families and well-wishers cheered them on their way, maybe accompanying them a short distance as they crossed the River Seine. At this point, in the early Middle Ages, pilgrims would have passed a colossal building site where gantries and wooden scaffolding were enclosing a building far taller than everything around it, topped by twin soaring towers and at ground level a triple portal of huge proportions swarming with builders and stonemasons hauling on ropes to assemble row upon row of carved figures around and above each of the three doors. The Cathedral of Notre Dame was nearing completion.

Then, once on the Left Bank of the river, they would take the straight corridor of a road which is still called the Rue Saint-Jacques[1], making their way through the heart of the old city, past the recently-built Church of Saint-Julien-le-Pauvre, then on up the slow hill past the celebrated university, the Sorbonne, until finally they reached the southern walls of the city and another church bearing the name of their saint, Saint-Jacques-du Haut-Pas, St James of the High Step.

From here, once through the southern gate of the city, it was the open road – and the beginning of a 700-mile trek into the totally unknown.

Not that they were likely to be on their own. 'Thanne longen folk to goon on pilgrimages': so wrote the English poet Geoffrey Chaucer in the fourteenth century in his Prologue to the best-loved of all accounts of a pilgrimage, *The Canterbury Tales,* his collection of stories of a party of pilgrims setting out from London to the shrine of

1. See Plate 1.

the murdered Archbishop of Canterbury Thomas à Becket. As Chaucer makes clear to our delight, medieval pilgrimages could be colourful and convivial occasions. However disparate the company might be – like Chaucer's spicy hotchpotch of humanity – whether for security, for comfort, or simply for companionship, pilgrims generally chose to travel in bands – as early accounts and illuminated manuscripts show. It was the Italian poet Dante, a century before Chaucer, who wrote in *The Divine Comedy* that people would describe the 'Way of St James' as the Milky Way on account of the huge number of people who travelled to the saint's city. In Dante's day, and in the two preceding centuries, more than half a million travellers are said to have used the roads to Santiago every year. And even if not all of them were *bona fide* pilgrims, but merchants and itinerant craftsmen, or merely adventurers and vagabonds, this is still an astonishing volume of humankind to be on the road to a remote corner of Spain, far away under the mists and Atlantic skies where there was little except a tomb, a church and a small community assembled round it. And yet half a million travellers! And this at a time when the total population of the region we now know as France was barely more than twelve million.

What was it that drove them? And what was the story that lay behind so demanding a journey?

*

The pilgrimage to Santiago was one of the most dynamic social movements of the Middle Ages, and it is one that has managed to retain its profound appeal in the radically different social climate of our own day. Even if it can seem sometimes to have become a bauble of the modern tourist industry much of its core of meaning and purpose has survived the long passage of more than ten centuries. In that time the Santiago pilgrimage has been a creative force, a spiritual force and a political force, as well as a triumphant testimony to the enduring power of legend.

And the legend is this.

James the Apostle (sometimes known as James the Greater, not to be confused with James the Lesser who was the half-brother of Jesus) was a fisherman on the Sea of Galilee. His father was Zebedee; his mother was Salome, believed to have been the sister of the Virgin Mary. James therefore seems to have been Christ's first cousin. He was recruited by Jesus as one of his twelve apostles, then after the Crucifixion he responded to Christ's last command that his disciples fan out across the earth to spread the gospel far and wide. Accordingly he voyaged to Spain where he spent a couple of years, until the Virgin Mary (still living at the time) appeared to him in Zaragoza raised on a pillar between twin choirs of angels. Inspired by this miraculous event James proceeded to erect round the pillar the first church ever to be dedicated to the Virgin. Shortly afterwards he returned to Jerusalem where he was beaded by a Roman sword wielded by King Herod Agrippa.

Had the legend ended at this point there would have been no pilgrimage to Santiago, indeed no Santiago at all. Everything rested on the second chapter of the story, treating events that immediately followed James' martyrdom. His body (including the head) was first carried by disciples to Jaffa on the coast of Palestine, then borne by stout ship down the length of the Mediterranean and up the Atlantic coast to the Bay of Padrón in north-west Spain, the voyage being accomplished in a mere week – proof of its miraculous nature. The party arrived thus far only to encounter Roman authorities once again who gaoled them, until in due course they were released by the intercession of an angel. Queen Lupa, who was neither a Christian nor remotely interested in the newcomers' unlikely tale, ordered the body of James to be buried on a remote hillside where a celebrated snake would be sure to polish off the disciples as well as the body of the saint. But the snake it was that died – on seeing the sign of the cross – whereupon Queen Lupa became converted to the Christian faith, and at last the body of the apostle was allowed to be given a decent burial, in a large stone coffin, and at a place where his disciples were themselves later buried.

It is the third chapter of the story which begins to anchor legend to historical fact – and dramatically so. But first there is a gap of six centuries in which there is no evidence that anyone knew of the existence or whereabouts of the saint's grave, or even that James had ever been in Spain at all, dead or alive. Church literature, from the *Acts of the Apostles* onwards, is entirely silent on the subject. In due course the Romans left Spain, the Visigoths took over, and Christianity inched its way into this outpost of Europe near the end of the known world. Then, early in the seventh century, copies began to appear in Western Europe of a Latin translation of a Greek religious text which became known as the *Breviarum Apostolorum*. The text attracted attention because it stated that Christ had awarded his apostles specific 'mission fields', whereas in the New Testament Jesus had merely instructed his apostles to make disciples of all nations (*St Matthew* 28: 19-20). More intriguing still, this Latin version included interpolations, or additions, confirming that James' mission had been to preach in Spain. Here, as far as we know, was the first written evidence of any connection between St James and Spain, though it may well be that these scribal additions expressed a long-standing oral tradition that the apostle had indeed preached in Spain. On the other hand, it may also be, as sceptics have pointed out, that the translator mistakenly wrote *Hispaniam* (meaning Spain) instead of *Hierusolem* (Jerusalem). Since the original Greek text no longer exists, it is impossible to establish the truth.

However, it was one thing to claim that the apostle had preached the gospel in Spain after the death of Christ; it was quite another to maintain that he was brought back to Spain and buried here after his own martyrdom. Here two historical events proved crucial in creating the framework of the St James legend as it has remained in the public's imagination ever since. Firstly, in the early eighth century the Saracens invaded from North Africa, and in a short time occupied and controlled most of the Spanish peninsula. Only the north-west corner remained unconquered – the Kingdom of the Asturias as it was known. It was an island of Christianity in a sea of Islam.

The second historical event was the appearance of one of the most influential religious texts of this era and of many centuries to follow. This was the *Commentaries on the Apocalypse*, the work of a Spanish monk and theologian known as St Beatus of Liébana. Beatus was born at about the time of the Saracen invasions, and therefore spent his youth and manhood under the shadow of Islam, which gives a special poignancy to his writings. The district of Liébana where he settled lay in the Cantabrian mountains in northern Spain within that Christian pocket unconquered by the Saracens: nonetheless it would have felt an area under siege, and the concept of a Holy War and the dream of Reconquest would have been constantly present in his mind. Christian Spain desperately needed a saviour, and it was Beatus who made a key contribution towards finding one. In his celebrated *Commentaries*, which began to be circulated in the third quarter of the eighth century, he became the first to claim in writing that St James had not only evangelised in Spain but was ultimately buried here. It was a giant step towards establishing the legend surrounding the saint. After all, if St James was indeed buried here then his grave must surely exist. Somewhere there must be a shrine to be discovered; and the shrines of saints, as was well known, could perform miracles.

We can do little more than speculate, but even in a prevailing climate of religious make-believe and self-deception it seems most unlikely that Beatus would simply have invented the story of the saint's body having been returned to the country where he had evangelised. He is much more likely to have been voicing a conviction rooted in some long-standing local tradition, whatever its origin, that the body of St James had indeed been brought here. In any event the effect of Beatus' pronouncement was dynamic. Even if a belief in the saint's grave being in Spain may hitherto have been for the most part a wishful tale, now it had acquired the stamp of Church authority. And in the context of a continuing Saracen threat, and the resulting siege mentality of the Church and local rulers in that Christian pocket of north-west Spain, Beatus' statement would have created a mood of high excitement and expectation which was the ideal breeding-ground for what was to follow. And it did not take long.

It is tantalising not to be able to draw back the curtains of history and witness what actually occurred in north-west Spain during these early years of the ninth century. Was there a widespread search for the grave? Were there constant rumours – hopes continually being raised? Was there a suspicion that it was only a fairy tale? How credulous were people? As it is we are restricted to a few surviving records. The first written evidence we have of the saint's grave having been discovered comes from a list of Christian martyrs that was being compiled at about this time by a monk named Florus de Lyon. Referring to this area of north-west Spain, in the year 838 he noted an 'extraordinary devotion being paid by the local inhabitants' to the bones of the apostle St James. Six years later comes the first record of a pilgrim actually visiting the site: ironically he was an Arab traveller, Ibn Dihya, who observed that visitors to the saint's tomb included Normans. How he knew this, and how they managed to communicate, he did not disclose, nor why he chose to be there at all. What is clear, though, is that even before the middle of the ninth century the shrine was well-enough known to be attracting pilgrims from far and wide. The word had got around with remarkable speed.

The story of the actual discovery of the supposed grave has an air of romantic improbability about it, while at the same time containing some intriguing elements of proven fact. There is a further confusion: the earliest written account of the tale of the grave's discovery dates from two hundred years later in a letter purporting – falsely – to be by the hand of Pope Leo II. That aside, the contents of the letter would appear to be a sincere account of events in north-west Spain early in the ninth century as they were now widely believed to be. The story begins with a hermit by the name of Pelagius informing the local bishop, Theodomir, of a vision which had revealed to him the whereabouts of the saint's tomb by means of a guiding star accompanied by celestial music. The seat of Bishop Theodomir was at Iria Flavia (today Padrón), situated at the head of a deep bay opening out on to the Atlantic Ocean. It was in a deserted spot some twelve miles from here that a stone tomb was duly discovered containing the remains of three bodies. The bishop immediately pronounced these to be the bodies of St James and the two disciples who had brought his body from the Holy Land. The King of the Asturias, Alfonso II, then hastened to the tomb. He promptly declared that St James was henceforward to be worshipped as the protector and patron saint of Spain. And he had a small church erected over the tomb, and a monastery close by. It was the beginning of what was to become the city and cathedral of Santiago. A town grew up round the new church and monastery during the course of the ninth century, and this became known as Campo de la Estrella, or Campus Stellae, 'the Field of the Star', later to become shortened to Compostela.

Here, in the darkness of the ninth century, lie the foundations of the whole St James legend. And from those foundations grew one of the phenomena of the Middle Ages.

History and legend part company over several aspects of this story. Yet, setting aside the celestial music and guiding star, there is no doubt that a grave, or several graves, came to light about this time. Recent archaeological excavations beneath the present cathedral revealed an ancient tomb inscribed with the name of the bishop mentioned as the one led to the site of the grave by the hermit Pelagius. The long-buried tomb beneath the cathedral reads – very clearly – 'Theodomir'. Traces of further graves were detected, believed to date from the Roman or early-Christian period, and the prevailing view among scholars today is that here was an ancient cemetery, and the word Compostela is therefore likely to derive not from the Latin noun for a star but from the verb *componere*, 'to bury'.

The wide discrepancy between fact and fairy tale in the whole St James story is of trivial importance compared to its contribution in so many areas of life in the era following what has been described by Hugh Trevor-Roper as 'the darkest age of Europe'.[2] At some indefinable moment early in the ninth century it became widely believed among Christians that in their hour of need one of Christ's closest disciples was present in their midst. From that moment it was as though a climactic change took place in the hearts and minds of European Christians. The contribution of the St James story

2. Hugh Trevor-Roper, *The Rise of Christian Europe* (London: 1966)

began to make itself felt in so many areas of human activities – in an outpouring of religious fervour, in a widespread resurgence of the human spirit, in artistic achievements and church building on an unprecedented scale, in the field of politics, in the expansion of trade and commerce and, by no means least, on the field of battle.

And it was here on the battlefield – not surprisingly – that St James first of all made his mark, taking up arms in the cause of beleaguered Christianity. In the year 844, barely a few decades after the discovery of his tomb, the saint is said to have made his first appearance as a knight in shining armour at the side of a Christian army led by Ramiro I, King of the Asturias, who was facing an overwhelmingly superior Saracen force. The battle supposedly took place at a mountainous site known as Clavijo overlooking the fertile plains of northern Castile; and here St James is credited with riding to the king's rescue on horseback and personally slaughtering 70,000 of the enemy. Thereafter the saint became popularly known as *Santiago Matamoros* – St James the Moor-Slayer. And it is in this guise (as we shall see later) that he appears on so many churches along the Spanish *camino*, sword raised, banner aloft, crushing the forces of Islam beneath his stallion's feet.[3] After Clavijo the triumphant campaign continued: at Simancas in the tenth century, at Coimbra by the side of El Cid in the eleventh, at Las Navas de Tolosa in the breakthrough to Andalucia in the thirteenth – in all at least forty appearances in battle by the seventeenth century, according to the Spanish historian of the Santiago legend, Don Antonio Calderón. No good Spaniard in the Middle Ages, and for many centuries later, would have believed that his country could have been liberated from the Saracens without the flashing sword of their patron saint.

It was a whirlwind of events to have been generated by a pious claim first put about by a Spanish monk in the eighth century: St Beatus of Liébana deserves to be regarded as the true godfather of the Santiago legend. Nor was that influence short-lived: it extends far beyond the era when the shrine of St James was being established

3. See Plate 2

and the first pilgrims were flocking to Santiago. The long-term importance of Beatus' *Commentaries on the Apocalypse* lay in the fact that the work became so popular among Church leaders that in the centuries to follow artists in monastery workshops across Europe were busy illustrating it with fantastic and lurid imagery drawn from descriptions in the Book of Revelations. These illustrated copies of Beatus' text were widely distributed during the Middle Ages and became a primary source of many of the most powerful and disturbing carvings and mural paintings of the Romanesque period. Nothing expresses the doomsday vision of the medieval Church more eloquently than these apocalyptic images which snarl and leer out at you from church after church, assaulting the eyes of generations of pilgrims as they made their way to Santiago, just as they do today on the long roads across France and Spain.

*

Nowadays a brace of motorways heads south from Paris. The traditional road bisects the two, carrying quieter traffic, much of it local, as well as a regular procession of summer pilgrims on the first leg of their journey. For the medieval traveller this would have been a gentle introduction to life on the road, since this first stretch out of Paris is as flat as the famous local cheese, which is Brie. For at least thirty miles it is hard to imagine any distraction, either now or a thousand years ago. But then suddenly the old road passes the battered remains of an ancient fort before leading into a narrow strip of a town, Étampes, and here the modern traveller and the medieval pilgrim are on common ground. At either end of the town rise two churches, Notre-Dame-du-Fort and Saint-Martin, the former with its handsome tower and spire, both of them dominating the town only a little less than they would have done in the twelfth century when pilgrims paused here to refresh themselves from the local well and pray in one or other of these churches, both still in the process of completion.

Heading on south, less than a day's journey brought pilgrims to another narrow passageway of a town, then a mere hamlet. This was Toury, today somewhat larger than in the Middle Ages, but still centred on a chunk of medieval church with a stone colonnade extending from end to end, facing the town square. Then, from here it was only a short distance to the next objective – or, rather, a double objective. Principally this was Orléans, already a focus of pilgrimage more than 300 years before Joan of Arc brought glory to the city by driving out the English army, so launching the revival of the fortunes of France in the Hundred Years' War. A more symbolic objective was the great river that runs past Orléans. The Loire is the longest river in France, 634 miles of it, and from here it flows westwards across the lowlands of central France towards the Atlantic, guiding Santiago pilgrims – as it has done for a thousand years – along the next stretch of their journey.

2. Along the Loire

LIKE A LONG STRING OF PEARLS the medieval pilgrim's journey was strung with sacred places which had to be visited – not unlike the modern tourist ticking off a list of historic sites 'not to be missed'. The motive may seem to have changed, though less than you might think. The Middle Ages had a hunger for religious relics: we have a hunger for historical relics – cathedrals, castles, ancient monuments, ancient cities. The Middle Ages themselves have become part of our own store of relics.

The pilgrim road from Paris has now reached the River Loire. The numerous shrines 'not to be missed' lay along the river, east and west. But first there was Orléans itself. The town was a major stopping-place for pilgrims because it boasted two important relics. The lesser of the two was a chalice that had belonged to an early bishop of the town, St Euverte, about whom little is known except that a nearby abbey was dedicated to him. But the second relic was an object of the deepest veneration, a supposed fragment of the Holy Cross. It was the first of many such fragments which the medieval pilgrim would soon encounter on his travels, and one cannot help wondering if, even in an era of the most naive credulity, doubts would at some stage begin to creep in as to the likelihood of the Cross having been splintered into quite so many pieces and distributed across quite so many far-flung places. Nonetheless, at this early stage of the journey no doubt wonder and awe were uppermost; and in the Middle Ages this particular fragment used to be displayed in the church that was built in its honour. This is the Church of Sainte-Croix, now on the edge of the old town. Today only traces of the medieval crypt survive of the early church, concealed beneath a grandiose Gothic-style cathedral – but with no trace of the Holy Cross. Scepticism may in the end have triumphed.

The main pilgrim road as we know it heads west from here, following the flow of the Loire. Yet in the opposite direction, twenty miles upriver from Orléans, stands a place which had been a focus of pilgrimage several centuries before the cult of St James, and it was where a great many Santiago pilgrims would have made a respectful detour. This is the ancient abbey Church of Saint-Benoît-sur-Loire, one of the most striking Romanesque churches in France. Approached from the west it looks like a massive stone box punched through with gaping holes. This is merely the porch: the present church itself, and the former abbey to which it was attached, came into existence because it came to possess the body of St Benedict, founder of the Benedictine Order. And quite apart from the historical importance of the saint, it was the Benedictines who were prominent in promoting and aiding the pilgrimage movement. It would have been widely known that they were the pilgrims' friend.

St Benedict of Nursia was an Italian monk in the early sixth century who founded the great abbey of Monte Cassino in southern Italy. Here he composed the famous Rule of St Benedict, a humane and perceptive handbook setting out how monks should lead their daily lives. Accordingly he is generally regarded as the father of western monasticism.

Then, a century after St Benedict's death, Monte Cassino was sacked by marauding Lombards. News of the abbey's destruction reached the small monastery of Fleury, on the Loire. From here a party of monks set out for southern Italy in the brave hope of retrieving the body of the saint. On arrival they found that St Benedict's grave had miraculously escaped destruction; so in about the year 672 AD they brought the body back to their monastery in northern France. From this moment the abbey of Fleury acquired fame and wealth as a popular centre of pilgrimage, duly changing its name to the Abbey of Saint-Benoît, and acquiring a new abbey church whose west front is the imposing porch which confronts travellers today as they approach from the direction of Orléans. The porch originally supported a belfry, and it is the oldest part of the church, dating from the eleventh century. Now, as in the Middle Ages, it serves as an ideal assembly area for those attending or leaving mass, conveniently sheltered from the sun and from the winter gales hurtling up the Loire from the distant Atlantic.[4]

Travellers and pilgrims waiting in the porch found themselves surrounded by a forest of stone columns whose capitals are carved with images that will be repeated again and again on the pilgrim roads through France and into Spain. They are sermons in stone, designed to match the doomsday sermons delivered every Sunday from the pulpit. There are familiar bible stories – among them the Annunciation and the Flight into Egypt – together with inevitable reminders of the perils of sexual temptation and sin, all embellished by lurid scenes from the Book of Revelations, inspired by those illuminated versions of St Beatus' *Commentaries on the Apocalypse* described in Chapter 1.

What is particularly unusual at Saint-Benoît is that we know who carved these images. One of the Corinthian capitals in the porch bears the inscription UMBERTUS ME FECIT – 'Humbertus made me'. We know nothing else about him, but he must have been someone to be reckoned with. The vast majority of medieval church carving are anonymous, and the very few examples we have of signed work suggest that the sculptor in question was held in especially high regard – the outstanding example being that of Gislebertus at Autun, among the greatest of all medieval church sculptors (as we shall see in a later chapter).

The size of the nave of the abbey church itself is an indication of just how many worshippers flocked here to venerate the relics of the founder of the Benedictine Order. Traditionally his remains would probably have been contained in some form of gold or silver reliquary, handsomely engraved, and placed on the high altar during mass in full view of the congregation. Today those relics are kept

4. See Plate 3.

down below in the labyrinthine crypt, encased within the massive central pillar. Something of the drama of the original display on the high altar has inevitably been lost in the process.

Forms of worship have inevitably changed over the centuries. To Christians in medieval Europe the value of shrines and the relics they contained needs to be understood in the context of the religious climate of the times. In the Middle Ages the prospect of eternal damnation was preached relentlessly by a Church obsessed with the promise of the Second Coming and the Day of Judgment. The world as people knew it was believed to be coming to an end. This dark prophesy was preached just as vividly by the sculptors and painters who decorated the churches in which those hell-fire sermons were delivered. For the simple illiterate peasant, who knew nothing of the world beyond the fields he tilled and the church he attended on Sundays, this vision of the future was all he was offered. He had no means of knowing otherwise. From the day he learnt to use his eyes and ears to the day he died he was indoctrinated with the urgency of obtaining divine forgiveness for sins which he probably had no idea he had committed. It was in the very fabric of human nature to be sinful, and that was it. Doom sounded like a gong in his ears all his life. There was only one way out – to seek forgiveness – *remissio peccatorum*. And the surest way such forgiveness could be obtained was by making contact with the saints, who alone could intercede with God on his or her behalf. The surest way of getting God to listen was to go to them and ask.

The most powerful ingredient in medieval religious life lay in the cult of such relics. They were the essential go-betweens, and visiting the shrines where they were displayed was what pilgrimages were fundamentally all about. Even the great thirteenth-century theologian and philosopher St Thomas Aquinas, who might be expected to have held a more rational view of such things, was an unequivocal advocate: 'We ought to hold them in the deepest possible veneration as limbs of God, children and friends of God, and as intercessors on our behalf,' he wrote.[5]

5. From the *Collected Works of St Thomas Aquinas*, c. 397 AD (Oxford: 1999).

Much of the power of holy relics lay in the fact that they were universally believed to perform miracles, as an apparently limitless number of worshippers were eager to testify. Nothing could enhance the prestige and popularity of a shrine more than a reputation for healing the sick, curing blindness, or madness, or whatever human condition was associated with a particular saint. No one in medieval France would seriously have doubted that the relics of a saint could perform such miraculous feats. So closely was religious worship bound up with a belief in these powers that it even became a ruling by Church authorities that no new church could be consecrated unless it was in possession of a holy relic of some description. Nor was it confined to the Church. Monarchs and rulers also formed personal collections of relics. The Emperor Charlemagne early in the ninth century was among the first, having obtained them in quantity from Constantinople. The Byzantine capital, named after the first Roman emperor to convert to Christianity, Constantine I, became something of a marketplace for biblical relics, being relatively close to the Holy Land, which was of course their principal source. The later Byzantine emperors also acquired hoards of such items, and it was after the disgraceful sacking and looting of Constantinople by the Fourth Crusade in 1204 that the flood-gates were truly opened, and many an adventurer masquerading as a crusader returned home with sack-loads of stolen relics, most of them bogus.

Yet, in spite of the flood there were never enough relics to go round. This was the great age of church-building and of new monastic foundations all over Western Europe. With demand exceeding supply, fraudsters and dubious merchants were very soon doing a roaring trade in fakes. And in a credulous world, and where a relic might be nothing more than a fragment of bone or a splinter of wood, their job was an easy one: hence many of the – to our eyes – ludicrous examples of relics displayed for the benefit of the trusting faithful. Monks at the twelfth-century Abbey of Saint-Médard de Soissons, in northern France, claimed to possess a tooth of Jesus. Solemn theological objections were raised on the grounds that Christ had been resurrected, presumably with his teeth intact, to which the monks retorted artfully that this must be a milk tooth. That not everyone was taken in by such outlandish claims is made clear by Chaucer in *The Canterbury Tales,* scornfully mocking his Pardoner for carrying in his wallet a fragment of cloth which he swore was from the sail used by St Peter when he was a fisherman on the Sea of Galilee.

Genuine or make-believe, relics of the saints were enshrined in places it became obligatory for pilgrims to visit. Santiago de Compostela might be the distant goal, but almost every day there would be a shrine of some sort possessing relics to be revered. A pilgrim's journey became a continuous prayer that all would be well.

But there is another side to this journey from shrine to shrine. Whether by chance or good planning it was often the case that a summer pilgrimage through France would find travellers reaching a shrine around the time of a saint's day – with luck the very saint revered at this particular shrine. And these would turn into festive occasions. They might begin with moments of the deepest piety: there are accounts of crowds of pilgrims on the eve of a saint's day keeping vigil all night in the church where the saint's relics were displayed. And on the following morning a solemn mass for a packed congregation would be held. But then, duty done, the atmosphere would change. Secular life took over, and the saint's day became a feast day. The pilgrimage became a party, with music and dancing, acrobats and jugglers performing their acts, hawkers and food vendors plying their trades. Musicians would mingle with the crowds in the square outside the church even while a service was still being conducted inside. There is an account of a saint's day in Conques, in south-central France, when bawdy songs were sung so loud outside the great abbey church that they drowned the words of the litany. Nor was there anything new about such behaviour: as early as the fourth century St Augustine wrote of religious occasions being accompanied by 'licentious revels'.[6]

In all, what we see in descriptions of saints' days are the beginnings of carnivals, fairs and fiestas. Important Church occasions were the focus of public celebration as much as ceremonial piety. The

6. St Augustine of Hippo, *Confessions*, c. AD 397 (Oxford: 2009).

bucolic scenes of village celebrations immortalised in the paintings of Peter Brueghel in the sixteenth century owe their origin to those annual events when pilgrims, fellow-travellers, merchants and local folk, rogues and hangers-on came together to honour some long-dead saint for the good of their souls, then having done so would then step aside from the drudgery of daily life for just a single day, and cast caution to the wind.

The setting is often still there. If we stand by the great gaunt porch of Saint-Benoît's abbey church, it is not hard to imagine the scene as it might have been on a saint's day all those centuries ago. On the stone pillars above the crowd are those apocalyptic images of hellfire and damnation which pilgrims could never get away from. Yet down below in the square there is quite a different world: there is jollity, music and laughter, the singing of ribald songs, all washed down by gallons of sparkling Loire wine. And the party will go on deep into the night. Pilgrimages could be about enjoyment as well as piety.

Then in the morning pilgrims would make their way from Saint-Benoît, perhaps a little worse for wear, along the high bank of the Loire towards Orléans, where a few days earlier they had venerated a supposed fragment of the Holy Cross in the Church of Sainte-Croix. Before continuing westward to the next major stopping-place, the city of Tours, they would have joined up with local pilgrims preparing to make the same journey. Orléans was an important town, and we know that a considerable number of Santiago pilgrims came from here. Today a Renaissance mansion in a side street close to the river offers an insight into the medieval pilgrim's world. It is called La Maison de la Coquille. The name has survived from an older building on the site, which was probably a pilgrims' hospice, or simple inn, attached to a religious house close by. *Coquille* means 'scallop-shell', and most pilgrim hospices came to be identified by this insignia from the time when it became universally recognised as the emblem of the Santiago pilgrimage.[7]

7. See Plate 4.

How this came about is a complex tale. At least by the twelfth century scallop-shells from the waters of the Atlantic near Santiago were being sold outside the newly-built cathedral to pilgrims who would then proudly take them home as mementoes and as proof of having successfully completed the journey. Later the image of the *coquille* became a badge, often cast in metal and worn on a cord round the neck, or else stitched on to clothing, so distinguishing pilgrims from other travellers who might have less honourable reasons for taking to the road. Later still the French genius for gastronomy led to the creation of a delicious dish of scallops cooked in wine, cream and cheese, for which they appropriately invoked the name of the apostle by calling the dish *Coquilles Saint-Jacques*.

The Orléans hospice on the site of the Maison de la Coquille would have been one of many in this part of the town. A nearby street, which once led to the only bridge over the Loire, still bears the name Rue des Hôteliers. Here too stood a late-medieval pilgrims' chapel, the Chapelle Saint-Jacques, which remains largely in the memory today as a place where Joan of Arc prayed after her successful siege of the city. This was a chapel attached to a pilgrims' guild, known as a *confrérie*, or 'confraternity', which had been in existence since the thirteenth century. Anyone could join a confraternity – men, women, priests – provided they could provide proof that they had actually been to Santiago de Compostela. In the early days the word of the local priest would have been proof enough, perhaps supported by producing the scallop-shell which the pilgrim had brought back with him. Then from the fourteenth century the canons of the cathedral in Santiago took to issuing a certificate to arrivals. These were beneficial to the returning pilgrim, but also served as good publicity for the city of Santiago whose cathedral authorities were always keen to explore fresh avenues of fundraising.

In France alone there were more than 200 confraternities of St James in virtually all the larger towns. Collectively their members formed a genuine society of pilgrims: they were a distinct and certainly rather special body, with their own customs, folklore, dress, songs and poems, and of course possessing the powerful bond of a shared experience – the fact that they had all of them made that long journey on foot to Santiago and back, in a small tightly-bound community in which few others had ever travelled further than the next market town.

Confraternities were secular bodies run on charitable lines (to some extent at least), with obligations to help the poor and to sponsor those in their town who wished to undertake the pilgrimage themselves. Naturally they were also social clubs, with their own constitution and rules, as well as possessing a great fondness for banquets, especially on every 25 July which was St James' Day. The largest of these *confréries* was the one in Paris, founded in the thirteenth century, then greatly expanded early in the following century by the French King Philip IV (the Fair), under whose patronage the Paris *confrérie* built a new church, a chapel and a hospice near the Porte Saint-Denis at the northern edge of the city. The French monarch had recently succeeded in suppressing the Knights Templar and burning the order's senior members at the stake, so securing much of the knights' vast wealth – all of which made the king's lavish generosity towards the confraternity possible, bloodstained though it may have been.

As it happens records of the Paris confraternity have survived for the year 1340, just a quarter of a century later. These include the accounts for the 25 July banquet of that year. From these we learn that over one thousand members attended, each paying two sous. Whatever the chefs may have produced on this occasion, it accounted for five cows, twenty pigs, three hundred eggs, two barrels of white wine and three of red. Even so, at some stage a large body of members processed through the streets of Paris carrying banners depicting St James.

It was a far cry from the bread and mug of rough wine which a pilgrim might feel glad to receive in some wayside hospice after a 25-mile slog through forest and swamp. A pilgrim's life had many complexions.

*

No stretch of the pilgrim road has changed more dramatically since the Middle Ages than the section skirting the Loire. Within a few centuries it was to become the 'Royal Loire', studded with spectacular *châteaux* which we marvel at today – Blois, Amboise, Villandry, Langeais, Saumur, as well as those close by: Azay-le-Rideau, Chenonceaux, Chinon, Loches, Chambord. The modern traveller following in the footsteps of the medieval pilgrim needs to be blind to these glories of Renaissance architecture and instead to go in search of more humble places.

Heading west along the river from Orléans we are almost immediately reminded that it was not only the large towns which possessed a community of former pilgrims. Cléry-Saint-André is scarcely more than a village today and can never have been any larger, yet we know from a notary's document that as late as the early seventeenth century a pilgrims' confraternity here boasted a membership of thirty-two men and one woman. (Who was she, one wonders?) Whether they had all of them been to Santiago is not recorded. What seems clear is that *confréries* such as this one continued to play a social role even in small communities over a period of many centuries. The local church here also offers a reminder that pilgrimages often overlapped one another. Cléry, on the road to Santiago, also attracted pilgrims to a shrine of its own. This was a statue of the Virgin which had been discovered in the thirteenth century by a local ploughman in a nearby thicket. The statue was held to be a miraculous arrival in their midst, and a cult grew up which persisted for centuries. Hence when the church was rebuilt in the fifteenth century by King Louis XI he had it dedicated to the Virgin: and so strong was his attachment to the place that he instructed that he should be buried here. And yet his tomb rests in a chapel dedicated not to the Virgin but to St James. Saints could sometimes be interchangeable.

From Cléry the road continues south-west along the river. Pilgrims passed through Blois, already a city of some substance in the Middle Ages, whose ruler in the eleventh century had married the daughter of William the Conqueror, who bore him a son, Stephen, later to become King of England. Then onwards again to the most important of the cities on the Loire, and one of the oldest and most revered places of pilgrimage in France. This was Tours.

3. A Brave New World

At the city of Tours, the pilgrim road finally ceases to hug the River Loire, and heads south. But before continuing their journey pilgrims would linger here a while: there was no more sacred a place between here and Spain than Tours. Its importance may be measured by the fact that this road from Paris was actually known as the *Via Turonensis* – the Road from Tours. Furthermore, of the four main pilgrim roads to Spain in the Middle Ages this was held to be the principal one: it was the *magnum iter Sancti Jacobi*.

The first account of this network of four roads laid across the landscape of France comes from that celebrated twelfth-century document called the *Liber Sancti Jacobi*, the Book of St James, the fifth volume of which is more generally known simply as *The Pilgrim's Guide to Santiago de Compostela* (*Iter pro peregrinis ad Compostellam*). It forms part of a larger manuscript known as the *Codex Calixtinus* (named after Pope Callixtus II). *The Pilgrim's Guide* itself is a work with an undisguised agenda, which is to promote the Santiago pilgrimage, and it does so with the aid of barefaced deceit. The *Guide* is presented as having been written by the highest authority in the Church, Calixtus II, who almost certainly had nothing whatever to do with it since he had been dead for at least ten years before the manuscript was composed. (The reasons for this blatant pretence may become clearer later in this book when the political issues surrounding the pilgrimage come into focus.)

The Pilgrim's Guide makes clear the attraction of the city of Tours. 'One must visit on this route, on the banks of the Loire, the venerable remains of the Blessed Martin, bishop and confessor'[8]: so begins an account of one of the most revered saints in France, St Martin of Tours, whose name is invoked again and again in churches and abbeys along the pilgrim roads in France and in Spain. St Martin had been a soldier in the Roman army in the fourth century, then rose to become the leading bishop in what was still Roman Gaul, recently converted to Christianity. A rich corpus of legends and miracles are attached to his life and career, and a widespread cult grew up around him in the succeeding centuries, making Tours a centre of pilgrimage. With the emergence of the cult of St James the Tours pilgrimage, like so many other local pilgrimages throughout France, became attached to the greater adventure of the Santiago trail. Tours became one of the many pearls strung along the thread of that great journey. The first sanctuary was built over St Martin's tomb in the fifth century, only to be destroyed in the ninth century by the Vikings – 'the Norman fury' – at a time when they laid waste to much of the Loire Valley. The church which replaced it was then destroyed by fire in the year 997. A far larger church was constructed in the eleventh century, further expanded early in the twelfth century; and it is this great new basilica which *The Pilgrim's Guide* urges Santiago pilgrims to visit: 'The sarcophagus ... glitters with an immense display of silver and gold as well as precious stones. ... Above this a huge and venerable basilica has been erected in his honour, similar to the church of the Blessed James, and executed in admirable workmanship.'

Here the author touches on one of the most distinctive features of the Santiago pilgrimage and the architecture which it inspired. The great Basilica of Saint-Martin-de-Tours was one of a group of five huge churches all of which conform to the same architectural specification. They were designed specifically to accommodate huge numbers of pilgrims, one church located on each of the four French roads leading to Spain as described in the *Guide*. Besides Tours

8. The passages from *The Pilgrim's Guide* which I have quoted in English throughout this book are based on the translation I made for my earlier study of this subject back in 1974. My source was an excellent version in French made by Jeanne Vieillard in 1938, at that time the only translation from the original Latin available to me (see Selected Further Reading).

on the Paris road, there was Limoges on the road from Vézelay, Conques on the route from Le Puy, and Toulouse on the southern route from Arles; the fifth being in Spain, the Cathedral of Santiago de Compostela itself. The *Guide*'s author, dedicated as he was to promoting the glories of Santiago, seems to have fallen victim to his own propaganda in suggesting that St Martin's church was modelled on that of Santiago (possibly in response to pressure from the cathedral authorities in Santiago, as may become clear later in this book). In fact, it was probably the other way round: the Church of Saint-Martin-de-Tours is likely to have been the model and prototype for the four others. Tours was the mother-church of the great pilgrim routes. Revisionist scholars have recently struggled to downplay the importance of this grouping of five archetypal pilgrim churches: nonetheless, in whatever order they were built, together they made up some of the most remarkable ecclesiastical buildings ever created.

All five churches conformed to a common plan because they were designed for the same purpose: this was to accommodate huge congregations on special occasions when pilgrims could be expected in exceptional numbers not only to attend mass but to venerate a saint's relics which would be displayed on the High Altar. These requirements necessitated a vast aisle of double the normal width to ensure that all could participate in the elaborate services held on saints' days and at other special festivals. Then, since honouring the saint's relics was the climax of a pilgrim's day, there needed to be a broad ambulatory around and behind the High Altar so that the congregation could circulate freely. A further feature of these churches was a semicircle of five chapels which were set in the apse beyond the ambulatory so that pilgrims could offer prayers in relative privacy.

Such was the celebrated Basilica of Saint-Martin, where 'the sick come and are healed' – *The Pilgrim's Guide* assures us 'the possessed are delivered, the blind are restored to their vision, the lame rise, all sorts of illnesses are cured, and upon all those who ask for it a complete relief is conferred.'

Alas, no longer. Only three of the five great pilgrim churches survive, and Saint-Martin-de-Tours is not one of them. The history of destruction which preceded it was to continue. It was vandalised by a Protestant mob during the French religious wars in the sixteenth century; then most of what remained was finally demolished in the nineteenth century to make way for a market. Today, following in the footsteps of yesterday's pilgrims, we can walk down the market street, the Rue des Halles, reflecting that this was formerly the nave of the great church. As a reminder, a single broken arch has somehow survived, snapped off above our heads. Further down the street on the right stands the Tour de l'Horloge, once the south-west tower of the church. Further on still, the Tour Charlemagne originally rose above the north transept: now it overshadows the little shops, market stalls and half-timbered houses of the old town. The mother-church of the Santiago pilgrimage has become a venue for cabbages and cheese. As for St Martin's tomb and shrine which once drew worshippers in their thousands, it is – surprisingly – still there, deep in the ancient crypt hidden beneath a grandiose nineteenth-century basilica built in what is politely described as 'the neo-Byzantine style'.

And so, after a respectful bow to the ghost of St Martin's basilica, today's travellers follow the trail of their medieval predecessors, and move on – southwards.

For the pilgrim there was always the problem of rivers. Today we cross them without thinking, pausing perhaps to gaze down at the gentle flow of water combing the thickets of bulrushes and water-irises. But for the pilgrim in the Middle Ages each river was a potential barrier. There were few bridges, and unless there was a convenient ferry each crossing meant negotiating with a kindly boatman who – as *The Pilgrim's Guide* ghoulishly explains later – sometimes proved to be more murderous than kind. This area of central France was particularly hazardous because the Loire is fed by numerous tributaries splayed like the fingers of a hand across this fertile plain, not joined up into a single arm until further downstream.

On one of these tributaries, the Vienne, is the tiny village of Tavant. It lies a short distance to the west of the pilgrim road, yet like so many isolated settlements in this region it preserves its own record of the great pilgrimage which flowed close by for so long. The squat twelfth-century church is remarkable in possessing frescoes of the same period, including lively figures clearly drawn from life, among them – on the wall of the crypt – a study of what is apparently a pilgrim: and if he is indeed a pilgrim bound for Santiago, then he is among the very first of whom we have a picture. There are anomalies about his appearance. He has the usual leather pouch for carrying food, as well as the long pilgrim's staff. Yet in his hand he also carries a palm-branch, the traditional emblem of a pilgrim to Jerusalem (even though it was sometimes adopted by Santiago pilgrims). Then his headgear bears no resemblance to the wide-brimmed hat turned up at the rim generally believed to be part of a Santiago pilgrim's uniform: rather it resembles a turban of some sort, again suggesting a connection with the East. So, perhaps he was a palmer recently returned from the Holy Land in the wake of the First Crusade, maybe wearing a trophy on his head to impress his fellow-villagers; and the artist busy painting religious scenes in the church at the time decided to include a portrait of so decorative a local celebrity. Or there again, maybe he was a pilgrim about to set out for Spain wearing what he considered to be an appropriate outfit. After all, most images of Santiago pilgrims in their recognisable gear of hat, jacket, staff, wallet and scallop-shell are of a later date; and in these early centuries who knows what pilgrims normally wore?

Then, as if to demonstrate how the conventions of a pilgrim's dress became stereotyped to the point of caricature, a little further south along the pilgrim road, at Châtellerault, the Church of Saint-Jacques displays a seventeenth-century polychrome statue of the apostle whose hat and cloak are smothered with enough scallop-shells to have made a feast of *Coquilles Saint-Jacques*. This is pilgrim dress turned caricature.

A mile or so further still, close to the pilgrim road, lies a place so sleepily anonymous that only its name betrays it as the site of one of the most momentous events in the early history of Europe, with a strong indirect bearing on the Santiago pilgrimage. It is a village with the name of Moussais-la-Bataille. In other words it is the site of a battle. Somewhere in the lush fields around this village was where, in the year 732, the general of the Frankish army routed a Saracen force which was threatening to plunder its way through France at least as far as Paris. This was the first significant check to the repeated Moorish invasions from Spain which were threatening to overwhelm much of Christian Europe. It was the beginning of a tide being turned, and the first fragile pointer to a counter-offensive which was to culminate in the crusades and in the Reconquest of Spain. The general of the conquering Frankish army was Charles Martel, Charles 'the Hammer' , also distinguished as being the grandfather of the Emperor Charlemagne, Charles 'the Great', the first Holy Roman Emperor, who will feature prominently later in the Santiago story.

The road south now enters a region which brings *The Pilgrim's Guide* colourfully to life, in the process providing a clue as to who may have been responsible for writing it – or at least writing this section of it. The region is Poitou: that is, the area centred on the city of Poitiers. Here, we read, is 'a land well-managed, excellent and full of all blessings. The inhabitants of Poitou are vigorous and warlike, extraordinarily able users of bows, arrows and lances in times of war; they are daring on the battle-front, fast in running, comely in dress, of noble features, clever of language, generous in the rewards they bestow, and prodigal in the hospitality they offer.'

This effusive account of Poitou and its people is in startling contrast to the sketchy and impersonal nature of what precedes it in the *Guide*. The chapter continues at unusual length with a description of the places and people on the route ahead – some of it furiously hostile – which makes it clear that this section of the book at least was written by someone who had actually travelled the pilgrim road and is relating his experiences of it. Furthermore, his unashamed bias in favour of Poitou suggests that the author is likely to have come from here. His identity is something of a puzzle, though there are intriguing clues, as well as any number of false trails. In the latter category, besides the spurious attribution to Pope Calixtus II, there is a second name given as author and co-author of two of the other chapters. He is called Aimery the Chancellor, who is known to have been a cardinal and an adviser to several successive popes as well as a friend of the first Archbishop of Santiago, Diego Gelmirez.

There are other clues besides, and they point to another candidate who happens to share the same name – Aimery. A surviving letter purporting to be from Pope Innocent II states that the *Codex Calixtinus*, the manuscript which includes *The Pilgrim's Guide*, was donated to the Cathedral of Santiago de Compostela by a certain Aimery Picaud who made the pilgrimage in the company of a man named Oliverus and a woman called Ginberga who may have been Oliverus' wife. The same Aimery also appears as the author of a hymn written down immediately after the last words of the *Guide*. Furthermore this Aimery is known to have been a monk in the priory of Parthenay-le-Vieux, which lies in the heart of the Poitou region of France – the area effusively eulogised in *The Pilgrim's Guide*.

Suddenly, from these fragments of circumstantial evidence pieces of the puzzle seem to be falling into place. We have two principal authors of the *Guide*, both called Aimery. One is a high-ranking dignitary of the Church, friend of popes and of Santiago's archbishop, acknowledged as being responsible for a long description of the cathedral and city of Santiago towards the end of the *Guide*. The second Aimery is a lowly monk from the Poitou region, who remains anonymous in the text, yet his presence can be felt everywhere. The account of the landscape and people of his native Poitou, as well as of neighbouring regions, is so vivid and opinionated that it suggests he is most likely to have been responsible for at least the chapter entitled 'The Quality of the Lands and the People along the Road', and very possibly other chapters as well. And this same Aimery, as we are informed, was the man who later carried the completed *Codex* manuscript all the way to Santiago. He may even have undertaken the pilgrimage twice. In any case he was someone who knew sections of the different pilgrim roads extremely well.

Aimery Picaud's church at Parthenay-le-Vieux still exists, a short distance to the west of the main pilgrim road running south towards Poitiers, capital of the Poitou region. The church itself was built early in the twelfth century, at a time when the young Aimery may well have been a novice at the priory. Today the church stands solidly among trees and rough ground, its handsome octagonal bell-tower a prominent landmark in this flat countryside. A rounded apse fans out from the eastern end, while on the west side three sculpted portals greet the visitor with the customary admonitory figures of good and evil stretched along semi-circular bands of carving overhead – pairs of dogs representing Hell, and birds standing for Paradise. Then, in the centre of the left-hand portal is a powerful life-size mounted figure wearing a crown and trampling a foe beneath his stallion's hooves. Like the messages of good and evil, this would soon become a familiar figure to pilgrims travelling through this region. The crowned warrior was a symbol of the Church Triumphant, designed to represent the first Christian Roman Emperor, Constantine I, crushing the forces of paganism – a further reminder of the crusading aspect of the Santiago pilgrimage. As for the priory itself, all that remain are retaining walls that enclose fruit-trees and vegetable plots, and a fragment of the former cloister where Picaud would so often have strolled, discovered as recently as the 1920s embedded in the wall of a farmhouse close to the church.

In fact there are two Parthenays, a couple of miles apart. And it is this second Parthenay which remains one of the 'showcase' pilgrim towns of France, even though it stands only on a tributary pilgrim road. In this region there are so many threads of roads conveying pilgrims, including those from England, who had travelled directly from Normandy and Brittany, avoiding Paris and Tours, and gradually converging as they progressed south. Parthenay today is like a full-scale demonstration model of what a medieval town was like: indeed there is no town along any of the pilgrim roads, even in Spain, which more clearly shows how the Santiago pilgrimage made its mark on the local life and architecture in the Middle Ages. Travellers would approach the town from the north, and characteristically the northern outskirts of Parthenay became the Faubourg Saint-Jacques, the suburb for Santiago pilgrims, because here was generally where they found lodgings for the night. The *faubourg* was deliberately set outside the walls of the town, so enabling travellers to come and go after the gates of the town were locked at night. To this day hundreds of French towns, from Paris down to places smaller than Parthenay, retain an area still named Faubourg Saint-Jacques.

Here, in the heart of the *faubourg* of Parthenay, there survives the shell of a Chapelle Saint-Jacques, long ago incorporated into a domestic building and a neighbouring barn. Here pilgrims would offer their prayers on arrival before finding a hospice or lodgings of some sort close by. Then, barely a hundred yards further, the road opens up to reveal a prospect which has remained unchanged for more than three-quarters of a millennium. This is the thirteenth-century stone bridge – naturally called the Pont Saint-Jacques[9] – which leads across the gentle River Thouet directly to the principal town gate, the enormous fortified Porte Saint-Jacques; and from here into the main street of the town, called (not surprisingly) the Rue Saint-Jacques. On either side stand half-timbered houses formerly occupied by merchants and tradesmen who had grown prosperous supplying provisions and other services to pilgrims passing through the town in their thousands on their way south. The merchants gave their houses fine stone lintels with the appropriate year engraved on them, and overhanging gables in wood carved with corn motifs and human heads. Today's traveller then climbs up towards the remains of the town castle and, next to it, the Church of Notre-Dame de la Couldre. Only a particularly fine Romanesque west door survives as a witness to a historic occasion which took place here in 1135 in the lifetime of Aimery Picaud (who may well have been present). One of the most forceful and charismatic preachers of the Middle Ages came to this pilgrimage town and delivered a sermon of such hypnotic power that the local ruler, Duke William of Aquitaine, who was present, is said to have become a devotee on the spot.[10] The preacher was none other

9. See Plate 5.

10. Duke William's most significant contribution to European history is that he was the father of Eleanor of Aquitaine, whose inheritance of Aquitaine enabled her husband, the English King Henry II, to claim this large area of 'France' as belonging to England, a claim that led ultimately to the Hundred Years' War between England and France.

than St Bernard of Clairvaux, founder of the Cistercian Order and a guiding spirit of resurgent Christianity. Here, as elsewhere along the roads to Santiago, those passionate issues of the day, the Holy War and the Reconquest of Spain, were woven into the very fabric of the pilgrimage movement.

How much or how little of *The Pilgrim's Guide* was actually composed by a monk from Parthenay-le-Vieux is of far lesser importance than why it was put together and where the inspiration for it lay. Here a strong clue lies in its final words. The author concludes with a list of places where he claims it has been written. These include Italy, Germany, 'the lands of Jerusalem' (which sounds unlikely), then significantly 'mainly in Cluny'. So often in *The Pilgrim's Guide* claims of authorship and geographical location suggest propaganda rather than actuality. Attributions tend to act as smoke-screens. Yet 'mainly Cluny' has an altogether more meaningful ring. Whatever the extent of Picaud's contribution to the book, his priory of Parthernay-le-Vieux was a Benedictine house which had strong links to Cluny. The priory's own mother-abbey in the Auvergne, La Chaise-Dieu, had been founded in the mid-eleventh century by a monk of Cluny who had been an apprentice to one of its most forceful abbots, St Odilo, who had directed much of his abundant energy into supporting the Christian rulers of northern Spain in their campaign against the Saracens, and in doing so safeguarding the pilgrim route to Santiago.

As in so many twists and turns of the pilgrimage story the name of the great abbey is never far away. Cluny was the political powerhouse of the medieval Church, the most influential ecclesiastical body of its day, and for several centuries the spiritual heart of Christendom, shining 'as another sun over the earth', in the words of Pope Urban II. With its massive investment in Spain and in the Santiago pilgrimage, what more likely a guiding spirit could there be in the compiling of a book urging pilgrims to go there? Whether it was actually written or merely masterminded there, the *Guide* has the shadow of Cluny all over it – as we may see more clearly when this journey takes us there.

*

The first modern scholar of the Santiago pilgrimage, the American Arthur Kingsley Porter, wrote in the 1920s that 'the pilgrimage roads may be compared to a great river emptying into the sea at Santiago'. The image is a memorable one. The continuous flow of a river evokes the unbroken passage of pilgrims over the centuries, as well as the essentially peaceful and restorative nature of a pilgrim's journey. However hazardous, the roads to Santiago were felt to be the roads to heaven, the way to personal salvation. And from our perspective in the twenty-first century the art and architecture of those roads are the signposts which guided people there. Nowadays we travel to admire those achievements, much as medieval pilgrims travelled to venerate the shrines contained within them.

Less identifiable than buildings and works of art is the human element, which is what the pilgrimage is all about. What kind of people were they who undertook such a journey at a time when travel was liable to be dangerous at the best of times, and for most pilgrims a step into the unknown? *The Pilgrim's Guide*, popular though it became, copied and circulated widely over the following centuries, would still have been for a small minority of travellers: the vast majority of pilgrims would have been illiterate. Latin was not their native tongue even if they could manage to read it.

Above all this was the pilgrimage of Everyman. Santiago was the most popular goal for pilgrims throughout much of the Middle Ages, engendering an intensity of devotion and affection which under very different circumstances has been maintained to this day. Largely due to this universal appeal across a broad social spectrum, the route to Santiago in its heyday became a high-road of Christian teaching, Christian institutions and Christian art. And on that road all humanity was there. Chaucer's pilgrims were heading for Canterbury, not Santiago; yet even though they were a more varied and colourful bunch of travellers than one might have encountered on our road to Parthenay and Poitiers, they nonetheless illustrate a general truth about pilgrim bands, particularly in the later Middle Ages, which is that their journey could be a social occasion, pleasure-loving and sometimes raucous, as they whiled away the long hours between shrine and shrine, hospice and hospice.

Chaucer's Squire, 'a lusty bachelor ... fresh as the month of May' and 'syngynge ... al the day', may not have been the typical pilgrim; yet we know that singing was a popular feature of the Santiago pilgrimage. Special pilgrim songs have survived, and so have manuscripts depicting pilgrims on the road carrying musical instruments. Horns, tambourines and the zither were common, though the classic pilgrimage instrument was the hurdy-gurdy. This would have been far too cumbersome for the ordinary pilgrim to carry all the way to Santiago; but we know that there were poet-minstrels, *jongleurs,* who would entertain pilgrims on their travels, breaking off to sing at fairs along the route, or outside churches on special feast days, just as itinerant musicians today will earning an extra buck serenading tourists on market-days or doing the round of cafés and restaurants.

The pilgrimage was a world on the move: a floating population made up of a cross-section of medieval society. At the top end of the social scale there were aristocrats. In Jonathan Sumption's words, 'The annual or biennial pilgrimage became a recognised mark of aristocratic piety.'[11] And one suspects that the piety may have been largely for show. At the opposite end of the scale were the criminals sentenced to undertake a pilgrimage by the civil courts as punishment for a variety of offences, among the most serious being arson. Such sentences were relatively few, partly because offenders could be given the choice of paying a fine instead. This was calculated on a sliding scale depending on the severity of the sentence: the fine imposed as the alternative to going to Santiago was roughly the same as that for Rome, but only a quarter as much if the sentence was to go no further than to Saint-Martin-de-Tours. Then, in the middle of the social scale, was another category of traveller for whom piety was also not the primary incentive for setting out on pilgrimage. These were itinerant merchants and salesmen who posed as pilgrims as a

11 Jonathan Sumption, *The Age of Pilgrimage* (New York: 2003).

way of plying their trade *en route* while at the same time enjoying the exemption from taxes and tolls which was a pilgrim's coveted privilege.

Yet the overwhelming majority of pilgrims to Santiago in the Middle Ages would never voluntarily have undertaken so long and hazardous a journey far from home unless driven by a spirit of genuine piety. This was a Christian world obsessed with the expectation of a Second Coming and the imminence of the Day of Judgment. Accordingly it was a society plagued by a sense of sin, and by a desperate need to seek redemption if hell was to be avoided. To go on pilgrimage was one means of attaining such a goal. In our own day of rapid travel and easy communications it is hard to grasp just how isolated Christians in Western Europe could feel from the roots of their faith, especially since the Holy Land itself was now in the hands of the Infidel. By claiming to possess the body of one of Christ's apostles Santiago offered a bridge to the birthplace of Christianity; and by travelling there a pilgrim could feel his own footsteps touching that bridge.

At the same time the incentives to set out on the long road to Santiago cannot have been only the fear of hellfire. Pilgrims were not entirely blindfolded against the pleasures of daily life. Again the lesson of Chaucer is a salutary one: a pilgrimage could be fun. It offered possibly the one and only chance to escape the smallness and monotony of village life – and most people still lived in villages, and rarely moved far away from them. Piety and the freedom of the open road could be happy companions on a pilgrim's journey. Freedom of the road may also have brought a welcome escape from the authority of the parish priest. In the Middle Ages people belonged to their local church in a more total sense than parishioners may feel today. The church might offer spiritual guidance, but it also controlled people's thoughts and daily lives – just as the sheer size of a church with its tower or steeple dominated the mean cottages where most of the congregation lived. Churches delivered a double message: a demand to be obeyed on the one hand – but then, high above as if radiating from heaven itself, the sound of bells. In the words of that eminent scholar of the medieval world, Johan Huizinga, church bells were 'like good spirits lifting people's spirits into a sphere of order and serenity'.

Together with this sense of liberation from the daily grind, a pilgrimage to a distant land would also offer a unique glimpse of a broader life – a life full of strange sights and sounds. A modern tourist setting eyes for the first time on the Taj Mahal or the Egyptian pyramids would have some idea of the impact of a great abbey or cathedral on a French peasant who had never before left his native village. The shock of so many new experiences would have been accompanied by an exhilarating sense of romance which may have lifted the pilgrim's spirits even more than the sound of church bells. Here was an exciting and brave new world – besides which a short journey beyond the city of Santiago took the pilgrim to the end of the known world: Cape Finisterre, *finis terra*. It is difficult to imagine in our more pragmatic world a comparable feeling of spiritual achievement and sheer wonder. In so many ways a pilgrimage was a journey like no other.

In the words of one of the early abbots of Cluny, Abbot Mayeul, aristocrat and scholar, 'life itself is but a pilgrimage, and man lives as a fleeting guest on this earth'. Not for the first time the voice of Cluny echoes down the pilgrim roads. And we shall hear it again and again.

1. Paris, No. 1 St James' Street. The long walk begins. (Adam Woolfitt)

2. Santiago Matamoros – St Jacques the Moor – slayer and liberator of Spain: an illustration from the *Codex Calixtinus* manuscript – *The Pilgrim's Guide*. (Wikimedia Commons)

3. The porch of the abbey church of Saint-Benoît on the River Loire. Pilgrims came here to revere the relics of St Benedict, founder of the Benedictine Order, brought here from the abbey he founded, Monte Cassino, in southern Italy. (Prost.photo/Wikimedia Commons)

4. The ubiquitous scallop-shell, symbol of the Santiago pilgrimage and of St James, ‘the saint from the sea’: widely carved on churches, on the doors of wayside inns, and worn or woven on pilgrims’ clothing. (Adam Woolfitt)

5. Parthenay in south-west France approaching Bordeaux: the medieval bridge and Porte Saint-Jacques leading to the pilgrims’ street. (Adam Woolfitt)

6. Musical accompaniment on the pilgrim church of Aulnay in western France. The theme from the Bible of the Old Men of the Apocalypse playing their instruments was a favourite subject carved on churches along the pilgrim roads. (Adam Woolfitt)

7. The village church of Rioux, one of many richly-decorated churches in the Saintonge region of south-west France as the pilgrim road approached Bordeaux.
(Adam Woolfitt)

8. Pilgrims would scratch graffiti at the entrance to a hospice as they waited to be admitted at nightfall.
(Adam Woolfitt)

9. St James represented as a pilgrim in the village chapel at Harambels, near the Pyrenees: one of the earliest pilgrim churches in France, mentioned in the twelfth-century *Pilgrim's Guide*.
(Adam Woolfitt)

10. Meeting-point. A traditional Basque headstone now marks the place on a hillside near the Pyrenees where three of the four major pilgrim roads – from Paris, Vézelay and Le Puy – join to become one road leading to Spain. (Adam Woolfitt)

4. Churches 'more beautiful than before'

THE PILGRIM ROAD NOW CROSSES A REGION that is 'well-managed, excellent and full of all blessings'; so *The Pilgrim's Guide* assured the medieval traveller. Such praise is not surprising: this was the author's homeland of Poitou, and not a word was to be said against it, least of all against its inhabitants who were so 'prodigal in the hospitality they offer'. Aimery Picaud, if he was indeed the author, was never to be so kind again when describing those who lived in other regions. In his eyes the people of Poitou enjoyed a monopoly of all human virtues.

Today a motorway runs parallel to the old Roman road which the early pilgrims would have taken. The tributary road running east from Picaud's Parthenay joins it a little to the north of the regional capital, the city of Poitiers. To the medieval traveller this was the city of St Hilary, Saint-Hilaire, and his shrine was the most important for the pilgrim to venerate after that of St Martin of Tours on the banks of the Loire. Hilaire had in fact been St Martin's mentor, a bishop and doctor in Roman Gaul during the fourth century. So the road taking pilgrims from Tours to Poitiers would certainly have been known to him. The saint's principal achievement, according to *The Pilgrim's Guide*, was to have 'vanquished the Arian heresy', that famous theological quibble over the precise meaning of the Holy Trinity. One dissident by the name of Leo, it goes on, was most horribly punished for the error of his ways, 'dying abominably in the latrines, afflicted by a corruption of the belly'. The saint himself enjoyed an altogether more peaceful end, after which his tomb was 'decorated with abundant gold, silver, and extraordinarily precious stones, and its large and splendid basilica is venerated by virtue of its many miracles.'

The 'large and splendid' Church of Saint-Hilaire-le-Grand had been built in the mid-eleventh century, apparently by an English architect by the name of Coorland – a reminder of England's powerful influence in this whole area of western France known as Aquitaine, long before it finally came under English rule in the mid-twelfth century. This was to take place with the marriage of Eleanor, Duchess of Aquitaine, to Henry Plantagenet, Duke of Normandy and Count of Anjou, who soon became King Henry II of England, ruling a vast territory that stretched from Scotland to the Pyrenees.

The church still stands, more or less in its original form, in a southern suburb of Poitiers on the site of two former churches likewise dedicated to the saint which had been destroyed respectively by the Vandals in the fifth century and by the Normans in the ninth. Grand in name and grand in concept, Saint-Hilaire-le-Grand is vast. Without entirely conforming to the pattern of pilgrim churches that were modelled on Saint-Martin-de-Tours, it was nonetheless designed to accommodate pilgrims in extremely large numbers, and there is no church along the entire length of the road from Paris to the Pyrenees which gives so clear an idea of how a massed congregation of pilgrims could be contained for a special service held on the saint's day – which in this case, so the *Guide* informs us, was celebrated on 13 January.

Medieval Poitiers enjoyed an explosion of church-building during the years of religious fervour that followed the peaceful passing of the Millennium, when people began to believe that the world was not about to come to end after all – at least not just yet. Most of these medieval churches in Poitiers have survived. For pilgrims there was even a second saint to venerate. She was a woman by the name of Radegonde who founded an abbey here in the sixth century. The eleventh- and twelfth-century church dedicated to her stands tucked among old houses at the eastern edge of the city close to the river. Its splendid Gothic portal, intricately carved, evokes a later era when fears of the imminent ending of the world were long past: God was in his heaven and all was well down on earth. The pall of darkness hanging over people's lives had lifted; and with it some of the urge to go on pilgrimage to save their souls had by now weakened.

In contrast to the flamboyant portal of Sainte-Radegonde is a modest little box of a building a mere hundred yards away. This is a baptistery dating from the very first century of Christianity in Roman Gaul, the fourth; and it bears the special credential of being the earliest example of Christian architecture in the whole of France. It is a sombre thought that this place of worship was already eight centuries old when Aimery Picaud was setting off on his pilgrimage from here: and in truth he may not even have been aware of its existence. A more poignant question is – would he have known the greatest of all the medieval churches of Poitiers, Notre-Dame-la-Grande, which was almost certainly being built during his lifetime? This former collegiate church had no specific connection with the Santiago pilgrimage; yet no pilgrim passing through the city from north to south could have failed to notice it, and to wonder at it. Today's traveller may feel the same, because here is one of the glories of church building in France.

Notre-Dame-la-Grande stands in the very centre of Poitiers, on the site of what was once the Roman forum. As a fervent advocate of Poitou Aimery Picaud would have been especially proud of the twin pine-cone turrets which so handsomely flank the west front of the building, and were a particular feature of medieval churches in this region. But it is the west front itself which remains among the highest achievements of Romanesque architecture. If there are more than a few square inches of stone left uncarved it would be a surprise. Here is a sermon in stone, spelt out in images across the entire face of the church. Arch above arch, frieze above frieze, are decorated with fantastic creatures inspired as ever by the biblical Apocalypse. They lash and snap at each another, devour their own tails, while in between these zoomorphic nightmares are rows of gentle saints and apostles, all bound together by entwining images of flora and fauna, and by intricate geometrical patterns that lead the eye a dance across the face of this extraordinary church. We are gazing at a carved morality play. And high above this tussle for people's souls on the facade of Notre-Dame-la-Grande stands the figure of Christ in Majesty in his oval-shaped mandorla like a seal of office. Here was the promise of ultimate authority, and the reassurance that the struggle with the forces of evil was all worthwhile. Then, in the midst of all this heavy moralising we come across an endearing touch – a panel depicting the child Jesus being given his first bath, with Joseph looking awkwardly out of place and keeping a safe distance. Ordinary human sentiments did sometimes find their place amid the rhetoric.

The term 'Romanesque' was only coined in the nineteenth century. But it is used to describe a style of architecture which came into being in Western Europe from about the middle of the tenth century in response to an upsurge of religious fervour and self-confidence following centuries of anarchy and violence at the hands of Vikings, Saracens and Magyars – triple invasions from north, south and east which devastated much of the continent. Now the demand was for more spacious churches to accommodate swelling congregations. To satisfy these needs architects turned for inspiration to the most substantial buildings to have survived the long centuries of chaos and disruption. These were the monumental civic buildings which had been created during the Roman Empire as long as a thousand years earlier – temples, amphitheatres, bridges, aqueducts. Nothing so impressive or so enduring had been created in the dark centuries since. So the new churches were constructed in emulation of them, with architects and stonemasons learning afresh those engineering skills at which the Romans had excelled. Doors and windows were no longer narrow slots but broad rounded arches supported by solid columns on either side, while roofs were vaulted so that the weight of a stone roof could be borne on massive piers set on either side of a wide central nave. The result was more space, more light and, in particular, more opportunity for decoration.

For these reasons, especially the last, the Romanesque style of church-building became ideally suited to the kind of pictorial sermonising which is such a dominant feature of Notre-Dame-la-Grande, as it is of hundreds of other churches in this region and along the pilgrim roads in general. Every arch and every space offered invitations for stone-carvers to create a corpus of imagery designed to deliver the Christian message. The facades of these churches are like large-scale illustrated books, each chapter telling some aspect of the bible story for the benefit of a largely illiterate population, each story pressing home the perils of a sinful life and the rewards of a godly one.

It is these elaborately decorated churches which seem to set the tone of daily life at a time in European history when no other sources of teaching were available to most people. Churches held the key to all knowledge and all wisdom.

No modern historian has offered a sharper insight into what it was like to be an ordinary citizen in medieval Europe than the Dutch scholar Johan Huizinga. In his *The Waning of the Middle Ages* he wrote: 'So violent and motley was life, that it bore the mixed smell of blood and of roses. The men of that time always oscillate between the fear of hell and the most naive joy, between cruelty and tenderness, between harsh asceticism and insane attachment to the delights of this world, between hatred and goodness, always running to extremes.'[12] With Huizinga's words in mind, as we gaze up at the facade of one of these Romanesque churches along the pilgrim roads, it is as if we are reading an open book of the medieval mind.

These new churches, more spacious and elegant than the cramped little structures which preceded them, owed their design and craftsmanship to northern Italy. And as so often in these early years of revitalised Christendom the incentive for establishing them here in France came from the monasteries – chiefly from leaders of the Benedictine Order, and in particular from those formidable aristocrats who were the successive abbots of Cluny, in southern

12 Johan Huizinga, *The Waning of the Middle Ages* (London: 1967).

Burgundy. It was in the year 987 that Abbot Mayeul of Cluny persuaded one of the most remarkable churchmen of his day to come to Burgundy. He was William (or Guglielmo) of Volpiano, at that time a monk in the Piedmont region of north-west Italy. William was not only a monk: he was an aristocrat (like Mayeul) with social connections to just about everybody who mattered in Europe. In addition he was a highly-gifted designer and architect – which was principally why Abbot Mayeul invited him.

It was an invitation which proved to be a historic moment in the history of church building in Europe. William accepted, and duly arrived in the Duchy of Burgundy, never returning to live in his native Italy. In the course of his time here, and elsewhere in France, William became to a large extent responsible for establishing the first truly international style of church architecture in Western Europe. He was the father – or more appropriately the godfather – of Romanesque, which was to remain the predominant style of church building for more than two hundred years until the evolution of Gothic late in the twelfth century.

But churches on the scale which William planned required builders and craftsmen with skills far beyond those that existed anywhere in Burgundy or in the whole of France. William was aware, however, that those skills did exist in the region of northern Italy where his own powerful family held sway. This was in Lombardy, the area immediately to the south of the Alps and the Italian lakes. No doubt using the influence of his social position, William succeeded in bringing a body of these Lombard craftsmen to Burgundy for the express purpose of carrying out the work of church-building which Abbot Mayeul was proposing. Two immensely powerful men were now working together.

As a result Burgundy became the cradle of what has become known as 'the First Romanesque style' of church architecture. By the end of the eleventh century a number of monasteries, priories and parish churches, most of them within a short radius of Cluny, all bore the unmistakeable hallmark of these Lombard craftsmen: tall slender bell-towers, decorative blind arches set into the walls, saw-edged moulding round the roofline of the apse. The Lombard masons and craftsmen operated within a system of itinerant workshops which were part of an extended mobile community that would have included wives, families, servants and domestic animals. The community established itself 'on site' wherever the work was, remaining there until the particular job was completed, before moving on to the next. They were like a nomadic tribe with no permanent home, generation after generation. The Lombards possessed a store of specialist skills which kept them in constant demand over a long period, so that within the next hundred years their influence had spread far beyond Burgundy. Today the churches which bear their unmistakeable signature stand proudly in the European landscape as far afield as Germany, Sweden, the Pyrenees, Dalmatia and Hungary. They remain among the unsung heroes and pioneers of European architecture.

The Lombards were in the forefront of what has been described as a spiritual Renaissance in Europe, of which the pilgrimage movement was a vital manifestation. Right across the continent there arose an urge to build, to give thanks, and to celebrate. People had come out of the darkness to seek a new light. A monk from Cluny by the name of Raoul (Rodulfus) Glaber was keeping a chronicle at exactly the time when the Lombards were building their tall handsome churches right across Burgundy. And he made a memorable observation about the prevailing mood of the time: 'A little after the year one thousand there was a sudden rush to rebuild churches all over the world ... One would have said that the world itself was casting aside its old age and clothing itself anew in a white mantle of churches ... A veritable contest drove each Christian community to build a more sumptuous church than its neighbours .... Even the little churches in the villages were reconstructed by the faithful more beautiful than before.'[13]

*

13. Raoul Glaber, *The Five Books of The Histories,* c. 1026- (Oxford: 1989).

The old Roman road continues south-west across the low-lying pastures and vineyards of Poitou towards the Atlantic and the broad estuary of the Gironde, and ultimately to Bordeaux. If the medieval pilgrim imagined that after the churches of Poitiers he might be free of didactic sermons in stone, he was in for a shock: because within little more than a day's journey he was confronted – right beside the road – by the Church of Saint-Pierre at Aulnay.

The village of Aulnay itself is out of sight, well to the east. But then this was not intended as a village church. It was always for pilgrims. And if the Poitiers churches had been an illustrated book, Aulnay was an illustrated encyclopaedia. It is hard to imagine what the foot-weary traveller would have made of it. Everywhere we look a face looks back at us – a face designed to inspire terror or hope: birds, horses, mermaids, four-legged creatures with wings and beaks, couples entwined by their tails, beasts bound by vine tendrils, elephants, grimacing giants, moustached owls; and then saints, apostles, angels, knights, maidens. The grotesque and the serene live side by side: the light and the dark. The south portal of the church is the most intensely carved – one of the most glorious ensembles of Romanesque sculpture in Europe, with four semi-circular bands of massed figures curved above the door, one above the other. Four knights crush demons beneath their shields and spears. Below the knights, along the inner band, is a frieze of beasts caught within the tendrils of a climbing plant. The next tier depicts the twelve apostles and the twelve prophets of the Apocalypse bearing crowns of gold and musical instruments, and vials filled with odours, after the account given in the fourth chapter of the Book of Revelations:

> ...and, behold, a throne was set in heaven, and *one* sat on the throne. And he that sat was to look upon like a jasper and a sardine stone: and there was a rainbow round about the throne, in sight like unto an emerald. And round about the throne were four and twenty seats: and upon the seats I saw four and twenty elders sitting, clothed in white raiment; and they had on their heads crowns of gold.

Only here the sculptors, having already carved twenty-four figures on the band below, took the liberty of raising the number of elders to thirty-one. The precise meaning of these figures, with their crowns and their musical instruments, has remained a topic of debate and dispute for centuries, as to whether they are angels, saints in heaven or simply elders of the Church. But if the answer has been lost on the tides of history what remains is an endearing theme that is echoed over and over again on Romanesque churches in France, like a chorus-line forever coming forward to sing and play for us as if to offer a welcome relief from so much persistent gloom.[14]

But it is the outer band of carving on the Aulnay south portal which is the most extraordinary. Here is an illustration of the medieval mind at its most nightmarish: an evocation of chaos, of life without God, a world without love, made up of hideous creatures who do nothing but howl and grimace and chatter like the occupants of an imaginary madhouse. It is yet another dark and visual sermon, designed as ever to assault weary pilgrims making their way into the church to celebrate mass, only to endure an actual sermon delivered most likely on the very same theme. One begins to feel sorry for them. As if months of foot-slogging across unknown lands were not testing enough, to be reminded of hell-fire at every place of prayer would seem an undue extra burden. Today's traveller may enjoy the privilege of appreciating these apocalyptic nightmares as works of art. The medieval pilgrim would have possessed no such sophisticated detachment: the very concept of 'art' as we understand it would have been quite unknown to him. It is we who, in a sense, have become 'illiterate': ignorant of the meaning of these images, insensitive to medieval pilgrims' terrors and anxieties, and by and large unlikely to be sharing the naked simplicity of their faith.

The south portal at Aulnay was carved about the year 1130 – around the time St Bernard was drawing packed congregations to his sermons and converting the elderly Duke of Aquitaine at Parthenay; perhaps, too, at about the time when Aimery Picaud

14. See Plate 6.

was gathering material for *The Pilgrim's Guide* in his monastery at Parthenay-le-Vieux, as well as preparing to set off on his own pilgrimage to Santiago. It was a time of fervent energy in all matters of faith, especially in church-building. Within the next fifty years there would scarcely be a village within a short radius of Aulnay that would not have a new church decorated, to a great or lesser extent, by the same didactic school of stone-carvers.

It was almost two centuries since William of Volpiano had brought his troupe of skilled masons and sculptors from Lombardy to Burgundy to build the first Romanesque churches in France. Since then other workshops had sprung up all over the country: at least six different 'schools' of church architecture were operating by the time *The Pilgrim's Guide* was being compiled, each with its distinctive regional style of building and decoration. Today, if we follow those four principal roads listed in the twelfth-century *Guide*, one of the enduring pleasures of the journey is noticing how the appearance and the mood of those churches alters as we move from region to region.

A short distance south from Aulnay pilgrims once again found themselves being given firm guidance by the *Guide* as to where they should go next. 'One must visit the venerable head of the Blessed John the Baptist, brought by ecclesiastics from the land of Jerusalem to a place called Angély, for safekeeping in the land of Poitou.' This instruction comes from the chapter devoted to saints who should be revered along the route, and it immediately follows Picaud's chapter, already quoted, on 'The Quality of the Lands and the People along the Road'. While there is no proof that Picaud may have been responsible for this chapter as well, the pride with which the writer claims the head of John the Baptist to be in the safekeeping of Poitou suggests the two authors may be one and the same. Where else, he seems to be suggesting, would so holy a relic have found so safe a haven?

Today the small town of Saint-Jean-d'Angély retains its connection with John the Baptist, though only in name. The head is actually believed to have been brought not from Jerusalem but from Alexandria, where it was given to the Benedictines in the ninth century. They proceeded to build a great abbey to receive it, and where it was placed on display for flocks of pilgrims to venerate, 'worshipped day and night by a choir of one hundred monks,' so the *Guide* continues. Even at the time there was clearly some question as to its authenticity since the author felt the need to claim numerous miracles as 'the reason why one believes this one to be the true head of the saint'. His implied doubts were well-founded. Several other claimants to ownership of the Baptist's head began to dent the abbey's special prestige. Worse was to follow. Saint-Jean-d'Angély became a Protestant town during the sixteenth-century religious wars, and the Reformers duly burnt down the abbey along with the abbey church and – we musts assume – the sacred head.

There were saints galore to venerate in this region. A further short journey south along the Roman road took pilgrims to a town actually called Saintes. It took its name in honour of a third-century Christian martyr, St Eutrope, about whom *The Pilgrim's Guide* had an enormous amount to say. He is described as coming from a noble Persian family, converted to Christianity and then travelled widely preaching the gospel, arriving eventually at 'a city called Saintes' (presumably still known by some other name), which was 'prosperous in all goods and provisions, abounding in excellent meadows and clear springs ... provided with handsome squares and streets, and beautiful in many ways'. Again we can detect the familiar note of pride in Picaud's native region. Yet Eutrope and his Christianity were not welcomed here. He was driven out, and returned to Rome to lick his wounds. Later he returned, and settled himself in a hut outside the town walls, where he was befriended by a beautiful girl who became his devoted disciple, until a jealous father recruited a hostile mob who came to the hut and 'stoned the saintly man of God' and finally 'slew him by beating his head to pieces with hatchets and axes'.

The richly flavoured account of St Eutrope's life and death occupies more than twice the space of any other entry in the chapter on saints to be venerated along the pilgrim roads. Being a local saint Eutrope clearly meant much to the author. But his heroic tale also tells us a great deal about the nature of religious faith at this period of resurgent Christianity in Western Europe, and why it is that the pilgrimage movement epitomises the very spirit of that faith. Besides the story's central theme of a spiritual crusade in the face of barbarism and ignorance, a number of other threads are intertwined – a taste for adventure and exotic lands, the importance of myth and legend, belief in the power of miracles, and nostalgia for home and home comforts. Along with these threads is a strong sense of romance, even of romantic and impossible love, reminding us that this was the era of the courtly troubadour poets, and that the local duke at this time, William IX of Aquitaine, has been described as the first troubadour poet.[15]

As we look back at the social phenomenon which has been the Santiago pilgrimage, from the Middle Ages onwards, all these diverse elements would seem to have been present to some degree: and maybe it is the interweaving of these varied threads which accounts for the impact the pilgrimage made on the medieval imagination – and, in our very different world, does so still. A pilgrim's costume has been a coat of many colours.

*

St Eutrope's tomb still rests in the crypt of the priory church in Saintes which the monks of Cluny built in his honour during the eleventh century. The crypt is all that remains of the original church, which must have been enormous, certainly as large as the Saint-Hilaire pilgrim church in Poitiers, and was designed for precisely the same purpose, in order to accommodate huge congregations, many of them pilgrims on their way to Spain and Santiago de Compostela.

As the *Guide* makes clear the fame and popularity of the saint's shrine was to a great extent due to the healing powers it was believed to possess. 'The lame stand up, the blind recover their sight, hearing

15. Successive Dukes of Aquitaine were all called William. The troubadour poet, William IX, was the father of Duke William X, the Santiago pilgrim who was also the father of Eleanor of Aquitaine, who married Henry II of England (see Chapter 3).

is returned to the deaf, the possessed are freed, and all those who with a sincere heart ask for it are accorded salutary help.' A belief in miracles was central to medieval religious thought. Priests who were attached to a church fortunate enough to have obtained a relic with such powers would compile lists and detailed accounts of the miracles performed, which would then be circulated, thereby recruiting more sufferers eager to be cured, along with all manner of other hangers-on. As Jonathan Sumption has put it in *The Age of Pilgrimage*, 'Every major shrine was perpetually besieged by a motley crowd of pilgrims, hawkers, musicians, beggars and idlers whose appetite for new wonders was insatiable.' Shrines, and the miracles performed there, could promote a veritable industry of healing, and a highly profitable one, most of all for the church or abbey concerned, for whom donations made in gratitude for miraculous cures became its principal source of income. A holy relic that was stolen, lost or somehow discredited could bring financial ruin to a church or abbey.

The old town of Saintes remains overloaded with medieval churches. But across the River Charente lies a particular treasure of Romanesque architecture. This is among the earliest and most splendid in the region, the Eglise Sainte-Marie: it was attached to an abbey which would certainly have been visited by passing pilgrims, though only by a special minority of them, namely women. This is the Abbaye aux Dames, an immaculately blue-blooded institution headed by an abbess who was always chosen from one of the noblest families in France, and who also supervised a ladies' college that was likewise for the daughters of the rich. What the young ladies actually learnt is not on record.

The abbey church itself, Sainte-Marie, was built early in the twelfth century, and it offers one of the earliest examples of those sculpted bands of figures, arranged in tight ranks above the principal door in a series of semi-circles – six of them – all densely and intricately carved, the figures radiating outwards from the hand of God in the very centre. Apart from images of angels, suffering martyrs and symbols of the four evangelists the number of crowned elders from the Apocalypse has now grown far beyond the thirty-one at Aulnay to a veritable orchestra of fifty-four, all of them arranged intimately in pairs who face one another with an air of cheerful piety as they play their musical instruments. It is a delightful human touch.

The skilled craftsmanship in stone, which is such a feature of the churches along this stretch of the pilgrim road, was clearly in high demand, particularly at this time when it was thought vital by religious leaders that the message of Christianity be broadcast on the face every new place of worship. The Church was expanding greatly. A missionary spirit was abroad, and sculptors and stonemasons had become essential agents in a vast proselytising campaign. They became part of another travelling workshop in the manner of the Lombards in Burgundy a century earlier. Along with pilgrims they travelled the same roads. Hence the design of church facades in this region of France, typified by that of Aulnay and Saintes, became carried by craftsmen over the Pyrenees and into Spain, where a number of churches along the *camino*, even as far as Santiago itself, display the unmistakeable 'signature' of these skilled carvers and masons. And as a result many of these itinerant French craftsmen working on the churches of northern Spain built in the wake of the Reconquest then chose to settle in their new lands along the pilgrim road, as Spanish towns with names like Villafranca bear witness today.

'Then comes the country of Saintonge,' explains *The Pilgrim's Guide*. This was the region close to the Atlantic, with Saintes as its capital and administrative centre. The pilgrim road runs through the very centre of it, beckoning the traveller to larger objectives – Bordeaux, the Pyrenees and Spain. Yet in this rural backwater it is as though the dynamic of the Santiago pilgrimage spread out across the area like a ripple of the nearby ocean, depositing churches as exquisite as jewels in every village. The Saintonge remains one of the great treasuries of Romanesque architecture in France, with more than one hundred churches dating at least in part from the twelfth century, a great many of them magnificently decorated.

Making a selection is inevitably personal, so wide is the choice. One gem is the church at Corme-Royal, a short distance off the main road from Saintes towards the oyster-beds of Marennes. Here the west door of the Church of Saint-Nazaire, protected from the eroding sea-winds by a high wall, is a scaled-down version of the portals at Aulnay and Saintes. The carved images tell familiar stories, the parable of the Wise and Foolish Virgins, figures representing Virtue and Vice, various saints and apostles including one who can only be St James, represented as a pilgrim and carrying a staff – as he frequently is in church paintings and illuminated manuscripts: the apostle as a pilgrim travelling to his own shrine.

A few miles away is Notre-Dame in Rioux, one of the most perfect churches in the Saintonge. Now the decoration across the entire face of the church is geometrical: diamond patterns, shell shapes, floral motifs, zigzags, criss-crosses, curlicues, chevrons, dogs-teeth, stylised foliage twisting and entwining on and on, as well as numerous other motifs spread everywhere. Scarcely a block of stone is left bare. If a church could be embroidered, it is Rioux.[16] Then, unexpectedly amid all this geometry, set into the central arch above the west door, is a carving of a smiling Madonna and Child so touching it would grace any museum in the world.

Then, after Rioux – Marignac, and Saint-Sulpice, its facade weathered by the Atlantic gales, its three-lobed apse commanding a landscape of vines and crumbling stone barns; further east, Saint-Martin at Chadenac, with its elegant figures of archangels whose robes ripple and billow like those of a Botticelli Venus, and which the great American scholar of the pilgrim roads, Arthur Kingsley Porter, considered to be finer even than the figures on the west door of Chartres; a short distance further, Échebrune, where the Church of Saint-Pierre is tucked into the woods with another facade of geometrical tracery, and whose lower columns display crude graffiti of a procession of pilgrims recognisable by their hats and staves[17]; and Perignac, where another Church of Saint-Pierre is fringed today by Cognac vineyards, with its wonderful mandorla, or oval-shaped

16. See Plate 7.

17. See Plate 8.

panel, of Christ flanked by two archangels with flowing robes, and an extraordinary band of horses' heads high above the west window.

The Saintonge offers a banquet of the Romanesque. And Romanesque is quintessentially the architecture of the pilgrim roads. When the monk of Cluny, Raoul Glaber, wrote that 'even the little churches in the villages were reconstructed by the faithful more beautiful than before' he would have been thinking mostly of his native Burgundy, and at a time at least a century before these little churches of the Saintonge were created. Had he lived in the twelfth rather than the eleventh century Glaber would certainly have warmed just as fulsomely to these little jewel-boxes on the far side of France. And his celebrated observation about the world 'casting aside its old age and clothing itself anew in a whiter mantle of churches' would have applied just as vividly here near the windswept shores of the Atlantic as in the sheltered plains of Burgundy.

5. Battles Long Ago

A GREAT DEAL MORE EVIDENCE SURVIVES of where pilgrims prayed than where they slept. Occasionally, though, the pilgrim roads offer a surprise. Half a day's journey on foot from Saintes took travellers to Pons. Today a motorway bypasses the town, and so does the local main road which preceded it, the N137. As a result, what was once the Bordeaux road out of town appears abandoned in the past, which has happily enabled a unique treasure to be preserved. This is the remains of a twelfth-century pilgrims' hospice, described ironically as the *Hôpital Neuf*, the New Hospital. The main building was long ago converted to domestic and other uses; but what has survived is its stone entrance by the side of the old road, and that of the chapel facing it, as well as more than twenty yards of stone arches which linked the two and gave pilgrims protection from the elements while they waited to be admitted at nightfall. And here is where they sat, resting after the day's long slog in the heat, whiling away the time.

We can still feel their presence, because scattered around these handsome Romanesque arches and columns are the marks which those pilgrims left while they waited on the broad stone benches provided. They are travellers' graffiti scratched deep in the stone. Some are little stylised human figures, perhaps semi-comic self-portraits. There are a number of crosses of different kinds, and at least one heraldic shield, evidently of some passing nobleman not so proud as to spurn a humble hospice. But for the most part the marks are inverted horseshoes, many of them with a cross set within, and which would have been instantly recognisable to everyone as a pilgrim's symbol – a traveller with a mission. They are strangely moving, these personal autographs: they remind us how little there is along the pilgrim roads which speaks of individual people undertaking this journey. Gazing at this graffiti at Pons we are suddenly made conscious that pilgrimages were about human traffic – made up of vulnerable, hopeful people whose homes were far away, seeking a place to rest and feed, and the warm company of fellow-travellers. To be a pilgrim was to be a member of a rather special club. And these marks scratched into the wall were a kind of membership badge.

Most pilgrims would have been strangers – even foreigners – in every place they stopped. Their looks, and certainly their language, would have been locally unfamiliar. So, like their customary outfit of staff, wallet, hat and scallop-shell, pictorial symbols like these would help identify a stranger's purpose for being on the road, or asking for food and shelter for the night. They would also have contributed to the protection which the pilgrim was entitled to enjoy. An eleventh-century Archbishop of Lyon made this pronouncement: 'All those who travel to the shrines of the saints are safeguarded against attack at all time.' Early in the following century the Lateran Council in Rome decreed that anyone who robbed a pilgrim would be punished by excommunication. This decree was to prove of considerable benefit to Santiago pilgrims, and it can hardly be a coincidence that the pope who issued it was none other than Calixtus II, the very pontiff credited (albeit falsely) with being the author of part of *The Pilgrim's Guide*. Maybe it was a form of posthumous thanks by those who compiled the text to a Church leader who had done so much in his lifetime for the wellbeing of pilgrims.

Hence the pilgrim came to be protected by a form of international law: and the same legal protection also absolved him from paying tolls and tariffs on his travels, as well as entitling him to charity and to safe conduct. Anyone robbing or attempting to kill him was now liable to the severest of all punishments in a Christian world, namely the punishment of God who was held to be the pilgrim's divine guardian.

A further protection consisted of the credentials he carried with him. These would have been provided probably by his local priest; or possibly by the local lord to whom he was a vassal and who under the terms of feudal law effectively owned him, and whose permission to depart on pilgrimage would have been essential. Besides such documentation the pilgrim also benefited from the medieval code of chivalry as practised above all by the various religious orders of knighthood which were springing up at this time, in particular the Knights Templars and the Knights Hospitallers. The Templars, the 'Poor Knights of Christ and of the Temple of Solomon', had been established in the wake of the First Crusade in order to protect holy places in Palestine which had been 'liberated' from the Infidel; while the role of the Hospitallers, who were the Knights of St John of Jerusalem, was to protect Christian pilgrims visiting those sites. Both knightly orders were keen to extend their traditional duties to safeguarding the roads to Spain on the grounds that pilgrims to Santiago were seen to be engaged in the same Holy War as the crusaders by contributing indirectly to the Reconquest of Spain. Accordingly both the Templars and Hospitallers became as prominent as the Church itself in providing facilities for the welfare of pilgrims in the form of hospices and fortified garrisons – if necessary supplying armed protection against bandits and wayside robbers. They acted as benevolent hosts and a police force at the same time.

Hospices, like the one at Pons, were generally attached to some religious house, either an abbey, a priory or a fortified *commanderie* of the knights. They varied considerably in the services they provided. Most were fairly basic, offering the simplest of meals with maybe some sour wine if the pilgrim was lucky; otherwise it was just bread and water, followed by a bare room with a large straw mattress on the floor on which a varying number of people would be required to sleep, accompanied by an even larger population of lice and fleas. But there were also more comfortable establishments, particularly where the presiding monastery had grown wealthy through donations, or where the Christian ethic of charity towards the poor prevailed. And pilgrims were of course supposed to be poor, even if there were noblemen who made the journey accompanied by a retinue of servants. Besides the rudimentary hospices there were also inns, for which the pilgrim needed to pay. These were often identified by scallop-shell images fixed to the wall, or by some other traveller's symbol. What pilgrims received for their money evidently varied: if *The Pilgrim's Guide* is to be believed, medieval inn-keepers, along with ferrymen and toll-gatherers, tended to deserve all those punishments of Hell so gruesomely described in church carvings all along the pilgrim roads.

*

Those jewel-box churches of the Saintonge are never far from the salt spray of the Atlantic; but one of them is perched on the very edge of the ocean. This is the Church of Sainte-Radegonde at Talmont, high on a cliff-edge close to the broad mouth of the Gironde estuary. All buildings and walls that once surrounded it have long ago fallen into the water, leaving the church perilously alone, battered by the winds and tides. In the Middle Ages pilgrims coming to Talmont were those who had skirted the coast from Brittany, and now needed to cross the estuary before continuing their journey south across what today are some of the rich Bordeaux vineyards of the Médoc. But their immediate destination was a deep natural harbour on the far shore of the estuary. This was Soulac. And here they were liable to find themselves in unexpected company. Anchored in that deep harbour, long since swallowed up by the Atlantic, there would often be one or more trading vessels which had just reached these shores having survived a stormy voyage across the Bay of Biscay and, before that, the English Channel. The cargo they would soon be loading for the return voyage consisted of oak kegs of Bordeaux wine destined for the dinner tables of the well-to-do in London, Winchester and Canterbury. The ships would be capable of storing huge quantities since they were now emptied of the cargo they had brought here from England. That cargo was... pilgrims.

It was a profitable two-way traffic, particularly once England came to own this whole region of France in the mid-twelfth century.

The only losers in this busy trade were the English wine-growers who – largely for reasons of climate – could never hope to compete with those of Bordeaux: hence the long decline of the English wine industry. So the English gentry developed a taste for French wines, while English pilgrims took advantage of a short-cut on their way to Santiago.

The most popular sea route to and from England was from the port of Bristol, in the west of the country and therefore conveniently placed for access to the Atlantic. The number of English travellers undertaking the pilgrimage to Santiago is unknown, though some idea of its popularity may be gauged by the fact that there could be as many as six English vessels moored in the harbour at Soulac at any one time. Another clue to numbers is the fact that more than four hundred English churches are known to have been dedicated to St James during the Middle Ages. One of these churches, in the village of Stoke Orchard in Gloucestershire, even possesses one of the earliest known cycles of wall-paintings on the life and legend of St James: these date from the early thirteenth century and are more or less contemporaneous with the famous stained-glass windows on the same theme in the French cathedrals of Chartres and Bourges.

For English pilgrims to Santiago the golden age was the twelfth century, as it was for pilgrims in France and other countries. Numerous conditions made this possible. This was an era of relative peace in Western Europe. The institutions of the Church had grown stronger and more influential, creating a stabilising effect on society as a whole, and accordingly making people's lives generally more secure. Much of this sense of security was the product of the new feudalism which now controlled European society. Bred out of the chaos of the later Dark Ages, feudalism was a finely balanced ladder of legal obligations whose rungs stretched across every layer of society from monarch down to serf. Everyone was subject to the authority of someone above them, from the lowly to the highest. Feudalism had emerged in response to a desperate need to deal with foreign invasions that had repeatedly ravaged the continent of Europe since the eighth century. The lynchpin of the whole system was the local lord, to whom everyone on his lands owed allegiance as a vassal. He ruled and effectively owned them, and in return he was obliged to protect them. His castle was his fortress, paid for by the taxes he exacted. Yet the local lord had his obligations too: he was the vassal of some overlord. Only the king, or the pope, at the top of the ladder, were exempt – except that they needed to regard themselves as vassals too... of God.

Feudalism had been brought to England as a result of the Norman Conquest in 1066. Over the following centuries, and in France and elsewhere in Europe, it resulted in the kind of well-ordered society in which pilgrims in ever greater numbers could feel secure enough to embark on a pilgrimage for six months without the fear of their legal rights or their property being removed in their absence. Pilgrims were now protected by royal decree as well as by papal decree.

This was the social climate which enabled Chaucer's motley bunch of pilgrims to undertake their cheerful journey to Canterbury, telling stories as they went. One robust member of that company was the formidable Wife of Bath, who had been married in church to five husbands, not to mention enjoying 'oother compaignye in youthe'. She was a lady who had found the time and the means to travel to Jerusalem no fewer than three times, in addition to having made her own pilgrimage to Santiago, as Chaucer respectfully explains – though in what spirit Chaucer spares us the details.

The fact that England owned and ruled this region of France greatly facilitated the movement of English pilgrims embarking near Bordeaux before making their way south towards Spain. In any case, the Kings of England were at this time considerably more French than English: the ruling Plantagenet dynasty originated from the Counts of Anjou, on the Loire. The English monarchs spoke French as their first language and generally spent considerably more time in France than in England. And since they also came to own – through marriage – vast chunks of what is now France there was no meaningful distinction between 'home' and 'abroad'.

Equally important for the pilgrimage movement were the strong links which the Church in England had established with the monastic orders in France. These were orders deeply committed to sponsoring the Santiago pilgrimage, to a large extent for political reasons relating to the Reconquest of Spain. Pilgrimage and Reconquest were virtually synonymous in the minds of Church leaders. At the gateway of Spain the Augustinian monastery of Roncesvalles, high in the Pyrenees, kept a hospice in London, at Charing Cross. This London hospice also acted as an information centre for prospective pilgrims to Santiago, supplying names of places along the route in France and Spain where pilgrims could safely lodge. But chief among these monastic orders were the immensely powerful Benedictines of Cluny. In the years immediately following the Norman Conquest the great Burgundian abbey of Cluny supplied monks to a number of new monastic foundations in England, principally Lewes Priory (founded by William the Conqueror in 1077), Faversham (founded by King Stephen), and the royal abbey of Reading, founded by the Conqueror's son Henry I, whose daughter Matilda made the pilgrimage to Santiago in about the year 1125. Here she was presented with no less a holy relic than a hand of St James, which on her return she presented to her father's abbey, immediately making Reading the focus of the St James cult in England.

*

Such was the background to those English vessels moored in the harbour of Soulac, having shed their cargo of pilgrims who would now be heading south across the Médoc lowlands before joining up with the principal body of French, German and other pilgrims as they approached Bordeaux.

A short distance inland the main pilgrim road continued south from Saintes and Pons, keeping the broad estuary of the Gironde just out of sight until eventually it reached the water's edge at the old Roman town of Blaye. Here, a few miles north of Bordeaux, medieval pilgrims made their first encounter with an enduring legend which lies at the very root of the St James story. In a church on the seashore at Blaye, so *The Pilgrim's Guide* explains, 'the remains of the Blessed Roland the martyr rest. Belonging to the noble family circle of Charlemagne, he entered Spain in order to expel the Infidel.' The legend relates to the emperor's campaign in Spain in the year 778 in which Roland, Count of Brittany and nephew of Charlemagne, was killed in an ambush on the emperor's rearguard in the Pyrenees above Roncesvalles, having famously blown his ivory horn too late to alert the emperor. Accordingly a grief-stricken Charlemagne then built a church at Blaye in which to bury his beloved nephew and military commander.

The key to the legend is the first French epic poem, *La Chanson de Roland*, The Song of Roland. This survives in various versions first written down (in Old French) around the middle of the twelfth century, but was certainly recited by travelling poet-minstrels along the pilgrim roads long before that time. The *Chanson* is a highly romanticised account of Charlemagne's Spanish campaign culminating in Roland's three mighty blasts on his horn before he dies.

How the Charlemagne legend became attached to that of St James and to the Santiago pilgrimage has long been a subject of heated debate among scholars, kept permanently on the boil since there can never be a definitive answer. However, most eyes have been pointed in one direction as the place most likely to have been the key player in creating the link: and as so often in the story of the pilgrimage that place is the great Burgundian abbey of Cluny, which had a profound commitment to the Santiago pilgrimage as well as to the Reconquest of Spain. We know that passages of *La Chanson de Roland* were regularly recited, or sung, along the pilgrim roads by poet-minstrels for the entertainment of travellers. But they also sang *Chansons de Saint-Jacques*, Songs of St James, which told of the many miracles which the saint had performed, and his numerous heroic deeds against the Saracens in the cause of the Reconquest. A number of these pilgrims' songs are recorded in the *Codex Calixtinus*, the manuscript which includes *The Pilgrim's Guide*, one of these songs appearing in the name of the *Guide*'s likely author, Aimery Picaud. And since its final words are that it was written 'mainly in Cluny', it is hard not to see the Song of Roland and the Songs of St James as having been promoted, at least, by the abbey in order to add heroism and prestige to the Santiago pilgrimage, colouring it with the authority of history.

But the strongest link between the Charlemagne legend and the pilgrimage is again provided by the *Codex*. One section of the manuscript is the so-called chronicle of Archbishop Turpin, the *Historia Caroli Magna*, the History of Charlemagne. Turpin was an eighth-century archbishop who also features in the Song of Roland as one of Charlemagne's trustiest warriors in his Spanish campaign. And there is no doubt that he existed. Yet his chronicle, as it appears in the *Codex*, is generally described as the *Pseudo-Turpin* on the grounds that Turpin himself had nothing whatever to do with it, since it was written at least three centuries later. As with the attribution of *The Pilgrim's Guide* to Pope Calixtus II this is another case of imaginative name-dropping. The preface to the chronicle presents Turpin as 'archbishop of Reims and faithful companion of Charlemagne in Spain'. In this latter role Turpin becomes the eye-witness to Charlemagne's campaigns, during which the emperor has a mysterious dream of the Milky Way as a kind of celestial signpost directing him westwards. Its significance is then explained to him by the appearance in his dream of the apostle St James. The stars, he is told, are beckoning him to the saint's tomb (as yet undiscovered). But at present the road to the tomb is overrun by the Infidel, and urgently needs to be opened up and safeguarded in order that pilgrims may travel there and venerate the saint.

Such is the clear message of the chronicle. As it happens *La Chanson de Roland* also contains the story of Charlemagne's dream: but the account in the chronicle of Turpin differs from it in one crucial respect. In the Song of Roland the emperor is visited by the archangel Gabriel. But in the Turpin chronicle the visitor has become the apostle St James, so giving the story an entirely new slant. Now Charlemagne is not only the champion of Christianity and of the Reconquest of Spain, but has become specifically the champion of St James, the first man to be made aware of the apostle's tomb, and therefore destined to become the very first pilgrim to Santiago.

Whereas the Song of Roland hailed the triumph of Christianity over Islam, the chronicle of Turpin hailed the triumph of St James. The shift of emphasis is so deliberate that it can only have been written in order to boost the cult of St James and the Santiago pilgrimage. And in doing so it was hugely successful. More than two hundred manuscripts of Archbishop Turpin's chronicle have survived, either in Latin or in Old French, so matching the distribution of *The Pilgrim's Guide*, and offering a testimony to its extraordinary popularity throughout twelfth-century France. It became the basis of the widespread belief, held by churchmen and pilgrims alike, that the Emperor Charlemagne was indeed the founding father of the Santiago pilgrimage.

From now onwards all humble souls who trudged wearily across France and northern Spain in order to pray at the apostle's shrine did so in the footsteps of the very first Holy Roman Emperor. It was a psychological masterstroke. More even than the Song of Roland it gave the journey to Santiago impeccable historical credentials, and a welcome touch of glamour.

The chronicle of Archbishop Turpin was of course a fabrication. Yet it seems to have had its roots in popular legend. Its most likely source was those fanciful pilgrims' songs, *chansons de geste*, which had been recited along the pilgrim roads probably for centuries, passed orally from singer to singer, with appropriate elaborations along the way. Then at some stage, in the eleventh or twelfth century, these tales had been cobbled together and written down as a coherent story. But by whom? Theories abound. The cathedral authorities in Santiago have been named, as have various monasteries in France with vested interests in the pilgrimage, including of course Cluny. Copies were subsequently made by scribes in any number of abbeys which possessed a *scriptorium*; and we need to imagine that passing pilgrims, the majority of them illiterate, would have passages read out to them to cheer them on their way.

To what extent all this was a deliberate exercise in propaganda, designed to promote the Santiago pilgrimage, is peculiarly hard to judge. Seen through the lens of our own times it is tempting to envisage some proto-Machiavellian spirit at work conducting a skilful operation exploiting the susceptibilities of ignorant people. There have been scholarly voices claiming that the Turpin chronicle, along with the pilgrims' songs, even the Song of Roland itself, were all purposely sponsored by Church authorities with vested interests in the opening-up of Spain and the expulsion of the Muslims. But to adopt such a modern viewpoint may be a failure to comprehend the workings of the medieval mind, and in particular the essentially mystic nature of the medieval religious experience. When considering these distant legends, and the social context in which they were recounted from generation to generation, we are reaching back into a time when in the minds of ordinary people distinctions between fact and fiction, history and myth, truths and make-believe, were largely blurred. In the words of Johan Huizinga, 'in more than one respect life had the colours of a fairy-tale'.

The essence of all fairy tales, as of legends, is that they are not presented as historical fact, but as a kind of metaphor. Part of their appeal is that they cast a certain light on the human condition – which in the Middle Ages was perceived by and large to be bleak. Fear of damnation was rife, and those fears were stimulated by sermons from the pulpit and by sermons in stone carved on church portals all along the pilgrim roads. Beyond the Christian world the human lot was perceived to be even worse. The Roland legend and the legend of St James tell of people in Spain under the yoke of Islam and therefore living in darkness. These legends, relating the rich exploits of Charlemagne, Roland and St James offered the promise of release, both for the pilgrim personally and for those living under the shadow of Islam. The triumph of Charlemagne represented the triumph of Christianity, of light over darkness. His legend charted a path of bright stars, the Milky Way, by which people could move out of the darkness of their own lives into the enduring light cast by the Christian God.

These stories were metaphors for human salvation, and as such they answered a vast need: hence their popularity. The fact that the legends were – to our modern eyes – simply fiction, not historical fact, is beside the point. The poets who sang them, and those who wrote them down, copied and translated them, were not passing these stories off as literally true. This was not what concerned them. They were like parables, or morality plays. The truth in them lay in what these legends revealed, that God is the path to a better life, and that through worship and love of God human beings can lift themselves out of the miseries of this world into the glories of the next.

In other words, 'truth' is what lies embedded in these legends, not in their historical accuracy. This is a concept that modern consciousness may find particularly hard to grasp. Yet without doing so one of the most inspired social movements in history, the Santiago pilgrimage, runs the risk of being seen as merely the product of an unprincipled and exploitative Church manipulating its gullible congregation like sheep to further its own ambitions – which would be a sad and misguided distortion. This book, at least, would not be written if that was believed to be so.

The question remains: where should we look for the source of energy and inspiration behind the dissemination of these vivid tales which fed the pilgrimage movement with poetry, song and romance? Where was the fountain-head? Inevitably, we look again towards the heartland of Christian pilgrimage, whether in the form of the crusades, or the cult of Rome, or that of Santiago. And that place is Burgundy, and in particular the formidable abbey of Cluny – wealthy, immensely influential and politically minded, courted by popes and emperors, and patrons of both. The bejewelled hand of Cluny, and of its succession of gifted abbots, touches so many aspects of the Santiago story, as we have already seen. A driving ambition of those abbots, in the eleventh and twelfth centuries, was to establish the power and influence of the French Church throughout northern Spain. Support for the Santiago pilgrimage was a key element in that ambition, and it led to Cluny helping to establish hospices and priories along the Spanish pilgrim road, as we shall see in the final section of this book. But in order to safeguard the road, and the institutions that were strung along it, it was vitally necessary to provide support for the beleaguered Christian rulers in Spain. Cluny itself could not supply military aid; yet it can be no coincidence that the most successful campaigns against the Saracens were those led by knights from Burgundy, many of them no doubt related to the lordly monks of Cluny who would also have been their spiritual mentors.

This was feudal France: and the top echelon of that feudal society was like an elite club whose members all shared the wealth and privilege of high birth, and were made up of Church leaders, senior monks in the local monasteries and priories, and the various lords and landowners of the area. In this latter category were these Burgundian knights who raised local armies, consisting largely of their own serfs, then crossed the Pyrenees in order to drive the Moors from Spain – all of them riding in the wake of Charlemagne, with *La Chanson de Roland* echoing in their ears, and brandishing the avenging sword of St James in the spirit of Santiago Matamoros.

It was heady stuff. This was a multifaceted feudal world in which spiritual values and a life of violent action were inextricably bound together. And if in this confusing theatre of war and peace the abbey of Cluny was indeed the command-post, it is impossible to imagine those wise, and worldly-wise abbots experiencing even a shadow of doubt over the rightness of their vast enterprises. The pilgrimage and the Reconquest – they were twin paths in a single journey into the light.

Meanwhile, in Blaye, on the broad estuary of the Gironde opening on to the Atlantic Ocean, today's traveller may well feel that the story of Roland sounding his horn three times before dying in battle and being buried here by Charlemagne is yet another of those fairy tales; because nothing remains here which speaks of that tale. Charlemagne's church and Roland's body have long gone, victims of the English army during the Hundred Years' War in the fifteenth century. On another of the four pilgrim's roads the traveller will later be shown what is claimed to be the very horn Roland blew near Roncesvalles – his famous oliphant. But for the time being the traveller on this pilgrim road can do little more than sit on the shore and reflect on one of the most beguiling legends of the Middle Ages – one that lies at the very core of the Santiago pilgrimage.

6. To the Bad Lands... and the Good Lands

BORDEAUX WAS THE CAPITAL AND CHIEF PORT of this extensive region of France which belonged to England at that time, known as Aquitaine. In fact, one of the main attractions for Santiago pilgrims as they reached Bordeaux was a particularly well-equipped hospice dedicated to the apostle yet in the English version of his name, St James, rather than the customary French Saint-Jacques. The Hôpital Saint-James was an English endowment, the main donor being the English King Henry II in the year 1181. It had been Henry's marriage to Eleanor, Duchess of Aquitaine, which had brought this region under the English crown.

The Pilgrim's Guide has surprisingly little to say about Bordeaux beyond the observation that the region is 'excellent in wine and abundant in fish', with which any modern traveller would be happy to agree. By now it is beginning to give off a clear message to pilgrims, to the effect that the good times are by and large over, at least until they get deep into Spain. But then the likely author of this section of the *Guide*, Aimery Picaud, was a man fiercely parochial about his native Poitou and the larger region of Aquitaine of which it formed a part, to the extent of finding it grudgingly hard to write anything good about people unfortunate enough to live elsewhere. It is just as well that most medieval pilgrims were illiterate, or at this stage of their journey they would certainly not be looking forward to what was in store for them in the days ahead. Their immediate prospect was to tackle the Landes.

Today the Landes is a national forest, one of the largest in Europe, composed mostly of Maritime Pine. But in Picaud's day most of it was swamp, and about as inhospitable as a landscape could be. We know that he did this journey himself once if not twice; so his description of the Landes is unlikely to have been entirely coloured by prejudice. 'This is a desolate region deprived of all good,' he begins. 'There is here no bread, wine, meat, fish, water or springs; and villages are rare here.' He then manages to offer a few words of praise in passing. 'The sandy and flat land abounds none the less in honey, millet, grasses and wild boar. But if perchance you should cross it in summer, guard your face diligently from the enormous flies that greatly abound there and are called locally wasps or horse-flies; and if you do not watch your feet carefully you will rapidly sink up to the knees in the wet sand copiously found all over.'

Nobody is spared the wasps and horseflies today, though the knee-deep swamps of the Landes have long been drained. But we know Picaud was not exaggerating. The modern traveller keen to savour what life was really like here in earlier times would do well to take time off in Bordeaux to visit the Museum of Fine Arts. Here there are romanticised paintings dating from the early nineteenth century, not long before the swamps were finally drained; and they show local shepherds coping deftly with the swampy terrain by going about their work on immensely tall stilts like well-practised circus clowns.

The old pilgrim road slices through the centre of the Landes from north to south, now flanked mostly by pine- and oak-forest, with the occasional clearing where geese bred for *foie gras* wander around in the company of pigs whose distant ancestors Picaud described. A few survivors of the medieval pilgrimage remain, dwarfed by the trees. At Cayac stand the remains of a priory and ancient hospice reminiscent of the one straddling the road at Pons. Here and there on the route beyond Cayac the occasional medieval chapel still lines the old road, long battered by sea-winds; then an ancient stone preaching cross rises up by the roadside, and another former priory church huddled among trees; then on to Belin where a burial mound is traditionally believed to contain the bodies of Charlemagne's warriors killed alongside Roland near Roncesvalles. Belin possesses one further claim to historical fame: it was the birthplace of Eleanor of Aquitaine, the heiress whose marriage to King Henry II of England in 1152, as we have seen earlier, was very soon to bring this entire region into the possession of the English crown, where it remained for the next three centuries.

Finally the vast forest comes to an end, and the landscape softens and opens out into fertile meadows. Across the River Adour and the traveller is now in Gascony – about which *The Pilgrim's Guide* has suddenly a great deal to say. At first Aimery Picaud seems to have had a good experience of Gascony: 'rich in white bread and excellent red wine, and covered by woods and fields, streams and healthy springs.' But then he encounters the local people, and the tone changes. 'The Gascons are quick with words, loquacious, given to mockery, libidinous, drunk, prodigal in their eating habits, ill-dressed and rather careless in the ornaments they wear. However, they are well-trained in combat and generous in the hospitality they provide for the poor.' In other words, they were protective and kind towards pilgrims, which almost redeems them in Picaud's eyes.

As the journey towards Santiago progresses *The Pilgrim's Guide* becomes as much a twelfth-century social document as it is a guidebook. And if the chapter on the people and places along the route, as well as several chapters following, are indeed the work of Aimery Picaud, then we find ourselves building up a character-portrait of this cantankerous, pleasure-loving monk from Parthenay-le-Vieux whose abbey church we so recently visited back in his native Poitou. The strength and appeal of his writing lies in the way we are drawn into envisaging him like any modern traveller venturing into unfamiliar lands, noting whatever strikes him and sometimes being taken aback by how different people's habits can be. Hence his extremely mixed feelings about the behaviour of the Gascons: 'Seated around the fire, their practice is to eat without a table and to drink all of them from a single cup. In fact they eat and drink a lot, wear rather poor clothes, and lie down shamelessly on a thin and rotten straw mattress, the servants along with the master and the mistress.'

The eating and sleeping habits of the Gascons were probably the least of a pilgrim's concerns on the road towards the Pyrenees. This was a stretch renowned for being particularly dangerous, doubtless due to the greater concentration of travellers making their way to Spain across the few mountain passes. For all the papal threats of excommunication bands of robbers were everywhere, some of them canny enough to pose as pilgrims with the appropriate clothing. Travellers making the long journey to Santiago were especially vulnerable since they were likely to be carrying most of their worldly possessions with them, such as they were. There is even a record of a blind pilgrim travelling on horseback who was robbed of his money *and* his horse, to be found later wandering helplessly by the roadside.

The journey could be hazardous enough even without the threat of robbery, as Picaud's account of the Landes swamps makes all too clear. At the same time the idea of a hazardous journey was not entirely unwelcome. Whatever the personal motive might be, the pilgrimage was supposed to be a spiritual journey – an expression of penance and a quest for the remission of a person's sins. It was a path to salvation, and this was not a path that was ever intended to be rose-scented. On the contrary it was supposed to be stony. Mortification of the flesh was regarded as a passport to heaven. One of the attractions of the journey was that it was arduous and demanding: in the eyes of the medieval Church physical hardship was a necessary and healing aspect of that journey. In the early centuries of the pilgrimage at least, the long trek to Santiago was certainly not supposed to be a pleasure trip.

Parallel to the celebration of physical hardship lay the cult of poverty. Avarice was a cardinal sin in medieval Church teaching, and to hoard money was the act of a miser, or so ordinary people were told. Congregations were reminded in sermons of the teaching of Christ that it was 'easier for a camel to pass through the eye of a needle than for a rich man to enter the kingdom of God'. (The fact that churches and religious institutions frequently behaved otherwise was conveniently overlooked.) The personification of this poverty cult, early in the thirteenth century, was St Francis of Assisi; and it would have surprised none of his followers that St Francis chose to include Santiago among his numerous barefooted travels. There could have been no more influential a role model: the most celebrated pauper of the day became the most celebrated pilgrim of the day. By his own exalted example, and by his preaching of the virtue of poverty, St Francis greatly broadened the appeal of the pilgrimage – ironically among the rich as much as among the poor. Furthermore the Franciscan Order, founded by the saint, proceeded to contribute to the pilgrimage movement, adding further to the support already given by other religious orders, in particular the Benedictines and Augustinians, and later the Cistercians.

The Pilgrim Guide's suspicions of the Gascons grow darker the further the author travels from his beloved Aquitaine, and ventures deeper into what he considers to be 'barbarous' country in the approaches to the Pyrenees. How much his account of events derives from first-hand experience is impossible to tell; but there comes a point in his account when he feels it imperative to offer the severest warning to all pilgrims travelling this road. The place is the riverside village of Sorde, then a popular stopping-point for pilgrims on account of its important Benedictine abbey, today in a semi-ruined state draped in ivy (perhaps held together by ivy), but dramatically situated by the water's edge, with a long curving weir stretching away towards the far bank.

There was no bridge, and the only means of crossing this river was by raft. And here, Picaud explains ruefully, the pilgrim was at the mercy of the local ferrymen – 'and may they all be damned,' he fulminates.

> They have the habit of demanding one coin from each man they ferry over; whether rich or poor, and for a horse they ignominiously extort by force four coins. Now, their boat is small, made of a single tree, hardly capable of conveying horses. Also, when boarding it one must be most careful not to fall accidentally into the water. You will do well to pull

> your horses by the reins behind you in the river, outside the boat, and to embark with only a few passengers, for if it is overloaded it will soon become dangerous. Also, many times the ferryman, having by this time taken his money, now has so large a cargo of pilgrims in his boat that it capsizes and the pilgrims all drown; upon which the boatmen, having laid their hands on the spoils of the dead, wickedly rejoice.

Perhaps Picaud had observed such a scene himself, or more likely it was a favourite piece of juicy gossip being bandied about in the local inn over a jar of wine. We are reminded, reading his account, that it was intended only for the tiny minority of pilgrims who were literate, and in consequence likely to be better off than most, and probably making the pilgrimage on horseback – as Picaud himself would have done. They were, after all, supposedly a party of three pilgrims, the other two being a man and his (supposed) wife. Picaud's description of the ferrymen's murderous behaviour at Sorde raises the question of whether he made not one pilgrimage, but two. If the account is based on a personal experience, or at least on stories told to him locally, then the journey to present the *Codex Calixtinus* manuscript to Santiago cathedral must have been on a subsequent occasion, since the *Guide*'s account of evil-doings at Sorde are contained in the *Codex* itself.

From Sorde pilgrims had a choice of two roads leading south towards the Pyrenees, depending on whether they had risked the river crossing or wisely continued westwards until a bridge took them on to the old Roman road. Either route led them into the Basque Country, At this point Picaud offers some robust observations. 'This land whose language is barbarous, is wooded, mountainous, devoid of bread, wine, and all sorts of food for the body, except that in compensation it abounds in apples, cider and milk.'

Picaud regarded the Basque language as barbarous because it was incomprehensible to him. As a monk he would have understood Latin, and spoken any one or more of the local languages, or dialects, all of which derived from Latin – which Basque does not. It is one of the oldest languages in Europe, with its roots deeper than Ancient Greek and Latin and still largely mysterious. Picaud is quite likely to have thought of it as the language of the Devil. He may even have known the story of how the Devil, keen to win the Basques to his side, set himself to learn their language: and in seven years managed to learn three words. Today's travellers in the region may find themselves faring little better.

Village follows village very closely in the Basque Country, always with the snow-covered peaks of the Pyrenees drawn like a long curtain across the road ahead, drawing closer hour by hour. Here and there a house is still marked *Pelegrinia*; a reminder that we are now entering the region where pilgrim roads from far-distant parts of France draw closer together and finally converge. At the height of the Santiago pilgrimage, in the twelfth and thirteen centuries, virtually every house in these Basque villages would have offered accommodation – like a modern bed-and-breakfast. It was a regular source of local income during the spring and summer months, and innkeepers would compete with each other for trade, often posting their male children in the street to invite passing pilgrims in. Picaud was as suspicious of such innkeepers as he was of ferrymen.

They were not the only locals he despised. There was a third category of predator of whom the *Guide* warns pilgrims to be especially wary. 'In this land,' writes Picaud,

> ...in the town called Ostabat ... there are evil toll-gatherers who will certainly be damned through and through. In truth they will actually advance towards pilgrims carrying two or three wooden rods, and proceed to extort by force a totally unjust tribute. And if some traveller should refuse to hand over the money on demand they then beat him with the rods and seize the toll money while cursing him and searching even in his breeches. These are ferocious people, and the land in which they dwell is savage, wooded and barbarous. The ferocity of their faces and likewise of their barbarous speech scares the wits out of anyone who sees them.

He goes on to point out that pilgrims were, in fact, exempt by law from such tolls. This exemption was widely known, though not always widely observed, one reason being that it was also widely abused. Merchants, as well as other kinds of traveller, were well known to pose and dress as pilgrims precisely in order to avoid payments; and it was this practice which may have offered a slender excuse for the behaviour of the Ostabat toll-gatherers, at least in their own eyes.

But the main reason that they gathered in such predatory numbers in this small town was that Ostabat was the very first halt for travellers after the junction of three main pilgrim roads: the one from Paris and the Loire, the road from Vézelay and Burgundy, and that from Le Puy and the mountains of central France. Pilgrims would have collected here from every country in Europe, and for toll-gatherers they were easy prey. They were a source of easy profit for innkeepers as well: in the Middle Ages this small Basque town, hardly more than a village, contained at least twenty hospices. From spring through to autumn there would have been an exceptionally large number of pilgrims from all parts of Europe grateful for a roof and a bed of straw in Ostabat.

Today Ostabat gives out scarcely an echo of what the place must have been like in medieval times. For a more genuine sound of the past the modern traveller needs to leave the main pilgrim road for a short distance and head into the woodlands of the Bois d'Ostabat in search of a tiny community by the name of Harambels. Here survives a fragment of the medieval pilgrimage which the modern world has bypassed. The core of this tiny village consists of four houses and a rugged stone chapel dedicated to St Nicolas, a fourth-century saint widely associated with the giving of gifts (and often believed to be the original Santa Claus). The chapel of Harambels is one of the earliest pilgrim churches in Europe, recorded in documents as early as 1039, at least a century before *The Pilgrim's Guide* was written.[18] The tiny community was built as an extended hospice for pilgrims,

18. See Plate 9.

created by four lay friars who brought their families here. They were all of them Basques, named Salla, Borda, Etcheto and Etcheverry: and such is the timelessness of life in these Basque woodlands that the four houses they built are still owned by the same four families. And the small graveyard beside the chapel is where generations of them have been buried for a millennium.

After the solitude and silence of Harambels the main pilgrim road can seem like a bustling highway – which, relatively speaking, it has been for more than one thousand years. It has been the pilgrims' highway to Spain. The road crosses and re-crosses a fast-flowing river deeply shaded by overhanging trees; and close to one of the bridges is another witness to the history of the pilgrimage – one that is even more secluded than the Harambels chapel. At first it is merely an ordinary track cutting through the undergrowth. Then, as we descend towards the river the track is seen to lead to a line of huge stepping-stones, each well over a yard in diameter, which have been laid in a long curve across the fast current from bank to bank. How old is a stepping-stone? Who can tell? Though there is one thing we *can* tell: these stones must have been put in place at least a thousand years ago, because this simple track, cutting through the forest on either side of the river, is one of the four main pilgrim routes – the one from Le Puy and the Massif Central. The road descends to the river on one side, then on the farther side rises out of the woods to disappear round the flank of the hill to the west.

Where it is heading – out of sight from here – is one of the pivotal points of the entire Santiago pilgrimage. It is a site so understated that you might pass by without even noticing. We are on the crest of a hill the name of which, Mont Saint-Sauveur (Mount St Saviour), at least provides a hint that this is no ordinary hill. The only other clue is a modern *stèle*, a marker-stone, set on an ancient carved gravestone.[19] But then if we stand here and gaze southwards we can pick out three tracks threading their way towards us through the fields and the deep hedgerows from three different directions: and

19. See Plate 10.

from the point where they converge they are joined by a lane which runs down the slope to become a single broad track snaking its way through the rough terrain beyond and over the far hill towards the Pyrenees and the Spanish border now only a few miles away.

The three converging tracks are three of the ancient pilgrim roads – the first the road from Paris which we have been following, the second the road from Vézelay, and the third the road from Le Puy by way of the stepping-stones we saw on the far side of the hill. From this junction-point the three tracks become just one pilgrim road which leads over the Pyrenees – until on the far side of the mountains this will be joined by the fourth road, the one from Arles and Provence, from that point on to become the single Spanish road to Santiago, the *camino*.

But that must wait. Meanwhile today's travellers need to follow in the footsteps of their medieval forebears on the second of those 'four roads to heaven', beginning many hundreds of miles further north among the noble vineyards and fertile valleys of Burgundy, always the heartland of the pilgrimage movement.

II. Via Lemovicencis: The Road from Vézelay

7. The Magdalene and Sacred Theft

VÉZELAY IS THE GREAT CHURCH ON THE HILL – a beacon which has guided pilgrims and other travellers in northern Burgundy for almost a thousand years. Originally it was attached to one of the most renowned of Benedictine abbeys, founded by the local count in the ninth century. Today the abbey is no more, but the church remains. It is now the largest parish church in France, and a masterpiece of medieval art and architecture. Anyone keen to make a study of the Romanesque in France could do no better than to begin here. The former abbey church of Vézelay is quite simply one of the most beautiful buildings in the world.

Such was the prestige of Vézelay in its heyday that two crusades to the Holy Land were launched from here in emotional ceremonies attended by English and French kings. In addition, throughout the Middle Ages it was the starting-point for the second of the four main pilgrim roads to Spain and the shrine of St James in Santiago de Compostela.

The early history of Vézelay is as violent and stormy as that of all early abbeys in France. Founded in the mid-ninth century by Count Girard de Roussillon, it was first established in the valley below (now the village of Saint-Père). Within a very short time this first monastery was plundered by Viking invaders from what is now Normandy, whereupon Count Girard had it rebuilt in a location easier to defend, on the nearby hilltop, and here he installed a group of Benedictine monks. He also acquired the added security of making the new establishment a dependency of the papacy in Rome, so protecting it from grasping local landowners. Nonetheless barbarian invasions continued early into the tenth century, not only by the Vikings from the north, but by the Magyars from the east (the region of Central Europe which is now Hungary). It was the most anarchic period in European history, and the new Vézelay, along with much of Burgundy to the south of it, was repeatedly pillaged and wrecked.

The early fate of the abbey mirrors that of France as a whole during these years. This was the Dark Ages at its darkest. It is hardly surprising that few people ventured on pilgrimage in so unsafe a world. The Christian empire which Charlemagne established late in the eighth century out of the ashes of the former Roman Empire soon collapsed and disintegrated, resulting in a plethora of weak little European kingdoms which could do nothing to resist invaders hungry to pluck the flesh off the body of the old empire. France was especially vulnerable, being geographically placed to tempt Saracen invasions from Spain, Viking onslaughts from the north and the Magyars from the east. The economy was crippled: agriculture declined as villages became devastated and deserted, and arable lands returned to forest and wasteland. Life was at a standstill, at best a grim struggle, as people could do little more than rescue what they could from the flood-tide of anarchy. Nothing was safe, and nothing was sacred. Europe bled and burned.

What eventually turned the tide was a combination of various factors, all coming together at much the same time. Crucially, the Norman Vikings finally settled down: early in the tenth century a peace treaty was signed with the powers in France, and Normandy became Christianised, and a powerful independent duchy. One major menace was thus removed. Piety had taken over from piracy. Then, as outlined in Chapter 5, there was the impact of the new strict social order of feudalism. By structuring everyone's life from the highest to the lowest feudalism had the effect of stabilising society as a whole. People knew precisely where they stood, and what their duties and obligations were, from monarch to count to humble serf. For the first time since the centuries of the Roman Empire society became ordered. One of the duties of a local lord was to be able to raise an army whenever necessary from the serfs who were at his disposal. As a result feudalism created a military structure within that society which at last proved capable of dealing with Saracen and Magyar onslaughts. Force could now be met with force. In turn, protection from repeated attack brought about a revival of agriculture, and hence of the economy in general: farmers could now grow crops and graze animals without the fear of them being burnt or driven off.

By no means least, feudalism greatly strengthened the various institutions of the Church, supplying them with legal powers and with a moral authority which had the effect of making them pivotal to the day-to-day life and wellbeing of a community. Altogether life began to feel safer and more benign. A human condition scarcely enjoyed for centuries was suddenly available – a sense of peace. In the words of a distinguished medievalist, Professor Joan Evans, 'it seems as if Europe settled on an even keel'.

With relative peace and economic stability it became possible for people to travel without undue fear. Merchants could convey their wares. Craftsmen could ply their trades. And pilgrims felt able at last to visit the shrines of the saints.

From the earliest days following the arrival of peace Vézelay became an immensely popular venue for pilgrims. This was no doubt partly due to its location, dramatically placed on a hilltop in the heart of prosperous Burgundy. But there was always a special aura about the place. Its patron saint was the Virgin Mary, which endowed it with a special and feminine appeal. But then before long another female saint became associated with the abbey. She is perhaps the most intriguing saint in the entire Christian pantheon, as well as the most unlikely; one who has exercised the imagination of countless commentators, theologians, fantasists, artists and fiction writers. She is Mary Magdalene. And, improbable though it may sound, the abbey claimed for centuries to possess her body.

How this happened derives from a chain of events which veered from the naive to the shoddy. But it was a claim which in a remarkably short space of time brought a hitherto insignificant Burgundian abbey unimaginable wealth and fame, so much so that by the twelfth century only Jerusalem, Rome and Santiago de Compostela could match its appeal as a centre of pilgrimage. The poor gave their pittance, and the titled and the wealthy their gold and their lands. The chronicler Hugh of Poitiers, who was a monk at Vézelay, wrote at this time that 'all France seems to go to the solemnities of the Magdalene'.

The magical appeal of the saint, and the universal fame of Vézelay, made it not only a shrine to be visited but also a gathering-place for travellers heading elsewhere. Large numbers of pilgrims from north-eastern France, Germany and the Low Countries now regularly assembled here as they prepared to set off for other shrines, in particular that of St James in Santiago de Compostela. The road they would take was the *Via Lemovicensis*, the Way of Vézelay.

*

The association of Vézelay with Mary Magdalene was always tenuous and shrouded in mystery and concealment, perhaps deliberately so since there was no apparent evidence to support the claim. In the early days there seem to have been only rumours put about by the monks that the abbey possessed relics relating to the saint. Nothing was specific, just a half-veiled secret, though intriguing enough to arouse expectation and excitement. Before long these subtle whispers that relics of Mary Magdalene were held by the abbey had the effect of attracting pilgrims like bees to a honeycomb. Whether the abbot and his fellow monks actually believed their own story is impossible to establish. Nonetheless the result was a swift and dramatic improvement in the abbey's fame and fortunes.

Inevitably this vague association with the Magdalene soon required clarification, and this duly took place with the appearance, during the tenth and early eleventh centuries, of several lives of the saints which had been translated into Latin from the Greek, and which originated apparently from various monastic sources in the eastern Mediterranean or in Sicily and southern Italy.

The significance of these manuscripts was that they became vital to the creation of the Magdalene legend in France, and therefore to the fortunes of Vézelay abbey. Step by step they established an account of the life and travels of the Magdalene in the years following the Crucifixion and Resurrection of Christ, to which she had been a witness. The earliest of these manuscripts was the *vita eremitica*, a Life of the Hermits and early Desert Fathers, probably dating from as early as the ninth century. The list of hermits somewhat surprisingly included Mary Magdalene. It was claimed that she had fled Jerusalem after Christ's Resurrection to escape persecution and had spent the last thirty years of her life as a hermit in the desert.

This was the first chapter of her reinvented life. Next came the *vita evangelica*, a Life of the Teachers, which appeared about a century later. This manuscript consolidated the earlier account by offering a fanciful homily to the Magdalene, and was clearly designed to boost the prestige of the saint as the repentant sinner who was beloved by Christ, and who subsequently became in a sense an apostle to the other apostles. This was chapter two. Now Mary Magdalene was not only a dedicated hermit but a very special disciple.

Progressively a life – and a way of life – was being sketched out for the Magdalene, filling in the unknown years of which the Bible makes no mention at all. Only a number of apocryphal texts, including a Gospel of Mary Magdalene, make further reference to her. But the crucial group of manuscripts linking her story to France consisted of several Lives of the Apostle, *vitae apostolica*, which emerged during the course of the eleventh century. Now it was explained that Mary, together with several other followers of Christ including her brother Lazarus, escaped persecution in Jerusalem by fleeing on a vessel to the coast of France, arriving at what is now Marseille, whereupon they proceeded to evangelise pagan Gaul, at that time under Roman rule. Mary Magdalene was said to have preached near Aix, choosing the life of a hermit until at her death she was buried there by St Maximin, another of the former followers of Christ who had been a fellow-occupant of the vessel that brought them to these shores.

What these Lives of the Apostles successfully achieved was to transplant the scene of Mary's thirty years as a hermit from the deserts of the Bible Lands to Provence. And the story did not end there. In a further manuscript, almost certainly originating in Burgundy, it was claimed that in the year 749 the then Abbot of Vézelay had despatched one of his monks, a certain Badilus, to Provence for the express purpose of bringing the body of Mary Magdalene back to Burgundy, thereby safeguarding the saint's relics from Saracen invaders who at that time were regularly plundering much of Provence.

The legend was now complete. Vézelay had been the custodian of the saint's body for at least the past four hundred years, so people were led to believe. And for those who might question the likelihood of such a tale a commentator at the time had the perfect response. 'Many people,' he wrote, 'ask how the body of St Mary Magdalene, whose native land was Judaea, could have been translated to Gaul from a land so far away. To such doubters we may make a brief reply. All things are possible to God.' To this observation a scholar of our own day, Professor Francis Haskell, has wryly added: 'How Mary Magdalene's relics came to Burgundy, how she became a heroine of the church, and one of the most loved saints of the Middle Ages, is one of the great romances of the age of chivalry.'

The rise of Vézelay to become one of the foremost places of pilgrimage in the Christian world, and her position as a major starting-point for pilgrims to Santiago, more or less coincided. And one common factor of huge significance united the two roles. In the year 1026 the pope placed Vézelay under the authority of another Burgundian abbey a short distance to the south. This was Cluny. And Cluny had a direct interest in both the Magdalene legend and – in particular – the Santiago pilgrimage.

It was stated at the time that the reason for the pope's decision was disciplinary; that the monks of Vézelay had been guilty of 'wretched and lascivious behaviour', though discreetly no details were offered. Lapses from the Rule of St Benedict, the order's founder, were frequent at the time, and Cluny, as the champion of monastic reform, was the natural disciplinarian in such instances. In fact the pope's edict was relatively gentle, and Cluny's control of its junior house was never total, and did not last long. Even so, the partnership between the two abbeys was soon productive to an extent far beyond the expectations of either abbey. In 1037 Cluny appointed one of its own monks as Abbot of Vézelay. He was Abbot Geoffrey, and it was during the decades of his abbacy that the place flourished as never before. It was Geoffrey who specially promoted the cult of Mary Magdalene. As a result the flow of pilgrims soon became a torrent. Donations poured in from people in all walks of life. Among the powers attributed to Mary Magdalene was that of aiding prisoners who had been unjustly jailed: before long so numerous were the chains offered to the abbey in gratitude by prisoners released in response to their prayers that Abbot Geoffrey had them melted down and made into new altar rails placed round the shrine of the saint. Accounts of numerous miracles performed by her spread throughout France and further afield. The Magdalene cult was reaching a pitch of hysteria, and in the process the wealth and fame of the abbey continued to multiply.

The contribution of Cluny to this bonanza was incalculable. Geoffrey was in charge of Vézelay under the shadow of two of Cluny's most formidable abbots: the first was Odilo, described by Bishop Fulbert of Chartres as 'the archangel of monks', and the second Hugh the Great. Both men were later canonised. Between them they held office spanning the entire eleventh century, overlapping it at either end – fifty-five and sixty years respectively. Both abbots shared a messianic ambition directed towards Spain; this took the form of employing the resources of the Church to push back Islam and so reclaim the land for Christianity. As we shall see in Chapter 9, and in the final section of this book, a vital arm of this ambition was to safeguard the pilgrim road to Santiago by establishing a powerful network of religious house along the route, both in France and in northern Spain These would act as service stations for the benefit of pilgrims, offering a roof over their heads, a meal, a prayer, a psalm, the comfort of company, local information, even medical treatment. Santiago pilgrims were the Christian army without arms, but whose sheer numbers, and through the donations they generated, were a vital support for the beleaguered Spanish monarchs struggling to hold their territories against the Saracens.

No wonder Cluny, through the good offices of Abbot Geoffrey, did everything possible to promote Vézelay as one of the great Christian shrines which was also a major starting-point for Santiago. Cluny even used its influence with the pope to obtain a papal bull in 1050 acknowledging that the saint's relics were indeed at Vézelay, and that the Magdalene, and not the Virgin Mary, was the abbey's principal patron. The Magdalene had become at once icon and fundraiser. As for the pilgrims collecting here from eastern France and beyond, as they attended their last mass in the abbey church before setting out on their long journey to Santiago, it was Mary Magdalene who pointed them the way. She had acquired a unique role in the Christian world. Of all the New Testament figures whose relics were believed to have survived, she was the woman closest to Christ. She had been embraced by Jesus both figuratively and literally. The medieval Church made much of the fact that she had been a whore. But now, embraced by Christ, her sexuality had been made respectable. Alone of all the female saints in the Christian calendar, she stood for a purity that is also sexual.

In the popular view of Mary Magdalene as the prostitute-turned-disciple, it was maybe the example of her own reformed life which accounted for her enormous popularity among pilgrims. She offered the promise that they too, as penitent sinners, could be accepted by God.

With her body now declared to be safely in Vézelay the triumph of the Magdalene cult was now complete. By the mid-twelfth century *The Pilgrim's Guide* could confidently claim that 'the most worthy remains of the Blessed Mary Magdalene must first of all be rightly worshipped by pilgrims. She is that glorious Mary who … watered with her tears the feet of the Saviour, wiped them with her hair, and anointed them with a precious ointment while kissing them most fervently.' The author continued by corroborating the story of the removal of the saint's body. 'After a long time a distinguished and holy monk called Badilon transported her most precious earthly remains to Vézelay where they rest up to this day in a much-honoured tomb.'

By now her story had become official history, and Vézelay was the proud beneficiary. From the perspective of our own times the story seems bewilderingly improbable. Historians generally agree that the *vitae* on which the Magdalene legend is founded are works of pious fiction, either deliberately invented in the interests of generating support for the pilgrimage movement, or in the innocent belief that a story about biblical figures passed down from generation to generation must be of divine origin. The first *vita,* the Life of the Hermits, which established the Magdalene as a desert hermit, was likely to have been a confusion of identities between the Mary Magdalene of the gospels and a desert penitent known as Mary of Egypt. The subsequent *vitae* establishing her living presence in Provence relate to a popular legend dating possibly to Roman times of the Boat of Bethany which brought a crew of saints, including the Magdalene and her brother Lazarus, to these shores to found the first churches.

As for the story of Badilus, and how the Magdalene's body become transported to Burgundy, this seems likely to have been a tale put about by the parties benefitting most richly from the escapade, namely the abbey of Vézelay masterminded (as with the chronicle of Archbishop Turpin and the pseudo-history of Charlemagne's dream) by Cluny. The supposed removal of Mary Magdalene's remains from Provence to Burgundy was justified on the grounds that they had been saved from being destroyed by the Saracens. But in the eyes of the medieval Church there was a spiritual justification too, that the removal of her body must have been God's will. It was a practice piously known as *furta sacra*, Sacred Theft – to which there could be no answer or objection.

No doubt there were those in Vézelay who remained sceptical about the razzmatazz surrounding the cult of the Magdalene, and who viewed the accumulating wealth and glory of Vézelay as a triumph, not of Christian virtues, but of mammon. And maybe those sceptics found a certain justice in the fact that on the saint's day, 21 July in the year 1120, a disastrous fire broke out in the abbey church during mass, largely destroying the place and killing more than a thousand pilgrims, so it was claimed. Widely believed to have been an act of arson perpetrated by local people exasperated at being taxed to the hilt, the conflagration nonetheless brought about just one beneficial result. It necessitated the rebuilding of the entire abbey church – the result of which is the architectural and sculptural masterpiece we still have today.

*

Vézelay remains 'one of the most beloved and beautiful of mediaeval sites,' wrote the American medievalist and scholar of the pilgrim routes, Professor Kenneth Conant. The Basilique Sainte-Madeleine, as it is now known, proudly rides the spur of its hill overlooking the rich undulating landscape of northern Burgundy. To pilgrims making their way here from the north and east the great church may have looked like the stern of a mighty ship preparing to sail southwards towards Spain. Today's travellers are more likely to approach it from the west, making their way up the hill through the old town along a road studded underfoot with golden scallop-shells, symbols not just of the Santiago pilgrimage itself but of the golden wealth the abbey once attracted through the devotions of so many thousands arriving to worship here before setting off on the roads to Spain. The 'large and beautiful basilica' mentioned in the twelfth-century *Pilgrim's Guide* must have been only recently completed after the disastrous fire of 1120. Reconstruction had begun immediately, and the new church was inaugurated by Pope Innocent II in 1132 after twelve years of intensive construction work.

Today the abbey itself has disappeared apart from fragments of the former refectory. As for the true glory of Vézelay, the traveller who finally reaches the open square after following the trail of golden scallop-shells through the old town is not immediately aware of it The massive west front which dominates the square was constructed as recently as the mid-nineteenth century by the French state's official restorer of historic buildings, the architect Viollet-le-Duc. It is a worthy if somewhat soulless pastiche, the original facade having been wrecked during the wars of religion in the sixteenth century, and the vandalism completed in the French Revolution of the late eighteenth century.

Then comes the revelation. We pass through the outer door into the spacious narthex, or assembly area, its very size being evidence of the numbers of pilgrims who would assemble here awaiting their final mass before setting off on the road. Crossing the narthex to the inner door we stand at the entrance to one of the longest and most handsome naves in France, its roof vaulted in alternating colours of local sandstone – from white through yellow to dark green – supported by ranks of columns whose capitals, no fewer than 135 of them, have been carved to illustrate scenes from the Old Testament.

But this is now the moment to step back, and gaze upwards. Overhead, spanning the entire double-entrance to the nave, is the huge tympanum, carved early in the twelfth century, which is the ultimate expression of that triumphant statement which will be repeated to pilgrims on countless churches all the way to Santiago: the iconic image of Christ in Majesty. The Vézelay tympanum, almost twenty feet in width, is one of the most astounding sculptural ensembles in the Christian world. In the centre Christ stares straight at us, into us and beyond us, his imperious gaze suggesting an unchallengeable authority over all around him. From his outstretched hands and finger-tips a blessing is transmitted to the four evangelists who surround him, the blessing being described as so many rays of light which are carved as though they were ribbons floating windblown across the golden surface – a magical touch making the stone itself feel as light as air. It is sculptural alchemy.[20]

Only the greatest artists have been capable of making intractable stone touch the human soul. We do not even know who the artist was who created the Vézelay tympanum, though there are intriguing clues pointing to where he is likely to have come from, and where he could have honed his remarkable skills. And these clues we shall follow up in a later chapter as we head south along the pilgrim road into the Burgundian heartland.

The Vézelay tympanum would have had a special meaning to the scores of Santiago pilgrims gathering here for that final mass.

20. See Plate 11.

Those ribbons of light spreading outwards from Christ's extended fingers represented not only a last blessing to his apostles after the Resurrection; it was also a final instruction that they should spread his message to all corners of the earth. This was a mission which St James fulfilled by preaching the gospel in Spain, and by his body being returned there after his martyrdom to become the object of this pilgrimage. Christ's blessing on that carving above the heads of pilgrims as they left the abbey church was a blessing to them too – a blessing and a reassurance – as they set off for St James' shrine.

*

The Abbot of Vézelay at the time of the devastating fire of 1120 was a Burgundian nobleman by the name of Renaud of Semur. Like several of his predecessors Renaud had been a monk at Cluny. Furthermore he was the nephew of Hugh of Semur, canonised as St Hugh in this same year, who had been Cluny's all-powerful abbot for sixty years until his death eleven years earlier. Scarcely had the flames of the church fire been extinguished than Renaud launched a massive rebuilding operation. A church guaranteed to attract so many pilgrims needed to be built as swiftly as possible, with no expense spared. Renaud's plans for the new church were also on an ambitious scale, doubtless coloured by the fact that at Cluny, his mother-house, the largest and most richly ornamented church ever built had recently been completed. It was one of the wonders of the world, and Renaud would not have wished to be outshone. The cult of Mary Magdalene was at its height, and so was the Santiago pilgrimage: accordingly the first requirement of the new church was that it should be capable of accommodating pilgrims in huge numbers. The nave itself was planned to be more than two hundred feet long, and the entire church almost four hundred feet in length.

For the next eight years until his death it was under the guidance of Abbot Renaud that the great pilgrim church we see today began to take shape. Throughout those years of intensive rebuilding, and over the decades following, the Cluny connection remained unbroken. From the outset Abbot Renaud placed another Cluniac monk in charge of operations. He was Pierre de Montboissier. He held the position for only two years before being elected Cluny's abbot, known to us as Peter the Venerable, protector of the persecuted Peter Abelard, and alternately friend and combatant of the fiery St Bernard of Clairvaux. Meanwhile at Vézelay the Cluny connection continued. As the new abbey church was near completion it was Peter the Venerable's own brother who became Vézelay's abbot. For a while the two greatest abbeys in Burgundy ran in tandem.

Few periods in French medieval Church history have been as decisive as the mid-twelfth century: it was as though everything a resurgent Church had been striving towards came about at more or less the same time. These were days of triumph. The abbey church of Cluny, already being described as 'the greatest church in Christendom', was now completed. So for the greater part was Vézelay. Further north another ambitious building project was also on the verge of completion. This was the royal portal of Chartres cathedral, its west front, like the Vézelay tympanum, one of the greatest surviving treasures of medieval sculpture.

Then, in 1146, came another key event in the history of Vézelay. The French monarch, Louis VII, invited the most eloquent churchman of his day, Bernard of Clairvaux, to launch the Second Crusade to the Holy Land with a sermon to be delivered on Easter Sunday that year, in the presence of the king himself together with many of France's noblemen and leading churchmen. And the location selected was Vézelay. The choice could not have been more appropriate. The new abbey church, by now almost complete, was already the foremost centre of pilgrimage in France, largely due to the fervent cult of Mary Magdalene, whose relics the abbey was now widely believed to possess. It was also one of the major starting-points for the pilgrimage to Santiago, attracting penitents and adventurers alike from eastern France and far beyond. Both events, together with the charismatic presence of Bernard, assured a huge congregation and an auspicious launch for the new crusade, just half a century after the first one. Equally important was the fact that the two movements, the pilgrimage and the crusade, shared a vibrant common cause, the continuing struggle against Islam – the pilgrimage being directed towards Spain, and the crusade to Palestine. The launch of the Second Crusade in Vézelay brought the two movements close together, each giving strength and a sense of purpose to the other.

So great was the crowd gathered at Vézelay on that Easter morning that Bernard undertook to deliver his sermon not in the new church in spite of its size but in a natural amphitheatre on the northern slope of the hill below. The sermon was by all accounts a *tour de force,* and Bernard's passionate words brought overwhelming support for the new crusade. And at the climax of his oration Bernard tore a strip off his clothing to be made into a crusader's banner. It was Vézelay's finest hour. And afterwards scores of pilgrims would have set off on their journey south with the great man's words ringing in their ears. The appropriateness of Easter Sunday for Bernard's sermon would not have been lost on many of them. Here was a place dedicated to Mary Magdalene, who had been the first disciple to see Jesus after the Resurrection on that very first Easter morning. The event at Vézelay had a powerful ring of history about it

We can still savour something of that historic moment. A footpath leads down the north flank of the hill below the abbey church, finally emerging from the woods onto a natural platform projecting from the hillside. This was the scene of Bernard's famous address, today marked by a tall wooden cross mounted on a plinth of bare rock. Originally a stone cross stood here, destroyed like so many other religious symbols during the fury of the French Revolution. What does survive is a tiny chapel nearby, all but masked by trees. This is the Chapelle Sainte-Croix or the Chapelle de la Cordelle, touching in its perfect simplicity, erected here shortly after that Easter day to commemorate the occasion when the king and much of the nobility of France came to hear Bernard's passionate call to arms.

The fame of Vézelay as a place of pilgrimage lasted little more than a further hundred years. But it was to be a final glorious century. In 1190 the Third Crusade was also launched here, this time by the French King Philippe-Auguste, accompanied by the King of England

Richard Coeur-de-Lion. Half a century later the French monarch Louis IX (St Louis) came to the shrine of the Magdalene several times to seek her blessing on two further crusades which he led, and during the second of which he died.

But then, abruptly, it all came to an end. In 1279 the Count of Provence, Charles of Anjou, led an excavation in the ancient crypt of the Church of Saint-Maximin where, according to legend, Mary Magdalene had been buried after her thirty years as a hermit. The count was determined to prove that the saint's relics still remained within his domain, and that the story of her body being transported to Burgundy was false. Charles led the excavation himself, removing soil and stones from around ancient tombs in the crypt with his bare hands. His efforts were duly rewarded. With the aid of unsubstantiated evidence and several forged documents, including a letter purporting to be from the Emperor Charlemagne, it was established to the count's satisfaction that the Magdalene's relics were indeed still there. It transpired that in anticipation of Saracen raids in the ninth century the monks of Saint-Maximin had taken the precaution of removing the saint's remains from her own tomb, swapping them for another body in a sarcophagus close by.

How Saracen raiders were supposed to be fooled by such a ruse, even if they had heard of Mary Magdalene or cared a jot about her bones, was not explained. The crucial significance of Count Charles' discovery was that the monk despatched by Vézelay to obtain the Magdalene's relics had clearly arrived too late, and so had unwittingly stolen the wrong body. The mistake was soon confirmed by the pope, and Saint-Maximin re-established by papal decree as the guardian of Mary Magdalene's body. And the role of Vézelay as one of the foremost pilgrimage shrines in Christendom for so many centuries was suddenly over.

But if one of the most celebrated acts of Sacred Theft in Christian history had finally proved to be a case of mistaken identity, it had nonetheless resulted in centuries of colossal wealth and prestige for Vézelay. Now, after the 'departure' of Mary Magdalene, what remained was the abiding legacy of her cult, which by its very magnificence has continued to entrance and inspire pilgrims and visitors alike ever since. That legacy is Vézelay's incomparable abbey church – the great church on the hill – whose glorious carved tympanum depicts Christ extending his blessing to his apostles and to all corners of the earth, including of course that far outpost of Christianity in north-west Spain to which medieval pilgrims and their modern counterparts set off from here on the long road under the stars. The power of that imperious image, and that blessing extending like rays of light to all around, would have remained, as it does today, in the memory of pilgrims for every mile of the journey to come.

8. The Broader Picture

THE PILGRIM ROADS WERE RIVERS OF HUMANITY flowing inexorably west and south; and like all rivers they were fed by tributaries from far and wide, swelling their size and strength as they headed towards Spain and the far Atlantic. Besides the four principal pilgrim roads listed in *The Pilgrim's Guide* there were many others spread across the country like a giant spider's web, leading to innumerable local shrines. Pilgrims setting off for Santiago would make a point of visiting some of these local shrines along the way: they served as welcome diversions on a long journey: a pause for a prayer and a blessing to sustain their spirits on the road ahead – not altogether unlike the modern traveller making a diversion to take in Siena and Assisi on the way to Rome. As today, there was always an element of spiritual tourism about pilgrimages: celebrated and beautiful places had a natural allure.

By the twelfth century the number of such shrines in France attracting pilgrims was beyond count as the cult of holy relics reached fever pitch. We can even talk of a 'relics industry' as churches and monasteries vied with each other to possess and display the most prestigious objects for pilgrims to venerate. Donations by grateful travellers whose prayers had been answered became a major source of income for religious houses fortunate enough to own such items. Relics were 'realisable assets', as Professor Christopher Brooke has succinctly put it.

Not surprisingly, with such intense competition there were soon simply not enough saints to go round. And as demand outstripped supply, so theft, and faking of holy relics, became widespread.

Christian principles all too often gave way to greed and opportunism; and many a priest preserved his self-respect by conveniently turning a blind eye to unwelcome evidence of trickery.

In the midst of this relics 'fever' the crusades made a welcome and important contribution. Crusading knights, many of them adventurers in disguise, began to bring back as trophies whatever fragments of the Bible Lands they could lay their hands on, together with colourful tales of what these objects were supposed to be and where they were supposed to have come from. An impressionable Christian world eagerly awaited them, and for the returning crusader it became a profitable trade. This new source of holy relics was particularly exploited as a result of the Fourth Crusade of 1204 in which the flower of European chivalry, having taken the cross and set out with heroic ambitions, proceeded to sack and loot Constantinople, the capital of the Eastern Church. One outcome was that relics began to reach France and elsewhere in Western Europe in a veritable flood; and the number of churches and priories claiming to possess sacred objects from the Holy Lands increased proportionately. Sceptics calculated how many sailing vessels could be constructed out of the many supposed fragments of the holy cross. And Chaucer's Pardoner, as we have seen, carried with him a fragment of the sail which St Peter had 'whan that he wente upon the see'.

Of the numerous tributaries feeding the pilgrim 'rivers' to Santiago one of the most important ran south from the spectacular island shrine and abbey of Mont Saint-Michel, off the coast of the English Channel on the western borders of Normandy. Here, unusually, there was no holy relic to be revered. The popularity of the site as a place of pilgrimage was due to a mystical combination of geography and legend. According to local tradition early in the eighth century – a time when most of what is now Normandy was in the hands of Viking pirates – the Archangel Michael appeared to a beleaguered local bishop, instructing him to build a church on a rocky islet a short distance offshore. Before long a cult of St Michael grew up on the site, and after the eventual Christianisation of Normandy in the tenth century successive Norman dukes undertook to finance the building of a magnificent abbey on the sacred island. The man responsible for designing the abbey and its church was that remarkable architect-monk from Lombardy, in northern Italy, by the name of William of Volpiano (discussed in Chapter 4). In the late tenth century William had been invited to Burgundy by the Abbot of Cluny for the express purpose of rebuilding abbeys and churches which had been desecrated during the centuries of barbarian invasions, principally by the Vikings. Together with his team of masons and craftsmen from Lombardy, William established in Burgundy what has become known as the 'first Romanesque style' of church architecture. His reputation soon drew the attention of the rulers of Normandy, now an independent dukedom whose rulers, in the fervour of their new faith, were engaged in making Normandy the heart of Christian culture and monastic life.

Hence, early in the eleventh century William of Volpiano was given the challenging task of building an abbey on the bare rock of Mont Saint-Michel. William's courageous response was to place the transept crossing of the abbey church at the very peak of the rock, so necessitating the construction of underground crypts and chapels in the rock below in order to bear the weight of the new church.[21]

It was a daring and triumphant achievement, and it heralded the emergence of Mont Saint-Michel as among the most revered centres of pilgrimage in Europe. Its importance soon extended to England, and to English pilgrims setting out for Santiago, largely as a result of the Norman invasion and conquest of England by William the Conqueror in 1066. As a reward for its support for the invasion by Duke William – now also King of England – the abbey of Mont Saint-Michel was awarded lands on the English side of the Channel, among them a small islet off the coast of Cornwall which was a match for the abbey-island across the water. A Benedictine priory was duly built on the Cornish islet, which took the name of the mother-abbey, becoming Saint Michael's Mount. Soon English pilgrims, before embarking from Plymouth further along the coast, would begin

21. See Plate 12.

their journey by offering prayers to the Archangel Michael here in Cornwall, then repeat their prayers to the same saint on arriving at the far side of the Channel, at Mont Saint-Michel. Prayers in hope of a safe crossing were thus echoed by prayers offered in thanksgiving for having arrived safely across the sea.

From here in Normandy English pilgrims then headed south, some towards Chartres and Orléans, others keeping further west and finally joining travellers on the principal pilgrim road from Paris and Tours somewhere in the region of Poitiers, and before long linking up with the scores of other English pilgrims who had sailed from Bristol towards Bordeaux on those trading vessels soon to return home with a less pious cargo – wine.

Doubtless most pilgrims beginning their long journey with a visit to Mont Saint-Michel would have understood than an archangel had no earthly presence and hence no earthly remains. Even so, there are accounts of devout travellers arriving on the island fully expecting to be able to venerate the body of St Michael. By way of compensation there grew up a popular custom among pilgrims to the abbey of gathering rocks and pebbles from the sea-shore at low tide as mementos, much as children on a seaside holiday today will collect shells and coloured pebbles to take home.

An even more famous site attracting passing pilgrims was the cathedral of Chartres, some fifty miles south-west of Paris. Chartres is not situated on one of the main pilgrim routes, and it is not known when the cult of St James first became attached to the cathedral; but by the early thirteenth century it was well enough established for the most beautiful assembly of stained glass in the world to include two windows that relate specifically to the apostle and to the discovery of his tomb in Spain. The first window is devoted to the Life of St James, made up of thirty panels, one of which depicts Jesus giving James his mission to preach in Spain, the sequence ending with the apostle's martyrdom at the hands of King Herod. But it is the second window, in the choir of the cathedral, which is more directly related to the Santiago pilgrimage, and known as the Charlemagne Window. One of the twenty-four panels shows St James appearing to the emperor in a dream, urging him to return to Spain to defeat the Saracens. Another panel depicts Charlemagne departing for Spain, and in a third he is gazing up at the Milky Way which will lead him to the tomb of St James. Together the three scenes illustrate the popular variation of *La Chanson de Roland* in which Charlemagne's visitor in his dream is not the archangel Gabriel but St James himself. In other words the Chartres window faithfully follows the version of the Song which was almost certainly conceived as a deliberate boost to the cause of the Santiago pilgrimage, probably on the initiative of the abbey of Cluny (as described more fully in Chapter 5).

That this version of the tale should have become enshrined in France's greatest cathedral nearly two centuries after it was composed is a testimony to how successfully the Charlemagne story had been adapted for public consumption. The medieval imagination lent itself to reinventing legend and presenting it as reality: it was a gift which supplies a key to the creative genius of the age – a gift manifest in its painting, its sculpture and, as here, in the magnificence of its stained glass.

Chartres had already enjoyed a long tradition of pilgrimage dating back at least to the early Christian era. The principal focus of veneration is made clear by the most celebrated of all the medieval windows at Chartres, one which would probably get the popular vote as the most beautiful example of stained glass in the world. This is the Virgin window with an incomparable intensity of lapis-lazuli blue. The cathedral itself is dedicated to the Virgin Mary (as is Notre-Dame in Paris), and it became a centre of the Marian cult as a result of possessing the most revered of all the supposed relics of the Virgin, known as the *Sancta Camisa,* or Sacred Veil. This consists of about sixteen feet of cloth (today preserved in a reliquary in an apsidal chapel), believed to have been worn by Mary at the birth of Jesus. The origin of the garment is as obscure as that of most holy relics, though it was probably stolen from a Jewish community in Jerusalem and brought to Constantinople, where it was offered as a gift to the Emperor Charlemagne by the Byzantine emperor of the Eastern Church. Charlemagne's grandson, Charles II, then presented it to the Bishop of Chartres in about the year 876. In the succeeding centuries it became an object of fervent adulation by pilgrims, especially by women, in the widely held belief that prayers offered here would ease the pains of pregnancy.

The far-fetched superstitions attached to sacred relics like the *Sancta Camisa* may be deeply alien to rational minds today, as is the gullibility of the medieval pilgrim; yet the modern traveller might prefer to reflect that without the deep passions and huge popular support generated by such holy shrines a great many of the places we now throng to visit and admire would simply not exist.

Chartres itself is as case in point. The era of the great cathedrals had a quite different feel about it from that of the monasteries which preceded it. Cathedrals themselves performed a largely different role within a community. Monasteries were created to be isolated from the social world: the monastic ideal had emerged at a time when Christianity could only survive in sealed pockets within a largely hostile environment – or at least an environment which had no need of monasteries and to which they did not belong. They were the product of a siege mentality. But by the time the great cathedrals were being created, in the twelfth and thirteenth centuries, Christianity had won. The world was no longer alien. Hence cathedrals were built in the very heart of a community, and for the needs of that community. They were the most important buildings in a town, and accordingly played a substantially different role in people's social and spiritual life from that of an abbey. Townspeople used them for a variety of purposes other than religious services and private prayers. Because of its sheer size and dominant position a cathedral became the natural venue for such events as local markets, each of its huge carved entrances becoming the focus of a wide range of commercial activities. In Chartres there were four annual fairs which were held in the area around the cathedral; and these coincided with the four feast days in honour of the Virgin – the Presentation, the Annunciation, the Assumption and the Nativity. Pilgrimages were a key entity on such occasions: the commercial success of these fairs was assured by the presence of large numbers of pilgrims who had come to venerate one of the most revered holy relics in Europe. While the majority of pilgrims may have been poor, there was invariably a minority with money to spend.

As the new cathedrals became 'people's palaces' it was natural that ordinary people should wish to play their part in maintaining them – particularly after the disastrous outbreaks of fire which were a perennial hazard in medieval churches where naked candles and torches provided the only artificial light, and roofs were often still of timber. Chartres suffered a sequence of devastating fires, necessitating constant rebuilding between the ninth and the thirteenth centuries.

It was precisely in response to such disasters that the widespread public affection for the local cathedral became demonstrated in spectacular fashion in what has become known as the 'building crusades'. In the year 1145 more than a thousand pilgrims arrived at Chartres dragging carts filled with building materials along with provisions for those who had lost everything when one of the fires spread through the town. It was recorded that for months, men and women hauled heavy wagons of stones up the slope to the cathedral site.

This degree of public involvement in the construction and life of a cathedral had the effect of altering to some extent the very nature of pilgrimages. Now that cathedrals themselves had become corporate institutions, so too were the pilgrimages which they attracted. The notion of a pilgrimage being one person's private journey in search of salvation was being replaced by an essentially collective exercise whose benefits might be described in today's jargon as a form of group therapy. Jonathan Sumption has described this change in the following words. 'Building crusades reflected the view that pilgrimages performed *en masse* were more meritorious than those performed alone. We find the pilgrim-builders forming themselves into sects, or brotherhoods, performing their penitential rituals in common, and solemnly expelling those members who showed signs of returning to their old ways.'

So a note of self-righteous intolerance creeps in at the same time. But it is the image of the wandering band of travellers, cheerful and high-spirited, which springs to mind most readily when we think of medieval pilgrims on the way to some distant shrine: a journey that has freed them from the toil and drudgery of daily life, and where penitence may count rather less than the enjoyment of good company and the pleasures of the open road. Chaucer may be partly responsible, with his motley crew setting out for Canterbury from the Tabard Inn, where many of them had no doubt spent a thoroughly jolly evening, then entertaining each other with robust stories along the way. A similarly colourful picture of the collective pilgrimage gazes out at us from illuminated manuscripts of the same era as Chaucer's great poem. Among the most delightful is contained in a fourteenth-century Burgundian Book of Hours now in the Musée Condé at Chantilly (illustrated on page XX). It shows a band of pilgrims returning from Santiago with all the time in the world to enjoy themselves, laughing and joking and playing games as they make their easygoing way through the pleasant country. In this bucolic scene we could hardly be further from the image of the solitary sinner plodding grimly to some holy shrine in the hope of being spared eternal damnation. It seems most unlikely that any of the pilgrims represented in the Burgundian Book of Hours had considered for one moment the possibility of hellfire.

Such records of pilgrimage as an enjoyable enterprise, whether from Chaucer of from illuminated Books of Hours, are both from the later Middle Ages. And inevitably they feel much closer to the spirit of the present-day cultural tourist than to that of the early centuries of pilgrimage when the journey to Santiago was still fraught with dangers and few physical comforts were to be found along the way.

It is tempting to make a further comparison with the modern traveller, and speculate on how much medieval pilgrims would have been struck by the beauty and sheer magnificence of the places they visited. Most pilgrims were from small communities where the only buildings of any size and grandeur would have been the church and perhaps the castle of the local lord. Few would ever have travelled far from home. Suddenly a great abbey, or a soaring cathedral, even a bustling town with tall mansions and cobbled streets, would have been quite unfamiliar. More bewildering still would have been the gold and glittering jewels decorating the shrines they had come to venerate. It is impossible not to believe that a sense of wonder and awe would have overwhelmed pilgrims, sustaining them on their journey, and remaining with them as a collection of golden memories for the rest of their lives.

*

After Chartres, the second of the magnificent Gothic cathedrals of France to honour St James was that at Bourges, further to the south and situated on the main pilgrim road we have been taking from Vézelay. The two cathedrals, Bourges and Chartres, are more or less contemporaneous, the former's main structure as it exists today having been started in the final decade of the twelfth century.

With its five elaborately-carved portals, soaring nave and flamboyant flying buttresses, Bourges cathedral must have been another awesome sight for pilgrims. They would have made their way down from Normandy, perhaps taking in Chartres, then crossing the Loire at Orléans before heading south into the dukedom of Berry, of which Bourges was the regional capital. And at this point they became united with other travellers who had been heading south from Vézelay.

Unlike Chartres, Bourges offers no open propaganda for the Santiago pilgrimage itself: in its stained-glass windows there is no re-telling of the Song of Roland with St James beckoning the Emperor Charlemagne in a dream to follow the Milky Way into north-west Spain. In Bourges the tributes to St James are more low-key: he is just one apostle among others. A thirteenth-century window in one of the chapels relates the customary legend of his life, concluding with his decapitation by Herod. In another chapel he appears as a bystander witnessing the Annunciation. And in a tall window on the south side of the cathedral, high up, his full-length figure is flanked by those of St Philip and St Thomas. Nowhere in the cathedral is there a call to pilgrims to set off for his shrine in Spain. But by this time, in the later Middle Ages, perhaps the urgency of the Santiago pilgrimage had already become a little blunted. The Saracens had long been reduced to a small pocket in southern Spain; and there was no longer any need for a rousing call to arms.

Pilgrims joining the road from Vézelay at Bourges would have missed out on the drama and hysteria surrounding the worship of Mary Magdalene described in the previous chapter. They would have missed, too, the impact of that peerless abbey church with its uplifting valediction for pilgrims who were setting off into the unknown in the form of the carved tympanum over the main entrance.

Historic roads often display fragments of their past, like mementos pinned here and there along the way. Today's travellers moving south from Vézelay are everywhere reminded of the history of the road they are taking. Modern highways tend to cut corners, whereas the original pilgrim road still threads its way more peacefully at walking pace from village to village. Following it here in Burgundy is to make a journey into the past – a journey signposted with names that speak of distant times, like the village of La Maison-Dieu, named after a long-vanished pilgrims' hospice. Or another village, Asquins, close to Vézelay, with its little Church of Saint-Jacques, and where there was once a ninth-century priory until it was sacked by Viking marauders along with other religious houses in the area, so causing the local count to found a new abbey more securely on a nearby hill – which became Vézelay.

Echo follows echo along the old pilgrim road as it meanders from village to village, through forests that have never changed and over streams that have always flowed. The traveller may notice a half-buried church on a hill, or stone slabs which are the remains of an ancient ford now replaced by a bridge. One village is called Metz-le-Comte, the *comte* being a descendant of the very count who built Vézelay back in the tenth century. So the echoes resound. Then, back on the modern road we encounter another ancient forest, and suddenly an isolated chapel comes into view dedicated to a saint widely venerated in these parts, St Lazare – in other words Lazarus, the friend of Jesus whom he brought back from the dead, and who according to legend accompanied his sister Mary Magdalene on the open raft which brought them to the shores of Provence. This was a legend so closely interwoven with the Santiago pilgrimage that the worship of St James throughout this area of France cannot be separated from it – as we have already seen at Vézelay, and as we shall see again in the next chapter.

The pilgrim road continues south-west through more wooded countryside towards the western border of Burgundy. The boundary here is defined by the Loire, the longest river in France, soon to flow northwards past Saint-Benoît and Orléans, from where it will accompany pilgrims on the Paris road towards Tours (as described in Chapter 2).

On this upper stretch of the river pilgrims made their first direct encounter with the religious house whose invisible presence had been felt all along the way so far. This was the great Burgundian abbey of Cluny. The monastery itself lay some distance away to the south-west; yet here on an island in the river was a priory which had come to be described as the 'eldest daughter of Cluny'. The priory was La Charité-sur-Loire. As pilgrims made their way south it was one of the major landmarks along this stretch of the road – a handsome cluster of buildings which included a magnificent church capable of holding a congregation of at least five thousand. The priory was surrounded by well-tended gardens, orchards and vineyards, as well as numerous houses, workshops and outbuildings. To pilgrims weary from the long road it would have seemed a paradise island.

La Charité had been the first monastery to be established as a dependency of Cluny – the first of what was to become an expanding empire of dependent abbeys and priories throughout Europe. And as Cluny's 'eldest daughter', in the eyes of the mother-house, La Charité seems to have remained also her best-loved daughter. It was the greatest of Cluny's abbot, Hugh of Semur (St Hugh), who in 1059 founded the priory here on what was then an island. Within a century it had grown massively, both in size and influence. Donors included King Henry I of England, son of William the Conqueror. While remaining under the authority of Cluny the priory also acquired at least seventy dependencies of her own, including religious houses in Chartres, Paris, and even in England.

As a key halt on the road from Vézelay, La Charité naturally attracted an abundance of pilgrims, and not entirely for spiritual reasons. The generous hand of Cluny ensured that hospitality matched the appeal of the place itself. It was a reputation for providing the best food and Burgundian wines that pilgrims were likely to enjoy on the entire journey which earned the priory its name – which has stuck ever since.

Today La Charité remains one of the gems of Burgundy – a gem that has been painstakingly repaired and polished. Historical events did not always treat it as charitably as it treated travellers. Fire caused extensive destruction of the whole complex in the sixteenth century, followed by further damage during the French wars of religion when it became – ironically – a Protestant stronghold, and suffered for it. Finally, in the nineteenth century, the local authorities delivered the *coup de grâce* by proposing to drive a road right through what remained of the priory church. In the nick of time help arrived in the shape of that angel of mercy, Prosper Mérimée, the French government's inspector of ancient monuments. Mérimée not only put a stop to the road scheme, but set in motion a restoration programme for the church, his greatest triumph being to save the superb Romanesque tympanum belonging to the original west facade, which he discovered set into the wall of a local private house, and which subsequently found a new home in a surviving area of the church, where it remains today to the admiration of all.

The riverside town on its graceful sweep of the Loire has been lovingly restored along with much of the ancient priory. The whole town, which grew up round the priory, is still dominated by the proud Romanesque tower which has been a beacon guiding pilgrims on the road from Vézelay for more than eight centuries. The noble church towers of this region are among the glories of Burgundy. Rising elegantly from the centre of so many towns and villages, they are a testimony to those incomparable stonemasons from Lombardy who brought their Christian vision and their building skills from northern Italy to this part of France in the early years of religious revival. They are towers which remain symbols of a resurgent faith and resurgent hope after the dark centuries of anarchy and insurrection. They stand tall across the Burgundian countryside as if God had planted his own standard across a newly-won land.

The greatest of these Burgundian towers were those that crowned the vast abbey church of Cluny which was Abbot Hugh's ultimate dream, only realised after his death, and of which sadly no more than one of the lesser towers remains. Political events and human rapacity struck Cluny even more cruelly than at La Charité. Yet if all too little of Cluny survives today, its contribution to the cause of St James, and to the vast enterprise of the Santiago pilgrimage, remains inviolate, beyond the reach of vandals. Cluny is the great ghost that haunts the pilgrimage movement. And so, leaving the 'eldest daughter', this is an appropriate moment to visit the mother-house itself.

9. Cluny and Autun

THE BENEDICTINE ABBEY OF CLUNY was never on one of the main pilgrim roads: yet being equidistant between two of them – the routes from Vézelay and from Le Puy – its long arms seem to embrace them both, extending even further to include the other principal roads as well. Cluny was the powerhouse of the Santiago pilgrimage – or, perhaps more accurately – its godfather. In the words of one of the eleventh century popes, Urban II, himself a former monk at the abbey, 'Cluny shines like another sun over the earth'.

Today Cluny is mostly a memory, a hollow shell filled with whispers of a glorious past. A single tower presides over the wreckage of a church which for five hundred years was the largest and most sumptuous house of God in Christendom.[22] Its accompanying abbey was for more than two centuries the spiritual heart of the Christian world, and its abbots among the most powerful figures in Europe, friends and advisers to Holy Roman Emperors, successive popes and the kings of England, France and Spain. To be Abbot of Cluny in the eleventh and twelfth centuries was to hold a position in the world as prestigious and influential as any president, statesman or business tycoon of our own day. As if temporal power was not enough, they had God on their side too.

It had all begun early in the tenth century when Duke William of Aquitaine decided to found a monastery on his own lands. The site chosen was in a secluded valley a short distance from the town of Mâcon, strategically placed between two major rivers, the Loire

22. See Plate 13.

to the west, flowing north, and the Saône to the east, flowing south. Furthermore, in these lawless times its location made it relatively safe from raiders who posed a continual threat: Vikings from the north, Magyars from the east and Saracens from the south.

From the outset the young monastery benefited from the duke's decision to draw up a foundation charter which exempted it from all forms of local interference, secular as well as ecclesiastical. Neither the local bishop nor the local lord (including Duke William himself) would have any control over it. The duke placed it under the sole authority of the papacy in Rome. This shrewd political move sowed the seeds of a binding relationship between future popes and abbots of Cluny. It was a relationship which was to prove of inestimable value to both parties, especially in the years to come when two such leading figures of the Church would soon combine in a holy war against Islam – sponsoring crusades to the Holy Land, military action in Spain and facilitating the pilgrimages to Santiago. It was a triple campaign, in harness, with both institutions bringing their weight to bear on the most pressing issue of the day. It was a bond with Rome symbolised by the young abbey's coat-of-arms, composed of the twin keys of St Peter and St Paul.

From modest beginnings the abbey soon expanded in size and importance. Many monasteries had grown lax in discipline during the troubled centuries of lawlessness and insurrection, paying little respect to the Rule of St Benedict laid down by the order's founder, and even less to rules of celibacy. Some priories swarmed with wives, mistresses and male lovers. Increasingly it became the role of Cluny to implement reforms. Priory after priory, abbey after abbey, became subject to the authority of the mother-house.

The burgeoning success of Cluny stemmed to a large extent from another farsighted clause in the duke's foundation charter, which stipulated that the abbey's monks held the right to elect their own abbot. Since the monks who chose to enter Cluny tended to be from Burgundian noble families, the abbey not surprisingly proceeded to be governed by a succession of aristocratic abbots who wielded extensive local power within this tightly-knit feudal society, both within the Church and in the secular world at large. And with such authority wielded on two fronts, ecclesiastical and secular, Cluny began to attract handsome donations of property and land from lords keen to invest in so powerful an institution whose monks were believed to have the ear of God, and would therefore be sure to include them in their prayers. Once again mutual benefit served the abbey well.

Less than a century after its foundation one of those aristocratic abbots forged the first link with Spain and the cult of St James. He was Odilo (to become St Odilo), and he was elected Abbot of Cluny in the year 994. He was to hold the office for the next fifty-five years, filling those years with extensive journeys to visit dependent priories, as well as with building projects for the new and much larger abbey church, and with pursuing a lifetime's ambition – doing whatever lay within his power to bring about the Reconquest of Spain from the Saracens.

Two events took place at the very outset of his abbacy which gave that ambition a special urgency. In the year Odilo took office the historic monastery of Monte Cassino in southern Italy, which had been founded by St Benedict more than four centuries earlier, was sacked by Saracen raiders from Sicily. It would have seemed that the heart of the Benedictine movement had been plucked out. Then only a short while later came another devastating Saracen attack: this time the victim was Santiago, the church and community that had grown up round the apostle's tomb discovered almost two hundred years earlier. Santiago was devastated by the most feared of the Saracen warlords in Spain, Al-Mansur. It was the culmination of two centuries of Saracen assaults on the Christian kingdoms of northern Spain. And it was Abbot Odilo's' bitter inheritance.

Perhaps it was the shock and the pain caused by those two early disasters which spurred Odilo to devote so much of his boundless energy to supporting the Christian cause in Spain. It was under his abbacy that Cluny, with the invaluable backing of the papacy in Rome, began to use its weight to support the harassed Christian rulers south of the Pyrenees. And soon the tide began to turn. It was as if the passing of the feared Millennium without the world having come to an end had influenced events in favour of the Christian powers. In 1002 Al-Mansur died: and with his death the military power of the Saracens in Spain seemed to slacken, as though they were losing their self-assurance and their predatory will. Soon, with the backing of Cluny, the ruler of Navarre, the small kingdom bordering on the Pyrenees, felt able to extend his territory to include neighbouring Aragon, Castile and León.

It is hard to establish Cluny's precise role in the re-establishment of Christian authority in northern Spain. What is certain is that under Abbot Odilo the abbey had a hand in promoting numerous military expeditions against Saracen strongholds, using its lordly connections to rally Burgundian knights to fight in Spain. It even seems likely that without the contribution of Cluny these campaigns might never have taken place. A measure of the debt of gratitude felt by the Spanish monarch, Sancho III, was the quantity of gifts showered on the abbey, mostly from loot seized by the conquering Christian armies. Burgundian knights also rewarded the abbey in a similar fashion. Hence the benefits of Odilo's relationship with the Spanish ruler were mutual: Sancho strengthened and enlarged his kingdom, while Cluny greatly enlarged its wealth and its power. There was now a greatly expanded abbey and a greatly expanded abbey church. A Roman priest who visited Cluny about this time in the company of the papal legate recorded his astonishment at 'the great and vaulted church ... richly adorned with various precious things'.

The close relationship between abbot and monarch continued until Sancho's death in 1035. By this time, and largely through the efforts of Odilo, the French Church had begun to extend its influence right across northern Spain, now cleared of the Saracen presence. Sancho himself had invited Cluniac monks to Spain, and in turn Cluny received and trained Spanish monks. One of these, by the name of Paternus, then returned to Spain to become abbot of Cluny's first monastery south of the Pyrenees, San Juan de la Peña.

Odilo's passion for the Reconquest of Spain needs to be understood in the context of the Saracen threat to Christian Europe over the previous centuries, and its sheer magnitude. Like every well-informed churchman Odilo would have been all too familiar with such a relentless passage of events. The advance of Saracen armies had been dramatic and terrifying. The prophet Mohammed had died in the year 632. Within a century of his death a number of apparently disorganised Bedouin tribes in the desert had come together to form a disciplined military nation which proceeded to take over all the former Roman colonies in North Africa, cross over to Spain and put its Christian rulers to flight. They had occupied Sicily, harassed southern Italy and made pillaging forays deep into France as far north of Tours, within striking distance of Paris – all the time maintaining total control of the Mediterranean Sea to facilitate the passage of their armies. This in a mere hundred years.

Even after their historic defeat near Poitiers by Charles Martel in 732, Saracen marauding parties continued to raid Christian lands as strongly as before. In the mid-ninth century they repeatedly drove north over the Pyrenees, sweeping westwards across southern France as far as the Rhône Valley and Marseille, leaving burnt towns and wrecked churches and abbeys in their wake. Finally, late in the following century, came the humiliating sack of St James' city.

All this had been Abbot Odilo's dark inheritance: and it was a trend of history which he devoted much of his long life to reversing. By the time of his death in 1049 the Reconquest of Spain and the opening-up of the pilgrim road to Santiago had become a twin cause indelibly identified with Cluny.

But if the banner was waved vigorously by Odilo his military contribution bore no comparison to the scale of the campaigns mounted by his successor as abbot. Hugh the Great (St Hugh) was only twenty-four on his accession, and was to remain Abbot of Cluny for a further sixty years, during which time he became one of the most powerful political figures in Europe as well as the most influential churchman of his day – head of a vast monastic empire made up of almost 1,500 dependent abbeys and priories across the continent.

A number of the most important of these, both in France and northern Spain, were acquired by Hugh specifically in order to further the cause of the Santiago pilgrimage. They were situated along the various pilgrim roads in France, and acted as invaluable staging-posts for travellers: Saintes, Saint-Jean-d'Angély, La Charité and (most notably) Vézelay, we have seen already; others, including Limoges, Moissac, Toulouse and Saint-Gilles lay on the various roads to come.

They were all of them signposts to Spain. Hugh's personal connections with Spain, and with Spanish monarchs, were even closer than those of his predecessor. They were strengthened – in the familiar fashion among the European ruling classes – by family ties, in particular with the Spanish King Alfonso VI (grandson of Odilo's patron Sancho III). Alfonso's Queen Constance was a niece of Abbot Hugh. Their daughter and heiress, Urraca, at the age of eight was married to another member of Burgundian nobility, the immensely wealthy Count of Burgundy, whose brother became none other than Pope Calixtus II, the supposed author of part of *The Pilgrim's Guide*. In this way political power, money, family ties and unchallengeable religious authority all came together to create an alliance which proved to be of immeasurable advantage to all parties concerned.

Hugh's abbacy of sixty years began in what was the golden dawn of the pilgrimage movement. By the time it finally ended, in the second decade of the twelfth century, it was already high noon. The years immediately following Hugh's abbacy were those of the pilgrimage's greatest popularity: the era of *La Chanson de Roland*, of the Charlemagne cult, of the pilgrim hymns recorded in the *Codex Calixtinus*, and of course of *The Pilgrim's Guide* and the racy travelogue of the Cluniac monk Aimery Picaud on his colourful journey to Spain. And there was also the glorious finale of the cathedral at Santiago completed later in that same century. But that was all to come.

Meanwhile the dependent abbeys and priories which Hugh established in France were a prelude. They were part of a larger plan. Soon he set about extending a similar chain of religious houses right across northern Spain. These new outposts, strung along the pilgrim road from the Pyrenees all the way to Santiago, acted as service stations for the ever increasing flow of travellers heading for St James' city – now recovered from the assault by Al-Mansur.

Well-equipped and well-endowed, these new establishments offered pilgrims a degree of security and comfort, even medical attention, which had hitherto been lacking. They were now able to set off on their ambitious journey in the reasonable hope of actually getting to their destination without being attacked, robbed or starved. The pilgrimage was beginning to becoming almost genteel.

The financial rewards to Cluny and to the Church in Spain were proportionately rich. As facilities improved and the road itself became less hazardous the wealthy and the highborn began to undertake the pilgrimage, accompanied by their retinues of servants and attendants; and as a result donations and bequests began to pour in, swelling the coffers of the Church. For Cluny the Santiago pilgrimages was becoming not only a cause but a lucrative investment.

More directly beneficial to the Burgundian abbey was the prodigious gratitude of the Spanish monarch Alfonso VI, soon to become Hugh's nephew by marriage. Like his father and grandfather before him Alfonso committed himself to making an annual tribute to Cluny of one thousand pieces of gold. We have no means of knowing how much this meant, but it was clearly an enormous sum; and no doubt it contributed to Hugh's decision to cross the Pyrenees expressly to meet his royal benefactor. The meeting took place in 1077, and it was Hugh's first visit to Spain. No account survives of what actually took place between abbot and monarch: nonetheless a whole range of events was clearly set in motion. On Hugh's part the meeting was a confirmation of Cluny's unequivocal support for the strengthening of the Church in Spain in the wake of Saracen incursions. In parallel ran an equal commitment by Cluny to rally military support for continued campaigns against the Saracens. In return Alfonso offered lavish quantities of gold in addition to the annual tribute, and – especially welcome to Hugh – beneficent gifts of abbeys and priories in Spain, mostly set on the pilgrim route. These included the ancient abbey of Sahagún, already a key link in the chain of religious houses on the road to Santiago, and soon to become known as 'the Cluny of Spain'. Appropriately it was a

Cluniac monk whom Hugh appointed to be its abbot.

In an era when archbishops and even popes donned armour and rode into battle it is hard to assess precisely what contribution Cluny may have made to Alfonso's military campaigns. There is no question of Hugh himself, or indeed any of his monks, actually taking part; yet in the feudal world of which Cluny was a part Hugh's aristocratic connections would certainly have played a vital role in persuading local lords to assemble armies from among their serfs. Alfonso's most dramatic military victory came just eight years after Hugh's first visit to Spain, when his army captured the key city of Toledo after almost three centuries of Saracen rule. The man credited with having led the successful assault was a French knight from Burgundy, Eudes de Bourgogne, who as it happens was Abbot Hugh's cousin.

Alfonso's reaction to this military triumph was another overwhelming gesture of gratitude towards Cluny. Toledo was once again the seat of the Primate of Spain; and now, presumably at Hugh's request, the monarch agreed that the Cluniac monk by the name of Robert, who was then Abbot of Sahagún, should become Archbishop of Toledo and head of the Church in Spain.

At a stroke Cluny had effectively become the spiritual ruler of Christian Spain.

Alfonso's gratitude did not end there. He decided to double the annual tribute paid to the abbey, from one thousand gold pieces to two thousand. The immediate effect of this vast increase in Cluny's fortune was the realisation of a dream which Hugh had cherished ever since his election as abbot thirty-six years earlier. His dream was of a church that was larger and more splendid than any yet built anywhere. Now Alfonso's tribute made it possible. Hugh wasted no time. The first stones of Cluny's new church were laid in 1088, just three years after the capture of Toledo. In spite of the nave roof collapsing at one stage, work on the enormous building progressed steadily over the following decades. In 1130, after forty-two years, it was finally completed – almost 600 feet in overall length. It was the greatest church in Christendom, and would remain so for many centuries. One of Hugh's biographers described it as 'so spacious that thousands of monks could assemble there, and so magnificent that an emperor could have built nothing finer'.

Hugh never lived to see his dream fulfilled, the abbot having died in the year 1109 after sixty years at the helm.

There are surviving drawings and engravings of the abbey church, made before almost all of it was destroyed in the angry wake of the French Revolution. They manage to convey something of the sense of awe and grandeur it must have inspired. It was not only the largest and most magnificent church ever seen at the time; it remained a true wonder of the world right up to its destruction in the 1790s.

It is easy to see the mighty abbey church as Abbot Hugh's outstanding legacy. Yet the sheer scale of the achievement too easily overshadows other developments relating to Cluny which arose directly out of the fruitful relationship between Abbot Hugh and King Alfonso, several of which had a powerful bearing on the Santiago pilgrimage. Like the roads in France, the Spanish pilgrim road was a venue for many interests and many kinds of traveller. Once free of Saracen attack, and with bridges, hospices and other services now in place, the road attracted a growing number of merchants and tradesmen of widely varying skills, all of whom found lucrative work along the way. In a hitherto impoverished land they brought skills which were sorely needed, and soon the Spanish road became a flourishing trade route as well as a vehicle for pilgrims. Suddenly there was new wealth, much of it generated by these craftsmen and merchants from north of the Pyrenees who had travelled with their goods and their skills along the pilgrim road. That it became known as the *camino francès* was not only due to the pilgrims being predominantly from France: the craftsmen who found work opening up the road were mostly from north of the Pyrenees too. King Alfonso recognised their value and saw to it that these skilled foreigners were encouraged to stay and settle down: as a result a number of towns along the Spanish pilgrim road became to a large extent French settlements – among them Estella, Logroño, Burgos and (as its name suggests) Villafranca.

In all this rapid social change taking place in northern Spain Cluny had a firm hand. The abbey was a presiding presence. Already in Hugh's day Santiago had a Cluniac monk as bishop. Now Cluniac abbeys and priories were dotted along the pilgrim road as far as Santiago itself; and the hospices where pilgrims and other travellers found food and rest were for the most part attached to those same religious houses. With Alfonso's benevolent encouragement the abbey had come to control the Church in the whole of northern Spain. And since the Church was the only organised body in the land Cluny effectively administered the entire area. The power of the French Church shored up Alfonso's fragile kingdom, while the Spanish monarch's patronage of Cluny made the abbey rich.

In the perspective of our own time it is hard to grasp how a monastery could exert quite so much political power and influence on an international scale. The monastic tradition was vastly different: the early monasteries had been enclosed cells established as far away as possible from the materialistic world which was regarded as 'Babylon', godless and corrupt. Monks were walled in, isolated with their prayers, their rituals and their holy texts. The contrast with eleventh- and twelfth-century Cluny could hardly be greater: from a remote cell in the desert to a sumptuous Burgundian abbey at the heart of a new feudal world, with its aristocratic connections and its abbots esteemed as power-brokers to kings and popes.

The transition from desert hermits to rulers had its roots many centuries earlier. It was the monasteries which produced some of the first thinkers in the Christian world, applying their intellect to explain and define the nature of their faith and its practice. They were men who began to make an impact on the wider world beyond monastery walls by setting out to establish basic rules on how a Christian life should be led: men such as St Martin of Tours in the fourth century, St Augustine of Hippo and St John Cassian in the next century, and above all St Benedict of Nursia, founder of the Benedictine Order and author of the *Rule of St Benedict*, in the sixth century. But it was not until after the dark centuries that followed, and the establishment of a new political order in Europe, that the intellectual role of the monasteries could find its key position within a refreshed Christian world.

By the eleventh century feudalism, with its clear definition of everyone's position and responsibilities in life, had supplied a social structure to Christian Europe in which the new monasteries played an invaluable part. They harboured an intellectual elite within those protective walls, as they had always done; except that now their role as men of learning had a vital political dimension. Because the leading monks were literate, and spoke Latin, they could communicate with each other right across the Christian world. Unlike their rulers, who were mostly illiterate, they enjoyed the gift of tongues. This made them invaluable to those rulers as ambassadors, political advisers and (as we have seen) as the sponsors of armies.

Add to all this their spiritual role, and it becomes clearer why the monasteries, Cluny above all, should have enjoyed such spectacular success. Its abbots had not only the ear of God, but that of the pope and of just about every political leader in Europe. And within their own world they presided over an empire so regulated that it imposed a structure – a sense of stability and order – in which religious practice could flourish. The pattern of how a Christian could lead his life was now clear. And without that structure it is impossible to imagine how a social phenomenon as sophisticated and widespread as the Santiago pilgrimage could possibly have taken place. Cluny's empire laid down a vast network of tracks across the continent of Europe along which pilgrims could set forth, in confidence, and in good faith.

They had become the roads to heaven, drawing travellers magnetically from shrine to shrine, each with its own story to tell – its own legend, its own special magic. Medieval society made little distinction between truth and folklore. The concept of 'evidence', or 'proof', was largely unknown or considered unnecessary. Doubts could easily be quelled if some dream or miracle revealed that God had willed it so. Accordingly legends were widely accepted as historical facts; and in medieval Christian Europe the most popular legends were those which brought people closer to the source of their Christian faith – already more than a thousand years ago and far away geographically. Legends relating to events in the life of Christ and his followers bridged those gulfs, extending a hand of comfort and reassurance to those living in a bleak world, as well as bringing a certain moral structure to people's lives. The pilgrimage movement of the Middle Ages was to a large extent the expression of a widespread yearning for such reassurances.

Legends relating to the birth of Christianity confronted pilgrims wherever they travelled. Those beginning their journey at Vézelay found themselves immersed in one of the most poignant of them. The convoluted tale of Mary Magdalene and her supposed life and death in France was told in Chapter 7. The intense popularity of her shrine as a place of pilgrimage was undoubtedly why *The Pilgrim's Guide* could list Vézelay as one of the four natural starting-points for those setting off to Santiago. Once again two Christian legends had intertwined – that of St James and that of Mary Magdalene – each enhancing the popular appeal of the other.

But the Magdalene legend had a further appeal to pilgrims travelling through this region. The miraculous raft (or boat) which had borne Christ's persecuted relatives and followers safely to the shores of Provence had also carried Mary Magdalene's sister Martha and her brother Lazarus, Christ's friend whom he had brought back from the dead in Bethany. The various legends relating to Lazarus are even more confused than those surrounding the Magdalene; nonetheless the one most widely circulated was that on arriving at these shores Lazarus became the first Bishop of Marseille and subsequently the city's first Christian martyr. Meanwhile his sister Martha evangelised elsewhere in Provence, performing astonishing deeds including the taming of a man-eating monster, the Tarasque, on the banks of the River Rhône – an event still celebrated in the town named after the beast, Tarascon.

Thereafter the story of Martha and Lazarus, like that of Mary Magdalene, appears to have lain dormant for many centuries, until the new blossoming of Christian faith in the early Middle Ages led to widespread church-building and a fervent quest for shrines and holy relics which the faithful could venerate: in other words, the arrival of the age of pilgrimage. The event which seems to have re-awakened the legend of Lazarus took place early in the eleventh century when the Duke of Burgundy made a public display of presenting what he claimed to be the head of Lazarus to a collegiate church in Avallon, in the northern region of his duchy.

There followed an immediate and indignant response from the cathedral authorities of another Burgundian city further to the south, Autun. The saint's entire body, they insisted, had been in their possession for many centuries. The age of ecclesiastical rivalry had begun. Pilgrimage was becoming big business, and Church authorities all over France were now vying with each other to attract the lion's share of it.

For Autun the principal rivalry was never with Avallon, but with a far more important establishment, the great abbey of Vézelay. Here, by the end of the eleventh century the cult of Mary Magdalene had firmly taken hold, and the news that the abbey was in possession of the saint's body was attracting pilgrims from far and wide. The cathedral authorities at Autun decided to follow suit, having no wish to be outdone by Vézelay. They too had holy relics, equally prestigious. The decision was made, early in the following century, to build a new cathedral dedicated to St Lazarus, whose body would in the course of time be placed in a magnificent tomb to be set behind the high altar.

The story of Autun in many respects runs parallel to that of Vézelay. Both religious houses rose to become among the most popular pilgrimage centres in France. The romantic legend of the saints from the sea landing on these shores made a powerful impact on the medieval mind: it was as though the miraculous raft guided here from the Holy Land by the hand of God symbolised the arrival in France of the true faith, and the whole land was moved to celebrate the event. There was a distinctive difference between the popular appeal exerted by the two saints. At Vézelay the Magdalene was the repentant sinner beloved by Christ, whose feet she had washed with her tears and dried with her long hair. At Autun the appeal of Lazarus was altogether more stern. Not only was he Lazarus of Bethany, friend of Jesus, but he was also an early martyr at the hands of the Romans. As if this was not credit enough the identity of Lazarus had by now become confused with the figure portrayed in Christ's parable of Lazarus (in St Luke's gospel) of the beggar living outside the rich man's gate whose sores are licked clean by dogs. Hence Lazarus became cast as the patron saint of lepers, who soon began to flock, or hobble, to Autun to receive the saint's blessing.

It must have been inevitable that pilgrims assembling at Vézelay before setting off for Spain and Santiago would have become drawn into the highly emotional cult of Mary Magdalene. The saint herself may even have been seen as a key figure guiding them on their long journey ahead. How many pilgrims, having left Vézelay on the road, then felt compelled to seek out the shrine of the Magdalene's brother Lazarus, who had been a fellow survivor of that miraculous raft, is impossible to know. But Autun was no more than a two-day trek to the east of the main pilgrim road as they travelled south: besides, any traveller who had made the longer diversion to Cluny is almost certain to have paused at Autun on the way.[23]

Today's travellers are more likely to embrace all three sites – Vézelay, Autun and Cluny – as a single group. Together they represent a trio of incomparable artistic masterpieces. Even though so little remains of Cluny itself, without the imaginative vision of its abbots and its school of carvers and stonemasons there would have been no Vézelay and no Autun. Cluny was the birthplace of some of the finest medieval art and architecture ever created. And in the case of Autun we have the rare experience of knowing the name of its creator.

It was an uncommon mixture of luck and prudishness which brought about this discovery. Early in the nineteenth century the local authorities responsible for the maintenance of Autun's medieval cathedral decided to remove an innocuous slab of plaster which in the previous century had been laid over the original tympanum above the cathedral's west door. The eighteenth century had been an era which

23 See Plate 14.

was happy to regard medieval art as crude, even barbaric, entirely inconsistent with the prevailing taste for elegance and good manners. Ironically, by covering over the entire area above the west door these eighteenth-century fathers of the church managed to preserve what would very likely have been wrecked by the anti-clerical mob during the French Revolution a few decades later. When the nineteenth-century restorers set to work they revealed a vast sculptural panel on the theme of the Last Judgment, with the figure of Christ in Majesty seated imperiously on a throne, his arms outstretched towards the damned on one side and the saved on the other. And below the feet of Christ emerged a Latin inscription, boldly engraved in the stone, which read *Gislebertus hoc fecit*. 'Gislebertus made this'.

Only an artist held in the highest esteem would have been permitted to trumpet his achievement quite so proudly, and in such a place where it would catch the eye of every parishioner and pilgrim entering the cathedral – right above their heads as they gazed up at the majestic figure of Christ in Glory. Here was self-congratulation writ large, endorsed what was more by the highest possible authority. And yet, but for that inscription the identity of a sculptor of genius would never have been revealed. Curiously, the effect of that name – even of a man about whom we know absolutely nothing else – does more than simply banish anonymity: it manages to impose a distinctive personality not only on this remarkable tympanum but on to the vast body of work which we know the same sculptor undertook throughout the cathedral.

Few artists in any era have been solely responsible for decorating an entire house of God. Gislebertus was one of that rare breed. His spirit inhabits the cathedral of Autun much as Michelangelo's inhabits the Sistine Chapel in Rome. The world of Gislebertus is one of extremes – of light and dark, joy and pain, gentleness and cruelty, pathos and tragedy. It is a restless world, populated by people who seem constantly on the move, expressed by the sculptor's simple device of making their clothing ripple and flow as if caught in a wind. Stone is made to appear light and fluid, as if moulded and caressed by the human hand rather than carved. Pressed together into one expanse of stone are so many little stories, each one a cameo, and with so many perceptive touches of humanity it is easy to imagine pilgrims gazing up at such a rich panorama of life and recognising it as a world they knew.[24]

Autun's great cathedral, and the way Gislebertus has humanised it, explains as movingly as any place in Christendom the nature and spirit of pilgrimage and people's urge to venture forth and follow their star. At Autun we come to realise that not all religious art of the Middle Ages was a punitive sermon in stone, and that human love and compassion, even ribaldry and laughter, had their place alongside prayer and punishment.

As it happens pilgrims entering Autun's cathedral were generally spared Gislebertus' vision of the Last Judgment. The west door was rarely used as the main entrance for the understandable reason that it opened directly on to the city's main graveyard. On the other hand it may be that the bishop realised that the north door would always be the preferred entrance, which is why he commissioned Gislebertus to create here a second tympanum on the theme of the saint to whom the new cathedral was dedicated, St Lazarus – whose relics were the main reason why pilgrims came here in such large numbers. Sadly only a few fragments of it remain, the tympanum having fallen victim to the same mindless iconoclasm by the eighteenth-century cathedral authorities as the west portal; except that in this case they were not content merely to plaster it over, they destroyed it – or most of it. From a brief description in the fifteen century we know that on the central supporting pillar the sculptor carved a tall standing figure of the saint, while the theme of the Raising of Lazarus from the Dead occupied the main area of the tympanum itself. Alas, neither has survived.

It may seem surprising that the heads of the cathedral chapter should take such violent exception to images of their own saint, and one who attracted so many pilgrims. But the true reason may lie elsewhere. At the base of the tympanum, right above the central pillar, Gislebertus carved the lintel as a horizontal frieze depicting

24. See Plate 15.

the Temptation of Adam in the Garden of Eden, one of the favourite themes of the medieval Church. It spanned the entire width of the north door, making it necessary for the two figures of Adam and Eve to be horizontal – approaching one another head to head at the centre by the Tree of Knowledge, Adam from the left, Eve from the right accompanied by the serpent and grasping the apple. It is an extraordinarily interpretation of the Temptation – vivid and distinctly erotic. Furthermore, because of the width of the lintel both figures were virtually life-size, and except for a few stray wisps of grape-vine entirely naked. In other words pilgrims making their way into the cathedral to celebrate mass would be required to pass beneath a startlingly realistic enactment of mankind's primal sin, which looked far too enjoyable to be regarded as sinful. And while such a scene was clearly acceptable to Bishop Etienne and his fellow-churchmen in the twelfth century it was evidently too much for their eighteenth-century successors in an age of periwigs and buckled shoes. Accordingly, in the interest of propriety and good manners they had it ripped it out.

The figure of Adam disappeared, along with that of Lazarus and most of the entire north tympanum. Eve – by the skin of her teeth – has survived. She was discovered by chance in the middle of the nineteenth century during the demolition of a house which had been built in 1769, a mere three years after the cathedral authorities had torn down the north door. They had not even bothered to clear away Gislebertus' wrecked tympanum, but had left the various sculpted panels lying around to be taken away for some nominal fee. Eve had become useful building material – a fate matched a few decades later and on a larger scale by Cluny's abbey church.

Eve is unlike any other medieval carving. She is enigmatic and entirely unforgettable. Her sexuality is presented as dangerous (as religious teaching of the day would have insisted), but also as irresistibly appealing. In this respect Gislebertus made her transcend the prevailing misogyny of the medieval Church; and she becomes a forerunner of a great European tradition of the female nude in art. Today she is the prime exhibit in Autun's Musée Rolin only a short distance from the cathedral which she graced for more than six centuries.

10. On the Miracle Trail

IT WOULD BE HARD TO EXAGGERATE the impact of sacred places such as Vézelay, Cluny and Autun on the ordinary pilgrim in twelfth-century France who in all probability had never experienced any religious ceremony more splendid than Sunday mass in the local village church. The opulence of the abbey buildings themselves, the grandeur of the church services with their elaborate liturgy, and of course the shrines of the saints with their jewel-studded reliquaries and so many vivid accounts of miracles performed there: all of these, put together, would have amounted to an overwhelming experience imbued with mystery and magic – an introduction to a totally unfamiliar world, even a glimpse of heaven on earth.

Now, after so many highly charged events, those pilgrims who had gathered at Vézelay only a week or so before might have anticipated a less demanding stretch of road as they left Burgundy and headed south-west along the fringes of the central mountains in the direction of Limoges, Périgueux and the distant plains of Gascony. But it was unlikely to be so. Protected though they might be by their scallop-shell and their status as spiritual travellers, pilgrims were still exposed to the political climate of the day; and towards the end of the twelfth century those hoping to make their peaceful way south from shrine to shrine would have found themselves drawn into two of the major social upheavals of the day – the crusades to the Holy Land on the one hand, and on the other the burgeoning war between England and France over the English-held territory of Aquitaine.

The pilgrim road had become a battle zone as well as a sanctuary for returning crusaders who had been captured or wounded in battle; and for travellers at that time there were reminders of both events everywhere they went. At Issoudun, just a few miles along the road from Bourges, the main street today known as the Rue Saint-Jacques leads to the Tour Saint-Jacques which originally formed part of a massive fortress built by the King of England, Richard the Lionheart, on his return from the Third Crusade in the last decade of the twelfth century. The tower was a bulwark in his heavy-handed campaign to secure his territories against the French King Philippe-Auguste, who had laid his hands on them in Richard's absence. The pilgrim road passes through the very town where the English monarch was fatally wounded by a bolt from a crossbow. Nearby, in the small town of Neuvy, pilgrims would pause to offer their prayers in a church dedicated to St James which had been built by an earlier returning crusader as a copy of the Church of the Holy Sepulchre in Jerusalem on the site of Christ's tomb. A few miles further still another small settlement, Cluis, lay on the very frontier between territory ruled by the Kings of France and the Duchy of Aquitaine which was ruled by England.

Altogether this was hardly the tranquil progress through the gentle countryside which pilgrims may have expected. In addition to the customary hazards of the road they would have found themselves continually assaulted by echoes of crusading fervour mixed with the roar of battle. Today's traveller in this historic region of France can still hear those same echoes rebounding from the medieval churches and castles that survive along the road, overlaid by further echoes of the great pilgrimage itself as it took place throughout these troubled centuries.

Relations between the English and French kings had for a time seemed amicable. Richard and Philippe-Auguste were united in their commitment to the Third Crusade, and had spent months together in 1189 at the abbey of Vézelay planning the great adventure in which they were to lead their respective armies. It was during the course of their campaign in the Holy Land against the Muslim leader Saladin that the two monarchs fell out. The French king decided to return early, to the contempt of Richard, leaving the English king to continue the campaign. After conducting a peace pact with Saladin Richard set sail for home, only to be shipwrecked on his return journey and held captive by the Duke of Austria until a vast ransom was raised to obtain his release and return to England in 1194.

This precis of one of history's most famously romantic melodramas would have little relevance to the Santiago pilgrimage had Richard quietly remained in England. But he was English only in name. Neither of his parents, Duchess Eleanor of Aquitaine and King Henry II, was English; and Richard himself did not even speak the native language: Where he was born, and where he mostly lived, was France: and now, as soon as possible on his release from captivity his ambitions turned to France, and in particular to the security of Aquitaine which his mother's marriage to Henry had placed under English rule. And as he led his army to secure its borders, his opponent was naturally his former fellow-crusader and companion at Vézelay, King Philippe-Auguste of France. The ensuing conflict turned the pilgrim road into a battlefield. And one longs for a traveller's eye-witness account of how pilgrims fared in such threatening circumstances.

Today Richard the Lionheart's presence is never far from this stretch of the pilgrim road. One of the most striking landmarks in the region is the slender spire and bell-tower of the Church of Saint-Léonard-de-Noblat, rising high above the river valley to the east of Limoges. The English monarch is known to have contributed to its building costs in thanksgiving to St Leonard for having facilitated his release from prison in Austria on his ill-starred return from the Third Crusade, so the king believed. In fact the connection between Saint-Léonard and the crusading movement dated back to its foundation a century earlier in the aftermath of the First Crusade, when one of its chapels was sponsored by a returning crusader and named after the Holy Sepulchre in Jerusalem.

Christian saints in the Middle Ages tended to rise from obscurity in response to particular needs and circumstances of the day; and St Leonard seems to have been a case in point. There is no record of his very existence until the eleventh century: then his emergence as a focus of popular veneration coincides with the beginning of the crusading movement as well as with the military campaigns of Reconquest in Spain that was heavily supported by Cluny. In both spheres of operation the saint was reputed to have performed numerous miracles in which prisoners captured in battle were released: From nowhere Leonard became widely recognised as a patron saint of prisoners; hence Richard the Lionheart's gesture of thanks in Aquitaine following his release from captivity.

Characteristically the fame of St Leonard soon attached his name to the list of saints whose shrine were required places of veneration for pilgrims generally, in particular those bound for Spain, where many cases of prisoners miraculously released from Muslim hands had been reported. *The Pilgrim's Guide* includes a fulsome entry on St Leonard, who is reputed to have been a sixth-century nobleman who abandoned a life of riches for a hermit's existence in the forests around Limoges, 'enduring cold, nakedness and unspeakable labours [before] passing away in a saintly fashion'.

The overheated style of writing suggests that the author may well have been the same Benedictine monk from Parthenay-le-Vieux, Aimery Picaud, whose ribald earlier comments on the behaviour of the Gascons we encountered in Chapter 6. His account of St Leonard's legacy continues in the same rich vein: 'His extraordinarily powerful virtues have delivered from prison countless thousands of captives. Their iron chains, more barbarous than one can possibly recount, joined together by the thousand, have been placed in testimony of such great miracles all around his basilica.'

One of the saint's miracles mentioned in the *Guide* concerned a crusader by the name of Bohemond, Prince of Antioch and son of the Duke of Apulia, who had been taken prisoner by the Turks in the aftermath of the First Crusade. The author attributes his release from captivity entirely to a miracle performed by St Leonard, In fact the 'miracle' consisted of the emir being moved to accept a huge ransom for Bohemond's release – a fact omitted from the *Guide*. Such was the universal belief in the power of miracles that Bohemond himself attributed his release to the saint's intervention, even travelling halfway across Europe to the newly-founded Church of Saint-Léonard-de-Noblat in order to offer his effusive prayers of thanks.

The pilgrimage movement was founded on a cult of the saints; and in turn the cult of the saints rested on a widely held belief in miracles. The canonisation of a new saint by the pope would only take place if the proposed candidate could be shown to have performed an impressive number of miracles. And since a church or abbey in possession of relics of a newly canonised saint stood to gain massively as a result by donations and bequests of land, not surprisingly there grew up, as in the case of relics, something of a 'miracles industry' in eleventh- and twelfth-century Europe. Candidates for sainthood were virtually queuing up. Centuries later, at the time of the Counter Reformation, Protestant jibes induced the Vatican to appoint a canon lawyer specially to mount an argument against the canonisation of a candidate – a role popularly known as the 'Devil's Advocate'. But in the Middle Ages no such corrective system existed, and papal judgment was a more haphazard affair depending largely on the strength of each case as presented to His Holiness, and on the pope's personal inclinations.

In modern terminology it all sounds like an exercise in skilful public relations. Priests and monks who were guardians of an important shrine are known to have taken pains to maximise its profitability by drawing up lists of miracles which their saint was claimed to have performed. Sometimes the eagerness of an abbey to claim a miracle led to an outcome at odds with public interest as well as the rule of law, as when the monks of Vézelay keenly supported the release of a prisoner due to the miraculous intervention of Mary Magdalene, in spite of the fact that the man was a convicted murderer.

The process of claiming and authenticating a miracle was not always as naive or grasping as it may appear to our eyes. Any number of events which today would be attributed to some identifiable natural cause did not appear so to the medieval onlooker. If there is an eclipse of the sun we know without hesitation what shadow has caused it, and that it will duly pass. If there is a severe flood in the plains we know that excessive rainfall in the mountains has caused rivers to burst their banks. If there is an outbreak of malaria we know that mosquitoes are the cause, just as that the Black Death was brought by fleas carried by the black rat. But in those times there was no such understanding of the workings of the natural world. Our life on earth was full of wondrous and fearful mysteries many of which lay outside the natural order of things, and could not be explained except in terms of divine will: that God – and sometimes a punitive God – had willed it so.

But God was also perceived to be merciful: hence it seemed natural to appeal to Him for forgiveness and help. What He had willed He could be persuaded to ameliorate; and here a channel of communication existed through which such an appeal could be made. That channel was through the good offices of the Christian saints, who had God's ear. They were the essential intermediaries: accordingly their shrines were of supreme importance in the medieval order. They were God's listening-posts. An appeal to divine authority through the intercession of His saints could lead to a radical transformation of human fortunes, whether in matters of illness, some natural disaster, an unjust imprisonment or personal misfortune, a crisis in battle, or whatever. And that divine intervention *was* the miracle.

Belief in miracles lay at the heart of Church teaching and of the Christian faith in medieval Europe. It was a belief universally held, and tended to invite scenes of public celebration that were sometimes far from godly. Yet, for all the trappings of funfair and fairground, without an unquestioned core of belief in the miraculous there would have been no such occasions: there would have been no cult of the saints, and no shrines to attract worshippers. And of course without those shrines there would have been no pilgrimages; and those of us today who love majestic church architecture, and the masterpieces of painting and sculpture which accompany them, would be sorely deprived. For many centuries the pilgrim roads in France and Spain were the inspiration for some of the most glories achievements of western civilisation; and it is places like Vézelay, Autun, Aulnay, Chartres and Santiago de Compostela itself which to our eyes may be seen as the real 'miracles' of the Middle Ages, whose magnificence transcends all cults and matters of faith. They lift the human spirit, bearing witness to the soaring power of the creative imagination.

*

This stretch of the pilgrim route along the edge of the central mountains was the frontline in territorial battles between England and France for more than three hundred years. As a result it is hardly surprising that so many of the saints revered in this region should have been honoured for miracles in which victims of war were healed of their wounds or released from captivity. In the medieval church at Saint-Leonard-de-Noblat, with its massive bell-tower and spire pointing so confidently to heaven, kings, dukes and countless more humble soldiers came to offer prayers of thanks to the saint whom they believed to be responsible for their deliverance from enemy hands.

Medieval pilgrims who paused here to pay their respects to those miraculous events then set off westwards across the valley to the city which gave its name to this road. The city was Limoges, and in *The Pilgrim's Guide* the road is named the *Via Lemovicensis*, and two thirteenth-century bridges still lead the traveller along the ancient trail. Limoges was the city of another miracle-worker, St Martial, who surprisingly gets no mention whatever. The little we know about Martial is that he was a preacher in pre-Christian Roman Gaul who defied persecution and achieved popular acclaim for his miraculous powers. It is reasonable to suppose that he might have been forgotten like St Léonard but for the fact that seven centuries later the newly-founded monastery of Cluny began to extend its influence south-west from Burgundy, sponsoring abbeys and priories which serviced the pilgrim road to Spain. And the Abbey of Saint-Martial was one of them.

With the growing popularity of the pilgrimage movement, spurred by the legend of St James and the emotive cause of Reconquest in Spain, the Abbey of Saint-Martial soon became richly endowed, and by the eleventh century the abbey church could offer pilgrims the dramatic sight of a reliquary of the saint as a seated figure entirely encased in gold, with hands outstretched in a gesture of blessing. The impact on pilgrims entering the candlelit church after days and weeks on the road in this war-torn countryside must have been hypnotic. Here was the golden saint himself, the master of miracles, arms extended in welcome to the weary traveller. It would have been close to being blessed by God. Alas, the reliquary-statue no longer exists, but travellers on the third of these pilgrim roads, the one from Le Puy, will soon come face to face with a similar reliquary which *has* survived, the extraordinary Majesté de Sainte-Foy at Conques, about which a great deal will be said later.

The Church of Saint-Martin in Limoges was one of the five archetypal pilgrim churches which conformed to the same plan, designed to accommodate large congregations capable of circulating freely along the broad aisles and behind the high altar in order to venerate the relics placed in full view on the altar itself (as described in Chapter 3). Such was the power and appeal of the great Church of Saint-Martin, with its iconic reliquary-statue, that pilgrims threw themselves to the floor before the miracle-working reliquary in the most extreme states of self-abasement. There is even a record in the fourteenth century of pilgrims arriving at Saint-Martial and stripping off their clothing in order to appear before the saint entirely naked and therefore bereft of all worldly trappings. Yet late in the same century devotional practice shifted from the dramatic to a more prosaic form of veneration: the golden statue with the outstretched hands was removed (and presumably the gold melted down) and replaced by a mere box with a little door which pilgrims could open in order to observe a hand of the saint. It is hard not to think that a certain magic had been sacrificed in the interest of being able to set eyes on the relic itself. Miracle-working had come down to earth.

Today almost everything here has gone – golden statue, reliquary box, saintly relic, church and abbey too – for the most part victims of the furious iconoclasm of the French revolutionary mob with its loathing of all monastic institutions in the late eighteenth century. But then in 1960, during building work in the city centre, a small but important discovery was made. Excavations revealed the crypt of the original church, part of which dates from the fourth century barely a hundred years after the death of St Martial, in the very first phase of the conversion of the Roman Empire to Christianity.

Like so many places along this pilgrim road Limoges bore the scars of battle from the protracted conflict between England and France known as the Hundred Years' War – which actually went on for three hundred years. In 1370 Edward the Black Prince, son and heir of the English King Edward III, occupied the city after a siege and proceeded to massacre three thousand inhabitants in an act of reprisal, or so it was claimed by the French chronicler Froissart. The fact that the figure may have been a considerable exaggeration scarcely alters the picture we have before us of a brutal time and place when the ordinary traveller or harmless citizen constantly feared for his life. Not surprisingly, miracle-workers were greatly in demand, and through much of the Hundred Years' War the Abbey of Saint-Martial, like that of Saint-Léonard-de-Noblat a few miles to the east, was the scene of numerous appeals and prayers of thanksgiving on behalf of prisoners miraculously released from captivity on both sides of the conflict. And if little remains in Limoges itself as witness to those violent times, today's travellers continuing south along the pilgrim road soon find themselves in the small town of Châlus where a gaunt stone tower stands as a monument to another grim event in that conflict between England and France. It was from this tower in the year 1199 that the English King Richard the Lionheart was fatally wounded by a bolt from a crossbow. The monarch who had survived a crusade and years of imprisonment eventually fell to the unlikely shot of a distant marksman.

Echoes of the crusades continued to follow pilgrims on their journey southwards from Limoges and Châlus. The next major halt on the road was the city of Périgueux. And here the modern traveller may be confronted by the same sense of disorientation as the medieval pilgrim would have experienced; because the huge sprawling cathedral of Périgueux, built in the twelfth century, is likely to make any visitor feel transported far away to the eastern Mediterranean. The building is crowned by a huge white dome, quite unlike any other cathedral in France, its design having clearly been drawn up at the behest of French crusaders or merchants familiar with the churches of Byzantium. Opinions vary as to its precise origin, but the consensus favours either the Church of the Holy Apostles in Constantinople, or possibly that it may have been conceived as a copy of the Basilica San Marco in Venice.

To the medieval pilgrim this was the shrine of another miracle-working saint. The appropriate entry in *The Pilgrim's Guide* makes this quite clear: 'After the Blessed Léonard one must visit in the city of Périgueux the remains of the Blessed Fronto'. The saint whose name now translates as St Front is reputed to have been the first Bishop of Périgueux, and the *Guide* gives a colourful account of his life. It seems he was ordained in Rome by no less a figure than St Peter himself, who then sent him to preach in newly conquered Roman Gaul together with a colleague by the name of George. When the latter died Front returned to Rome and was given Peter's staff which had the magical power to restore a man to life. 'And so it was done,' we are assured. Front proceeded to convert the city of Périgueux to Christianity, 'rendering it illustrious through many miracles, and died there in all dignity'. It was a story widely enough circulated for the scene of St Peter presenting the saint with his staff to have been carved in stone for the main portal of the original cathedral, the carving now displayed in the local museum.

This account of St Front's life is an eloquent illustration of how the medieval Church sought to link the shrines along the pilgrim roads to the era of Christ and his apostles: it was a continual process of bridge-building, designed to bring the pilgrimage movement close to the fountain-head of the Christian faith across a gulf of more than one thousand years. Whatever the origin of the *Guide*'s version of the St Front story, we know that there were other versions in circulation at the same time. From as early as the eleventh century St Front's companion, George, is named as one of the early Bishops of Le Puy in the late fifth century, almost five hundred years after he was supposed to have been brought back to life by St Peter's magical staff. The vast discrepancy in dates between the two versions is

11. A masterpiece of medieval sculpture, the central figure of Christ above the entrance to the former abbey church of St Mary Magdalene at Vézelay – starting-point of the second road described in *The Pilgrim's Guide*. (Vassil/Wikimedia Commons)

12. Mont Saint-Michel, off the Normandy coast: among the most revered centres of pilgrimage in the Middle Ages. English pilgrims bound for Santiago would pause here to offer prayers of thanks for their safe crossing before heading south to join one of the main pilgrim roads. (Adam Woolfitt)

13. An important diversion for pilgrims: the powerful Burgundian abbey of Cluny, prime sponsor of the Santiago pilgrimage, and probably responsible for *The Pilgrim's Guide*. (Michal Osmenda/Wikimedia Commons)

14. A major shrine on the road from Vézelay: the twelfth-century cathedral of Saint-Lazare at Autun. The sculpture throughout the cathedral is the work of one of the few medieval artists we know by name: Gislebertus. (Adam Woolfitt)

15. Autun rivalled Vézelay in popularity with pilgrims for supposedly possessing the relics of Lazarus, brother of Mary Magdalene and Christ's friend whom he brought back to life in Bethany. (Adam Woolfitt)

16. Starting-point for the third road: Le Puy-en-Velay – city of rocky hills and pinnacles. To reach the church of Saint-Michel d'Aiguilhe pilgrims needed to climb 267 steps. (Adam Woolfitt)

17. Golden majesty. The statue reliquary of Sainte-Foy, studded with precious stones: together with other treasures displayed in the abbey of Conques regarded as among the wonders of the Christian world.
(Robert Harding/Alamy)

18. Masterpiece of medieval stone-carving: a detail of the life-size figure of the prophet Jeremiah on the central column of the main entrance to the abbey church of Moissac.
(Adam Woolfitt)

19. Ancient stepping-stones led travellers across the River Bidouze in the Basque Country to where their road from Le Puy links up with the pilgrim roads from Paris and Vézelay.
(Adam Woolfitt)

20. A reminder to pilgrims as they passed by: a simple roadside cross in the Basque Country approaching the Pyrenees.
(Adam Woolfitt)

probably best explained by the relative requirements of two different Church bodies. The authorities in Le Puy, which was an important bishopric, would have been keen to establish a respectable list of early founders who had enjoyed close links with the Christian saints. The Cluniac promoters of the Santiago pilgrimage, on the other hand, would have been principally concerned to make a direct connection with the era of their patron, St James, whose shrine was the pilgrims' ultimate goal.

Resolving the discrepancy of five hundred years between the two versions required a small, but vital, twist in the story. In the Le Puy version St Front was merely given the apostle's staff on his return to Rome in order to bring his companion back to life; whereas in the *Guide*'s story St Front is given the staff by St Peter in person. Given the thread of propaganda running through the *Codex Calixtinus,* of which *The Pilgrim's Guide* forms a key part, it is hardly surprising that this should have been the version chosen by its compilers. Pilgrims arriving at the shrine of St Front in Périgueux could feel confident that they were walking in the footsteps of those who had been close to Christ and his apostles.

The story of St Front, dramatic as it is seen to be, is a variation on the tales told of so many of these revered early saints who were rediscovered by a revitalised Christian world after so many centuries in obscurity, and whose relics were now venerated all along the pilgrim roads in France and elsewhere in Europe. The saints themselves, as described in medieval texts, were generally isolated figures living in Roman Gaul, often hermits, who bravely preached the gospel in the face of persecution and who frequently suffered martyrdom. Crucially in the eyes of the medieval Church (particularly so in the case of St Front) for a religious house to possess the relics of these early saints provided a direct link with the time of Christ and his disciples, and thereby created an invaluable bridge between the 'modern' Christian era in Western Europe and the source of the Christian faith in the Bible Lands so very far away in time and place.

The pilgrim route from Vézelay is especially rich in shrines, churches and other monuments which offer that bridge between the early centuries of embattled Christianity and the medieval world, as well as a further bridge to our own time, a total span of more than two thousand years. Travelling along this rural stretch of road is a constant re-acquaintance with the past as we journey through different time zones – a trail of miracles and memories which threads its colourful way from Burgundy to the Pyrenees and Spain.

The shrines and weathered churches along this route are like signposts directing the pilgrim onwards. Soon after Périgueux the squat fortified tower of Sainte-Marie de Chancelade is a further reminder that here was an Anglo-French battleground. This was once another of the numerous abbey churches established by religious orders for the wellbeing of passing pilgrims. The former abbey was (for once) not part of the chain of religious houses set up by Cluny, but was Augustinian, following the Rule of St Augustine of Hippo, whose greatest contribution to the pilgrimage movement was to establish the great monastery of Roncesvalles high in the Pyrenees at the gateway of Spain (see Chapter 15).

A short distance further, and the village of Sainte-Foy-la-Grande can feel as though it fell asleep in medieval times and has scarcely woken since. And then, at La Réole, pilgrims reached the Garonne, the broadest river they would encounter on this route. River crossings, we have seen, were a constant hazard for pilgrims, since they were entirely at the mercy of local ferrymen, who were mostly not there for charitable reasons but to make money out of travellers who had no choice but to employ their services. Aimery Picaud's graphic account in *The Pilgrim's Guide* of the murderous ferrymen at Sorde, on the route from Tours and Paris, was quoted in Chapter 6. Here at La Réole, at least, travellers were relatively safe: between spring and autumn, when pilgrims were generally on the road, the River Garonne was shallow enough for them to wade across it. Picaud's lugubrious warnings would have been unnecessary. On the other hand, having crossed the river, pilgrims were now entering that region of swamp and vicious insects known as the Landes, about which his pronouncements were almost as dire. 'This is a region deprived of all good' was his blunt warning. Today this eastern area of the Landes is no longer the hostile swamp of earlier centuries, being largely forested or agricultural. But before setting out to cross it today's traveller is reminded that the miracle trail is still very much with us. On the edge of the Landes the handsome town of Bazas, small though it is, nonetheless possesses a cathedral which was modelled on the great Gothic cathedrals of northern France. Its surprising grandeur is due to its dedication to John the Baptist, a phial of whose blood was said to have been preserved here, unlikely though it may seem, and was the object of much veneration by pilgrims and – not surprisingly – the source of a great many miracles.

The Pyrenees are now in sight, and the road from Vézelay is drawing closer every mile to the Paris road, which at this point runs almost parallel only a short distance to the west; while closing in from the east is the third pilgrim road, from Le Puy, which we shall shortly be taking. Soon all three roads will converge in the Basque Country just this side of the mountains, while the fourth and most southerly road, from Arles and Saint-Gilles, will keep its distance and not join the other three until the far side of the Pyrenees.

Meanwhile the Vézelay road continues southwards across the eastern expanse of the Landes. One of the few human settlements of any size along this lonely stretch of highway is the small fortified town of Roquefort. And here, in a modest way, is the response of feudal lords to the scathing description in *The Pilgrim's Guide* of the Landes as a region 'deprived of all good' because Roquefort is an example of the 'new towns', known as *bastides*, which were established later in the Middle Ages specifically to bring together into viable communities those scattered inhabitants of the swamps with their pigs and waterlogged hovels. Aimery Picaud would have appreciated Roquefort with its massive ramparts and towers, and a hospice where pilgrims could enjoy 'bread, wine, meat, fish' and other delights of the flesh which the area, as he knew it, so sorely lacked.

After reaching the far side of the Landes yet another in the twelfth-century chain of abbeys founded by Cluny awaited pilgrims. This was Saint-Sever. All that survives today is the handsome abbey church, distinguished by a group of capitals startlingly painted in bright colours which seem incongruous at first until we realise that most stone carving in medieval churches was once similarly painted – even the great tympana of Vézelay and Autun. Then, a short distance beyond Saint-Sever an even earlier historical sight greeted the traveller. At Hagetmau in the year 778 the Emperor Charlemagne founded an abbey to house the relics of another early preacher, St Girons, who had suffered persecution in Roman Gaul. Though the abbey, greatly enlarged at the hands of Cluny in the twelfth century, was destroyed in the sixteenth-century wars of religion, the crypt with its fourteen magnificently carved capitals survives. And perhaps because we come across it unexpectedly in this unsung rural region it gives out an especially powerful echo of those times when medieval pilgrims would arrive at this same place after a long day on the open road, to admire these same carvings in this enclosed vaulted room and to offer their prayers.

Finally there was one more river to cross, the Gave de Pau. And today at Orthez a medieval bridge supports an imposing central watchtower which for eight hundred years has presided over the passage of pilgrims as they made their crossing. And from here it is less than a day's walk into the Basque Country, about which Aimery Picaud reserved some of his most vituperative epithets, as recounted in Chapter 6. And soon, on the crest of the gentle hill called Mont Saint-Sauveur, is a place where we have been before; because on this hillside with the broad flank of the Pyrenees not far ahead is where our road joins the road we took from Paris. It is also where we shall find ourselves yet again in a later chapter – because on this lonely spot, commemorated by a modern stone cross – is where the third of the four pilgrim roads also joins the first two.

And that third road is our next journey.

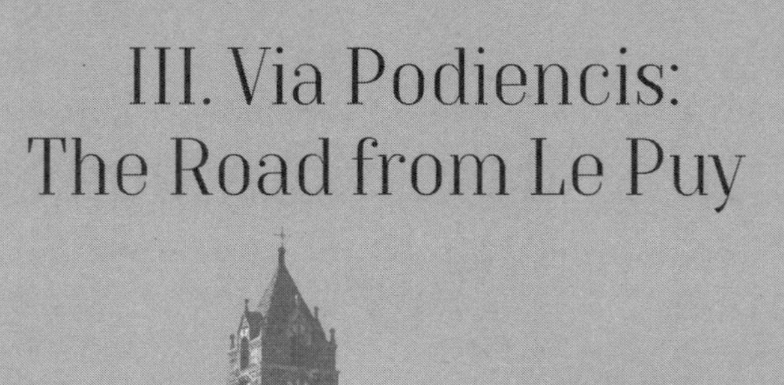

III. Via Podiencis: The Road from Le Puy

11. A Gift of Many Gods

OF THE FOUR PRINCIPAL PILGRIM ROADS IN FRANCE the one from Le Puy-en-Velay, the *Via Podiensis* is the least well documented geographically. A few key churches and abbeys along the route are recommended in *The Pilgrim's Guide*, but they are far apart from each other, and there is no Aimery Picaud to fill in the gaps and indicate which precise route travellers should take in order to reach them: neither are there any trenchant comments on the delights and horrors which pilgrims could expect on their journey. Wayside chapels and former hospices now provide invaluable markers of the likely route. As a result, the road from Le Puy has now become easily the most popular of the four roads for the traveller on foot, especially now that backpacking has become almost an industry. In the words of Robert Louis Stevenson, who famously travelled not far from here, in the Cévennes, with his donkey, 'I travel for travel's sake. The great affair is to move.' Today the track clearly marked GR65 has become generally identified as the original pilgrim road. And its popularity is understandable: the countryside of the Velay region, on the southern slopes of the Auvergne mountains, is wild and glorious; and as the traveller continues south-west several of the artistic gems of the pilgrimage are welcome staging-posts. Altogether, the pilgrim route from Le Puy is the walker's road to heaven.

Much of the landscape of the Velay was formed by volcanoes, and geologically this has given Le Puy an eccentric appearance, a city of sudden hills and surprising pinnacles of rock rising out of the plain, like gnarled fingers pointing to the sky.[25] It is a natural environment

25. See Plate 16.

which has always lent itself to myth-making, and Le Puy is known to have been a sacred place long before its association with the Santiago pilgrimage, and indeed long before the conversion of Roman Gaul in the fourth century. The Emperor Charlemagne celebrated mass here on at least two occasions, in 772 and 800. And a century and a half later, in 950, the local bishop by the name of Godescalc made a pilgrimage to the shrine of St James at Santiago. This was a little over a hundred years after the first reports of the discovery of the apostle's tomb; and we know from a visiting traveller's report that a sizeable pilgrimage from far and wide had grown up in the intervening years. Even so, Godescalc's journey seems to have been the first 'official' visit to the shrine by a senior churchman, and it is widely credited as a historic landmark in the story of the Santiago pilgrimage.

In 951 Bishop Godescalc commemorated his safe return to Le Puy by building a chapel on a tall pinnacle of rock within the city, and dedicated it to the Archangel Michael. It is unclear why his pilgrimage to Santiago should have prompted him to undertake such a thing, but in consequence the Chapelle Saint-Michel d'Aiguilhe became one of the earliest of the 'pinnacle' churches in Europe. In the centuries to follow a number of others would be raised on similar isolated hilltops. Not being an earthly being, and therefore having no relics to be enshrined, St Michael became traditionally venerated in chapels loftily perched and pointing to the heavens, Mont Saint-Michel in Normandy and Saint Michael's Mount in Cornwall being the most celebrated examples. Disciples of mystical geometry have found deep significance in the fact that shrines to the archangel are in a straight line from Cornwall and Normandy in the north, Le Puy in central France, and finally to his earliest known shrine on the slopes of Monte Gargano in southern Italy.

In Le Puy pilgrims to the Chapel of Saint-Michel d'Aiguilhe faced a formidable ascent of 267 steps. Worshippers in large numbers were clearly undaunted by this challenge, keen to express their devotion the hard way, and the chapel rapidly became a popular pilgrimage site. For several centuries it matched the appeal of the cathedral on a neighbouring hill only a short distance away.

The Cathédrale Notre-Dame dates from the late eleventh and twelfth centuries. Today's travellers, familiar with the glow and lightness of Chartres and Bourges cathedrals, may find it oppressively gloomy, being roofed by an almost windowless dome which seems to smother the daylight. The whole building has a distinctly oriental flavour, owing a great deal to the early churches of Byzantium, which are invariably dark. It was evidently inspired by crusaders returning from the Holy Land, and in particular Constantinople. What they wanted back in their own homeland was a place of worship which took them back spiritually to the Bible Lands which they had recently helped to 'liberate'.

At the same time there are equally powerful influences of that other crusading arena, Spain and the campaign of the Reconquest. The interior of the cathedral, and particularly the ribbed vaulting, carry strong references to that masterpiece of Muslim architecture in southern Spain, the Great Mosque in Córdoba. And here there may seem to be a startling contradiction – an important place of Christian worship inspired on the one hand by churches in the Holy Land that had been built in defiance of Islam, and yet inspired equally by one of the finest of all places of Islamic worship.

It is an enigma which perfectly illustrates the ambivalent relationship that existed between Christian Europe and Muslim Spain during these early centuries before the might of Christian arms eventually expelled Islam from the Iberian Peninsula. Until that moment Islamic Spain was the enemy which Christian leaders – at least the more enlightened among them – could not fail to admire, even envy. On the public level the appeal of a Holy War was irresistible to European leaders: the early military campaigns of the Reconquest and the burgeoning pilgrimage movement to Santiago carried huge political and emotional weight throughout the continent, boosting the morale of Europe and lifting Christian spirits so long battered by continual Saracen raids right across France.

At the same time there were other less demonstrative currents that flowed between the Islamic and Christian powers. From early in the tenth century the Muslim caliphate of al-Andalus (modern

Andalusia) in southern Spain, with its capital the city of Córdoba, became the wealthiest and most sophisticated political state in Europe, far outstripping the attainments of Christian civilisations in all the practical sciences, in mathematics, in philosophy and other intellectual pursuits. The library in Córdoba, with its Arabic treatises on medicine and the sciences, and its wealth of translations of Greek, Latin and Hebrew texts, was richer and far broader in scope than any library in the Christian world. As a result, even while armies in northern Spain were battling for territorial gain there existed a great deal of diplomatic and intellectual contact between the two regions of Spain, and even more so between the Muslim south and Christian scholars and Church leaders throughout Western Europe. Córdoba was something of an international city, open to foreigners, and many a Christian visitor returned from his travels with glowing accounts of what he had encountered. Islam might be the enemy in matters of faith and on the battlefield, but it possessed a priceless jewel – learning.

Then, at just the time when the present cathedral of Le Puy was being built, access to that Islamic world of learning was dramatically increased by one of the key events in the Christian Reconquest of Spain, the capture of the city of Toledo in 1085. Here was a city second in importance in Muslim Spain only to Córdoba, and it possessed a library equally rich. Now, with Toledo in Christian hands, that library was open to scholars from all over Europe, and free access became available to that rich store of learning and scholarship which travellers had hitherto only glimpsed in Córdoba. There began a veritable fever to explore those new fields of knowledge which had been opened up. Muslim scholars with an understanding of Latin were now in great demand as translators of Arabic texts on a variety of subjects from mathematics to medicine. One of the most enlightened churchman and theologians of the day became an enthusiast for Islamic writings. He was Peter the Venerable, the last of the great abbots of Cluny and a brave defender of Peter Abelard. He made a special visit to Spain in the year 1142 in order to seek out translators. The abbot had a particular ambition, remarkable for that time, which was to commission a translation of the Koran, though his primary motive for doing so was hardly ecumenical in spirit. It was in order that he could refute it. Unlike so many of his contemporaries in the Church he believed in the power of reasoned argument. Alas, it was an ambition he never had the chance to fulfil.

The cathedral of Le Puy is an embodiment of these contrasting influences – Byzantine churches on the one hand, Muslim mosques on the other. And it is far from being a lone example: other churches along the pilgrim roads, and this road in particular, send out similar signs of diverse cultures. In every case the result is magically harmonised; and it seems appropriate to speculate that a shared desire to create an environment designed for worship may transcend even the most profound religious differences. Indeed, maybe all places of prayer possess a key element in common, regardless of faith. If true, that is true ecumenicalism.

There are other gods, too, whose presence can be felt in Le Puy. Those preparing to climb the broad flight of sixty steps to the striking facade of the cathedral with its alternate bands of white limestone and black volcanic rock, might appreciate a charming story before they set off. It concerns a priest by the name of Voisy who was to become the first bishop of this cathedral late in the fourth century, and who made this same climb, at that time up the slope of what was a bare hillside. It was a midsummer day, yet to the priest's astonishment he found the crest of the hill to be blanketed in snow. Furthermore, on the snow-covered ground rose a solitary standing-stone, a menhir, which had been raised to some pagan god long ago. Voisy then noticed that encircling the menhir at a certain distance were the tracks of a deer. It was instantly clear to the priest that the deer had been a divine messenger, and that its footprints were meant to trace the outline of the church to be built on the site. And so, the legend goes, the first cathedral of Le Puy was erected here, and dedicated to the Virgin Mary. The menhir became Christianised in the process, and was given a place of honour in the sanctuary of the new cathedral, becoming known as the Throne of Mary. Hence Le Puy (together with Chartres) became the earliest shrine to the Virgin Mary in France.

By the ninth century the cathedral authorities had grown more purist, uncomfortable with this association of Christ's mother with pagan gods; and they broke up the menhir, incorporating the fragments into an area of the cathedral floor. Christian Europe was increasingly under threat by this time – from Norman invaders and Magyars sweeping across France from the north and east, and from Saracens in the new Muslim territories in Spain. Other gods were no longer to be tolerated by the Church, and the menhir had to go. But the older deities were not to be disposed of that easily, and the mystique of the menhir remained. The section of the church containing fragments of the ancient stone came to be known unofficially as 'the Angel's Room', and miracles continued to be reported. And when the present cathedral was constructed during the eleventh and twelfth centuries – a great deal larger in order to accommodate increasing numbers of pilgrims – it became part of the new narthex.

Thus Le Puy's long history of honouring many gods persisted across the centuries.

*

The four principal pilgrim roads listed in *The Pilgrim's Guide* all had points of departure which were traditionally centres of pilgrimage in their own right before the cult of St James took hold in France. It is easy to see why they were selected. They were all of them places which already catered for pilgrims: hence they acted as ideal platforms from which those preparing to undertake their long journey to Santiago could be sent on their way.

From the earliest days in the twilight of the Roman Empire the saint widely venerated at Le Puy was the Virgin Mary. It was to her that the first bishop, Voisy, had dedicated his church after the revelation of the deer's footprints in the snow. The subject of the Marian cult in the medieval Church is a contentious one which lies safely beyond the parameters of this book. It is relevant here largely because it came to contribute greatly to the popularity of Le Puy as one of the main starting-points for the Santiago pilgrimage. In the year 1254 the French King Louis IX, later canonised as St Louis, returned from the Seventh Crusade, of which he had been one of the leaders, bringing with him a number of sacred objects which he had obtained in Palestine. One of these was a statue of the Virgin Mary, believed to have been of Egyptian origin and perhaps carved in dark cedar-wood (probably from Lebanon), or, more likely, in ebony (from Africa). The king duly presented the statue to Le Puy, appropriately so since the cathedral was dedicated to the Virgin.

The carving was soon known as the Black Virgin of Le Puy. Dressed in gold brocade and set on the high altar, it immediately became the focus of intense devotion by pilgrims from far and wide. As so often with medieval shrines the cult of one saint became merged with another: pilgrims gathering at Le Puy before their long trek to Santiago would naturally attend their final mass in the cathedral, and find themselves offering their prayers not in the presence of a statue of St James but before this hypnotic black figure in gold on the high altar. Not surprisingly, so powerful an image remained with them on their journey, and the aura of the Black Virgin was carried by Santiago pilgrims westwards from Le Puy along the mountain route towards the Pyrenees, until the road became studded with wayside churches and chapels dedicated to Notre-Dame du Puy. In the minds of pilgrims the image of the saint was carried as a blessing on their journey, in much the same way as the blessing of Mary Magdalene was carried by those on the road from Vézelay.

The original statue of the Black Virgin brought back from the Holy Land by the French king was destroyed – like so many sacred objects throughout the country – during the French Revolution, and was replaced in the cathedral by a copy. The original statue seems to have been naturally black, or very dark, due to of the nature of the wood: yet it came to be associated with other effigies of the Virgin which were deliberately painted black.

It is these 'blackened' effigies which represent a puzzling variation of the Marian cult, one that attracted a wide following throughout the Middle Ages. It has been calculated that at least five hundred such statues of a Black Madonna existed in medieval

Europe, nearly two hundred of them in France. The most celebrated of these was the Black Virgin of Rocamadour, to the west of Le Puy in central France. This is a statue that still exists, and is still widely venerated, and in the Middle Ages it was the focus of one of the most popular pilgrimages in Christendom, King Henry II of England and St Bernard of Clairvaux being among those who journeyed specially to kneel before it. The statue was first mentioned in chronicles as a place of popular pilgrimage in the year 1235, just nineteen years before the French king's gift to Le Puy, though the Rocamadour statue is many centuries earlier, and the cult surrounding it was already long established. *The Pilgrim's Guide* makes no mention of it, presumably because Rocamadour was not on one of the four recommended roads. Yet the fame of the place, and its proximity to the route from Le Puy, must have beckoned many a traveller to make the necessary detour in the days ahead – and in a later chapter we shall follow them.

How the cult of the Black Madonna came about in the first place has exercised the imagination of theologians and historians for many centuries, giving birth to a variety of explanations of varying credibility. One favoured view is that she was a pre-Christian goddess, probably Isis the Egyptian goddess of rebirth, with whom the early Christians, especially the desert fathers, would have been familiar. And since the Le Puy statue is supposed to have originated in Egypt, the link is even closer. Another line of pursuit has led to the Old Testament, which has been widely quoted in order to identify her with the enigmatic figure in the Song of Solomon: 'I am black and beautiful, O daughter of Jerusalem.' More prosaic explanations that have been offered include the view that the figure was black, or at least dark, since this would have been Mary's natural skin colour in that part of the world. More humdrum still is the conclusion that these Black Madonnas had simply become darkened over the years by exposure to candle smoke in dimly lit churches.

Whatever the truth of her origin and identity, the Black Virgin of Le Puy hugely enhanced the popularity of the city as a place of pilgrimage, as well as the wealth obtained by scores of innkeepers, merchants, craftsmen and tradesmen who profited from the annual flood of pilgrims here to venerate the celebrated Madonna, as well as to equip themselves for the long trek across the hills of the southern Auvergne and the plateau of the Velay. And as travellers do today, they left the city of pinnacles and many gods through the medieval town along the cobbles of the old pilgrim road now appropriately named the Rue Saint-Jacques. Some of the most uplifting landscape in France lay ahead of them.

12. Golden Majesty

LIKE TODAY'S TRAVELLERS, medieval pilgrims gazing down from the plateau of the Velay could take a parting look at the impressive city they had just left, Le Puy. Those armed with a simple faith may have found themselves carrying confusing memories of the place where they had assembled a few days before. They would have been memories of a house of prayer which seemed to speak as much of Islam as of Christianity; of a chapel on a pinnacle reaching for the heavens and dedicated to an archangel; of a massive stone altar set within the cathedral yet erected originally in honour of some pagan god; and above all the memory of a painted wooden image of the Virgin Mary who was as black as ebony.

Who knows what they made of it all as they trudged westwards across the mountains? Maybe, like many of Chaucer's pilgrims on the road to Canterbury they were driven to go on pilgrimage by a spirit of adventure rather than by any pious urge, so all those strange and unexpected sights came as welcome offerings bringing colour to a monochrome life. Pilgrimage, after all, was perhaps the only permitted adventure of the day in which everyone could participate, regardless of rank or circumstance. Whatever the spiritual motive, pilgrimage was also the great escape and the great leveller.

Departing from Le Puy, pilgrims could choose one of several tracks across the high plateau. One road after barely an hour from the city led to Bains, where a priory (whose church still exists) carried the name of Sainte-Foy. Here was a foretaste of one of the great medieval abbeys of France, Conques, likewise dedicated to the martyred virgin, and which many pilgrims taking this road would have been anticipating as one of the highlights of their journey, now no more than three days ahead. The priory at Bains was one of the dependencies of Conques, and its monks had come from there, no doubt keen to fill travellers' ears with the wonders of the famous mother-house.

An alternative track led to Montbonnet, where there is still a medieval chapel originally dedicated to St James. The two parallel roads then join into a single track, becoming what is now the celebrated Grande Randonnée 65 (GR65). From now on modern travellers are constantly reminded of whose footsteps they are following. Every few miles another boxlike chapel meets the eye, where pilgrims would have paused to offer a prayer and refresh themselves from a stone water basin. It was always rough going on this road, in terrain with few creature comforts, a fickle mountain climate and persistent dangers which included wolves, bears and – in particular – bandits. Some of these made a habit of posing as *bona fide* travellers, even as pilgrims. And the fact that pilgrims tended to carry their few valuable possessions with them made them especially vulnerable. They might be protected by law, but bandits by definition lived outside the law.

So pilgrims needed all the protection they could get; and one body of men in particular took it upon themselves to provide it as an act of Christian duty. They were the feudal knights: not the knights who rode out to fight the infidel in Spain or led the crusading armies in the Holy Land. They belonged to one of the religious orders of knighthood which were emerging at this time, and whose members chose to observe a monastic way of life dedicated themselves to protecting vulnerable travellers as well as the sacred places where they worshipped.

In no other stretch of the French pilgrim roads were their services more urgently needed than in this wild mountainous region. The aptly named Domaine du Sauvage, now a farm, lay in a particularly rugged and inhospitable area a little further to the west along the road from Le Puy. Here in the twelfth century the Knights Templar established a hospice as a resting-place for pilgrims, together with a chapel dedicated to St James. The Templars, the 'poor Knights of

Christ and of the Temple of Solomon' had been established a century earlier in the wake of the First Crusade to protect holy places in Palestine. Now their role had been extended to providing safe passage to pilgrims, a sizeable proportion of whom on this road would have been making the journey to Spain and the tomb of St James. And in this capacity the Templars were joined even more prominently by their brother-knights, the Hospitallers, the Knights of St John of Jerusalem, whose fortified settlements, or *commanderies*, remain a prominent feature of the wilder upland regions of France today. The *commanderies* were half-monastery, half- barracks, but they were also 'safe houses' for pilgrims, usually established at strategic points along the road, such as a spring in the midst of a dry region, or – as at Les Estrets to the west of the Domaine du Sauvage – by a river crossing.

Here was the last fresh water pilgrims would come across for a while, because now the pilgrim road – the modern GR65 – climbs up on to the Plateau of Aubrac, an expansive stony region nowadays populated largely by imperious long-horned cattle as white as the snow which carpets the Aubrac plateau for most of the winter months.

In medieval times, however, there were less amiable residents of the plateau. This, even more than the upland closer to Le Puy, was bandit country. Ironically, this persistent menace to travellers was to a considerable extent the product of a new political stability and social order in France which had made it possible for people to travel as never before. Politically and socially, Europe was no longer the anarchic battle-zone it had been for the past two centuries and a degree of law and order now existed. The mass movement of pilgrims from shrine to shrine throughout the twelfth century symbolised this new 'settled' state of Christian Europe. Once pilgrims had obtained permission from the local lord, and a blessing from the parish priest, they were free to travel as never before in their lives, secure in the knowledge not only that they were protected by law, but that their property back home was likewise legally protected. Furthermore, being *bona fide* pilgrims they were temporarily released from a whole raft of feudal obligations of service to their lord. No wonder pilgrimage was becoming an attractive prospect, particularly to those who had spent a hard working life toiling in their master's vineyards. To be able to travel free as air from one hospice to another, punctuated by the occasional prayer, may well have seemed like the holiday of a lifetime.

On the other hand, to be free as a bird was also to be vulnerable to birds of prey. And in this new climate of social change and ease of travel there were plenty of predators waiting to swoop.

In the heart of the plateau of Aubrac the diminutive Romanesque church at Nasbinals is the surviving record of one of the first communities set up to safeguard pilgrims from such predators and offer them shelter. This was as early as the eleventh century, and the priory and accompanying church were established by monks from the ancient Abbey of Saint-Victor in Marseille, which had been founded by one of the key figures in the early Church, St John Cassian, early in the fifth century during the final decades of the Roman Empire.

The missionary tradition of the great Marseille abbey was legendary. Due to the teaching and zealous drive of its founder Saint-Victor became the fountain-head from which Christianity had spread throughout the southern region of Roman Gaul in the form of numerous far-flung priories. Now that missionary zeal was extended to the role of protector and watchdog. Along with the monks sent out by successive abbots of Cluny to found priories along the pilgrim roads, these monks of Marseille were among the first to establish a religious house and hospice specifically for the benefit of pilgrims, preceding the contribution of the Templars and Hospitallers by almost half a century.

Some fifty years after the arrival of the monks from Marseille a dramatic event took place a short distance to the west of Nasbinals. An eminent feudal lord, the Viscount of Flanders, was crossing this desolate region on his return from the pilgrimage he had made to Santiago. At the highest point on the Aubrac plateau he was attacked by robbers. It seems unlikely that so wealthy and important a man would have been travelling alone, but perhaps in the spirit of humble pilgrimage he was accompanied by no more than one or two attendants. Whatever the precise circumstances the viscount survived the assault, and as a gesture of thanksgiving set about building a priory and hospice for pilgrims at the place where the attack had taken place. It was designed 'to receive, welcome and comfort the sick, the blind, the weak, the lame, the deaf, the dumb and the starving'. The result of his vow was an elaborate cluster of fortified buildings – a typical knights' *commanderie* maintained by monks, nuns and knights, the latter becoming the nucleus of a new chivalric order of knighthood, the Order of Aubrac. This became closely associated with the Hospitallers, yet remaining proudly independent of their powerful brothers.

The Dômerie, as the principal establishment was called (after the title given to the head of the order), was attached to a church in which monks would ring the 'Bell of the Lost' to guide travellers when snow had fallen heavily across the surrounding plateau. Both monks and knights acted as a police force by patrolling the roads approaching the settlement, while the wellbeing of the *commanderie* and the travellers it cared for was maintained by large parties of lay brothers who supplied an extra labour force working in the fields and tending the hardy Aubrac cattle. It became a flourishing mixed community typifying the spirit of Christian charity represented by the new chivalric orders of knighthood. This was benevolent feudalism at its most humane. Here was a community with many diverse requirements, demanding a high degree of flexibility among its inmates, who might be required to tackle robbers one moment and milk the cows the next.

Much of this flexibility flowed from their observance of the Rule of St Augustine of Hippo. This code of conduct had been laid down by Augustine in a brief document written about 400 AD, more than a century before St Benedict set down his more precise and detailed Rule for how a monk should lead his daily life. St Augustine's more generalised vision of a religious community was what may have allowed Aubrac to accommodate the multiple demands of a mountain outpost more satisfactorily than would a Benedictine community more strictly bound by its unerring routine of liturgy and prayer. Even the great abbey of Cluny, ever among the most liberal of Benedictine houses, would have found it hard to interrupt the flow of Gregorian chant in order to deal with bandits.

Today, amid summer pastures alive with wild flowers and grazed by the ubiquitous long-horned cattle, Aubrac is a small mountain town and holiday resort which has grown up round the viscount's original settlement. Alongside sections of old cobbled street the medieval church has survived, and so has an impressive section of the former Dômerie which managed to withstand the ravages of the anti-clerical mob during the French Revolution. It seems that the banditry which led the Viscount of Flanders to found Aubrac as a safe haven early in the twelfth century did not die out with the Middle Ages.

*

The pilgrim road descends from the heights of Aubrac to cross the River Lot at Espalion. The handsome eleventh-century bridge in the heart of the medieval town creates a setting so unchanged that travellers may well wonder what century they have wandered into. The illusion of being a time-traveller is reinforced a short distance beyond the town when a church of the same period, resplendent in pink limestone, confronts the eye with an image so fundamental to early medieval Christian teaching that we are dragged back to that dark era when the compulsion to seek redemption resounded like a fearful gong in people's ears all their lives. These were the benighted years when fear ruled, and the Church maintained its power over people by offering the only slender ray of hope. The portal of this former priory church is carved with undisguised relish on the theme of the Last Judgment. And just in case those entering the church for morning mass were still unfamiliar with the precise meaning of Hell, here it was graphically spelt out, torture by torture.

Pilgrims who had taken other roads, particularly the Burgundian road, would have grown accustomed to more uplifting visions of human destiny. Among the outstanding achievements of the Burgundian school of church carving, at Vézelay above all, and certainly at Cluny before its destruction, was to give the Christian story a human touch, creating images which appealed directly to the onlookers' sense of hope, rather than despair; with the central figure of Christ in Glory replacing that of Christ in Judgment. It was a radical change in the prevailing religious spirit of the time – from darkness into light – inspired to a large extent by the dynamism of successive abbots of Cluny and subsequently that of St Bernard of Clairvaux as they set about revitalising a battered Christian world.

It was a change of heart and mind which altered the very nature of the pilgrimage movement: from being a journey undertaken in a spirit of penitence to becoming one of celebration and discovery.

Here in the southern Auvergne we are in a world still untouched by that Burgundian optimism. The eleventh-century church close to Espalion belonged to an earlier and darker era, and was attached to a priory founded as a dependant of the most celebrated monastery in this mountainous region of France – the historic abbey of Conques. This was the next major goal, just as it is today for those thousands who each spring and summer follow the GR65 across the highlands of the Rouergue.

*

No place on all the roads to Santiago offers quite so powerful a sense of a medieval pilgrimage as Conques. The village itself feels trapped in the Middle Ages as if a spell has been cast over it. Today's travellers arriving from the direction of Le Puy find themselves gazing down on a dense tangle of grey slate roofs clinging to the wooded hillside, a prospect that has scarcely changed since the earliest pilgrims trod this same path across the hills and caught their first glimpse of this hallowed place. In the middle of the jumble of roofs rises the massive abbey church on a scale quite out of proportion to the buildings that press round it. The houses and the embracing hill seem to close round it, holding it in their grip. *The Pilgrim's Guide* explains that 'in front of the portals of the basilica there is an excellent stream more marvellous than one is able to tell'. And there it still is, bubbling into its stone basin – a 'magic' spring like so many others round which holy shrines were established.

The particular character of pilgrimage towns is mostly lost: rebuilding, road widening and the destruction of town gates being largely responsible. A few survive, like Parthenay (see Chapter 3) and – pre-eminently – Conques. That special character is best appreciated today by an approach from the west, as travellers would have done on the journey home after completing their pilgrimage. From the ancient bridge over the River Dourdou the old road climbs steeply towards the village, appropriately named the Rue Charlemagne after the supposed founder of the first Benedictine monastery here. The winding cobbled road squeezes between half-timbered houses until passing through the fortified town walls at the Porte du Barry. From here it curves up into the centre of the village between low fan-tiled roofs on either side. Finally, around a sudden corner, it emerges into the open square in front of the vast rugged facade of the abbey church.

The impact is the greater for being out of scale with everything thus far. We step into a building that is labyrinthine and of colossal height. Conques is one of a group of five huge churches which all conform to roughly the same architectural design since they were built specifically to hold large numbers of pilgrims collecting at any one time, generally on a saint's day. An important requirement of these churches was that they possessed aisles of double the normal width so that pilgrims could process on either side of the nave towards the east end of the church where a broad ambulatory allowed them to view a saint's relics placed prominently on the high altar. As outlined in Chapter 3, these pilgrim churches were established on each of the four roads described in *The Pilgrim's Guide*, the fifth church being the pilgrims' final destination, the cathedral of Santiago de Compostela itself.

But here at Conques there is one noticeable difference from the other four churches: it is much shorter. And it is this relative horizontal concision which has the effect of making its vast height feel even more vertiginous. Arches are stacked in tiers one above the other in an intricate balancing act, until high up the palest of sunlight is filtered from invisible windows, falling in slender shafts to create patterns on the grey stone in an intriguing ballet of light. Down below we wander through a forest of columns, our eye always drawn upwards by the soaring height of those columns.

Outside, the massive west door of the church supports a carved tympanum which no medieval pilgrim would have been likely to forget. If there had been any scepticism about the nature of divine punishment then the Last Judgment of Conques would have dispelled it. The future of the human race is graphically spelt out. On one side is paradise, and on the other damnation. In the centre sits the figure of Christ in Majesty, an impassive figure of authority who calmly blesses with one outstretched hand and pronounces judgment with the other. The virtuous, who include Charlemagne, look a trifle self-satisfied, while the damned helplessly suffer – some are beaten, others cleft with an axe or hauled upwards by their legs. It is all somewhat matter-of-fact: an illustrated manual of official Church teaching, too impersonal to be horrifying, too stereotypical to be moving.

One significant figure is among the company of the blessed. It is a woman praying, and about to be touched by the hand of God. She is St Foy, to whom this abbey and its great church are dedicated. And thereby hangs an extraordinary tale. *The Pilgrim's Guide*, in its chapter on important saints to be revered, gives a brief and rather anodyne account of her life and death, omitting a number of essential facts. Those who 'proceed to Santiago by the route of Le Puy,' it explains, 'must visit the most saintly remains of the Blessed Foy, virgin and martyr, whose most saintly soul, after the body had been beheaded by her executioners on the mountain of the city of Agen, was taken to heaven in the form of a dove … At last [she] was honourably buried by the Christians in a valley commonly called Conques. Above the tomb a magnificent basilica was erected by the faithful.'

The author carefully leaves out how St Foy's body came to be in Conques at all. It is conceivable that he may not have known, although two written accounts dating from a century earlier than the *Guide* tell the story in full. Foy (meaning Faith, in Spanish Santa Fe) was a young Christian girl living near the town of Agen during the last century of the Roman Empire, and who openly refused to worship the official Roman gods. Like many a Christian martyr of that period she was accordingly tortured and finally beheaded. With the Roman conversion to Christianity shortly afterwards a cult grew up round her, and her relics held in the abbey of Agen became widely venerated and the source of numerous miracles – all of which helped to establish the fame and prosperity of the abbey, much to the envy of neighbouring abbeys, notably Conques, at that time a religious house of small importance buried away in a mountain village. Eventually, in the mid-ninth century the monks of Conques could stand it no longer, and hatched a plot. They selected a plausible member of their community to offer his services to Agen posing as a secular priest. The man's evident piety so impressed the abbot that he was appointed guardian of the abbey's treasury, which of course included the tomb of St Foy The story goes that he then waited ten years before seizing a unique chance of being alone in the church at night while the monks were all feasting in celebration of Epiphany. He duly smashed an opening in the marble tomb and made off with the relics of the saint – to be received with the utmost joy and jubilation at Conques.

In consequence Conques thrived, while Agen declined. It was another example of *furta sacra* – Sacred Theft, justified on the grounds that it must have been God's will. It was not as spectacular a robbery as that of the supposed relics of Mary Magdalene in Provence by the abbey of Vézelay at much the same time; nonetheless it was equally remunerative. Relics of the saints were by far the most rewarding investment a religious house could make, and the body of this martyred girl from Agen somehow possessed an aura which touched the hearts and the purse strings of Christians throughout Western Europe. In the words of Jonathan Sumption, 'A pilgrim was expected to be as generous as his or her means would allow, and there were some who asserted that without an offering a pilgrimage was of no value.' Stories of miracles at Conques abounded, and these were repeated enthusiastically as an inducement to further contributions.

They included tales of women failing to give their jewellery to the abbey and falling ill until the gift had been made.

One special attribute of St Foy was her power to release soldiers taken prisoner by the Saracens in Spain. The carved tympanum over the west door of the abbey church includes the image of iron fetters hanging from a beam right behind the figure of the saint. In a gesture of thanksgiving former prisoners presented their chains to the abbey in such quantities that in the twelfth century they were made into an iron grille which still separates the ambulatory from the choir. This is an exact repetition of the miracles attributed to Mary Magdalene at Vézelay, where prisoners' chains were likewise made into an iron grille for the abbey church (see Chapter 7). Here at Conques its original function was to protect the abbey's treasures which on special days would be displayed round the high altar for pilgrims to marvel at, and were visible to everyone in the nave.

The treasures of Conques were regarded in the Middle Ages as among the wonders of the Christian world. They were also glittering proof of the enormous wealth which St Foy had brought to the abbey over the past two centuries. Equally extraordinary is that the treasures have survived to this day, having been carefully hidden by the inhabitants of the village from the fury unleashed in the French Revolution which accounted for the destruction of so many sacred objects in other churches and monasteries throughout France.

Today the Conques treasure is housed in a special museum in an area of the former abbey cloisters. It represents centuries of gifts by feudal lords in gratitude for whatever miracles St Foy was believed to have performed. Among the earliest and finest pieces of craftsmanship is the ninth-century reliquary of Pepin, the first King of the Franks and father of the Emperor Charlemagne (the supposed founder of Conques abbey). The reliquary is a jewel-encrusted box bearing a crucifix in gold relief surrounded by intricate floral motifs in gold filigree. Another dazzling object is the so-called A of Charlemagne. This free-standing letter in gold and silver bears a significance which comes down to us in legend: Charlemagne is said to have ascribed each of his religious foundation with a letter, awarding A to Conques to indicate that it was the most important of them all.

But the object which pilgrims came principally to see – as travellers in their thousands do today – is the golden reliquary statue of the saint herself, known as the Majesté de Sainte-Foy. Here is her sculpted effigy. She wears a golden crown. She is robed entirely in beaten gold which is studded with precious stones. She is seated on a golden throne with her arms outstretched as if in blessing. And she gazes with a hypnotic stare into some other world. Jewels are all over her, emeralds, sapphires and opals among them, interspersed with polished chunks of rock crystals. Everything about her shines and glitters. She is both the source of the abbey's wealth and the boldest possible demonstration of it.[26]

So, what are we to make of her? And what did medieval pilgrims make of her? By any account the Majesté is one of the most striking and memorable of all religious artefacts of the Middle Ages. Here is an image that would turn heads anywhere, as it has done for the past thousand years. At the very least she is an astonishing example of opulent medieval craftsmanship. But she is also so much more. To the early pilgrim setting eyes on her on the high altar of a vast candlelit church the impact must have been stunning – bewildering and perhaps disturbing. Who, and what, was she? She was a queen on her throne. She was one of God's saints, adorned in the most precious materials this world could provide. She was a golden apparition gifted from heaven. She had the power to make miracles – curing the blind, healing the sick, releasing prisoners from their chains. Perhaps most important of all she may have embodied the sense of divine magic which was at the core of religious belief in the Middle Ages, a magical power that was capable of lifting people above the pain and dross of their daily lives.

And in this capacity the Majesté de Sainte-Foy symbolises what pilgrimages were all about: the search for a better life. Certainly there would be nothing quite as spellbinding as this golden image until the end of the road and the ultimate goal of Santiago de Compostela itself.

26. See Plate 17.

13. Tall Tales and Wild Beasts

Leaving Conques is like breaking a magic spell – though only slowly: the illusion of having wandered into the past lingers on. The old pilgrim road out of the village, the Rue Charlemagne, still belongs to the Middle Ages. So too does the fortified gate leading out into the countryside and down the wooded hillside into the valley. And even here the spell still holds as we cross the medieval bridge over the River Dourdou and prepare for the long climb up the mountain beyond, with a last glance back at Conques' abbey church rising from its cluster of grey roofs on the far hill across the valley.

There is one further link with events of almost a thousand years ago. The gold and bejewelled treasure of Sainte-Foy, which astonishes the modern traveller to Conques, is the very same assembly of glittering artefacts as medieval pilgrims marvelled at as they processed round the high altar of the abbey church on a saint's day mass all those centuries ago. The Conques treasure is unique in having survived wars and revolutions intact, while its centrepiece, the hypnotic Majesté de Sainte-Foy, makes much the same unforgettable impact today as it did when it was the most famous sacred reliquary in medieval Europe.

After a descent into the further valley the next halt for pilgrims was the riverside town of Figeac. Here there were once six hospices to accommodate them, a measure of the remarkable number of travellers regularly using these roads in the eleventh and twelfth centuries – many of them pilgrims, but also merchants, craftsmen and traders of one kind or another, and all contributing to what was an era of economic recovery in rural France after the long centuries of anarchy and insurrection. Provided you could escape the robbers, the toll-gatherers and the murderous ferrymen whom Aimery Picaud mentions in *The Pilgrim's Guide* these were good times to be out on the open road.

Besides the six hospices Figeac possessed an abbey dating back to the eighth century, and which in the eleventh century came under the capacious umbrella of Cluny, along with so many others across Europe. Like the six long-vanished hospices, nothing survives of the abbey, only a much battered and much restored abbey church, Saint-Sauveur.

From Figeac the pilgrim road followed the valley south-west until it joined the River Lot. Here the fortified town of Cajarc possessed a hospice much frequented since it was close to an important bridge over the river. There were few such crossings: the Lot flows through deep gorges, and the terrain to the north and south consisted of high plateaux even more inhospitable than the landscape between Le Puy and Conques. Pilgrims were wise to hug the river valley.

But there was one diversion which many would have taken, and it took them over the wildest of these bare uplands north of the River Lot. This was a limestone plateau at an altitude of more than three thousand feet, and known today as the Causse de Gramat. It was certainly a great deal more physically demanding than the diversion to Cluny which many travellers on the Vézelay road would have made, and only the most devout pilgrims would have undertaken it. Nonetheless theirs was a devotion that was widely shared, because their objective was one of the most popular shrines in the whole of Europe, attracting almost as many pilgrims annually as it does tourists today. The shrine was Rocamadour, set dramatically within a gorge of the Causse de Gramat.

A number of disparate threads have been woven together to create the mystique of Rocamadour. The principal focus of pilgrimage has remained the chapel of Our Lady of Rocamadour, the local variation of the cult of the Virgin Mary which swept through Christian Europe in the early Middle Ages. But there were other strands to the story which have contributed greatly to the emotional appeal of the shrine as a place of veneration. Its dramatic location has always helped, high on the wall of a river gorge, and which made the approach to it a physical challenge. Pilgrims often chose to respond to this challenge by stripping off their clothing and in a display of self-abasement climbing the 216 steps to the chapel on their bare knees. Pain and piety were good companions, as was frequently the case in medieval Christianity.

But the mystique of Rocamadour had a deeper resonance than this, due to an alluring legend which vastly enhanced the special appeal of the shrine. In the mid-twelfth century, when the local cult of the Virgin was at its fervent height, building works close to the chapel of Notre-Dame revealed an ancient tomb containing a body reported to have been miraculously preserved from decay. The events that followed read like an exercise in wishful fantasy. With the aid of numerous miracles the identity of the body was satisfactorily established as that of a biblical figure by the name of Zacchaeus, recorded in St Luke's Gospel as being a tax-collector from Jericho, a disciple of Jesus and believed to have been the husband of Veronica who wiped Jesus' blooded face with her kerchief on the road to Calvary.

How the chance discovery of a tomb on a French mountainside should have led to such an improbable identification can be explained by following the thread of a story put about at this time. Whether by coincidence, or possibly by a shared origin long lost, the story bears an intriguing resemblance to that of the supposed arrival of Mary Magdalene on these shores (see Chapter 7). And it is this. Following Christ's crucifixion Zacchaeus and his wife Veronica are said to have fled persecution in Jerusalem and left Palestine in a flimsy vessel which was miraculously guided to the shores of Roman Gaul, where the two vagrants sought the seclusion of the mountains. Then, after the death of Veronica some years later, Zacchaeus became a hermit known locally as Amadour, living high above a steep gorge where eventually he died and was buried beneath a rock. A religious community grew up around the hermit's tomb, incorporating his name into that of their priory: Rock of Amadour – which became Rocamadour.

So far the thread of the tale manages to make the gigantic narrative leap between the shrine in rural France and Palestine at the time of Christ. A further chapter in the story supplies a link of equal importance in establishing the aura of the place. At some date early in the Middle Ages, probably in the ninth or tenth century, the Benedictine community which now occupied a monastery on the site had come into possession of a wooden carving of the Virgin Mary seated with the infant Jesus on her knee. The statue may well have been the origin of the Virgin cult here in Rocamadour, though the cult only began to acquire fame with the discovery of the supposed tomb of Zacchaeus in the mid-twelfth century. From this moment onwards miracles galore were reported, and within a decade of the discovery *The Miracles of Our Lady of Rocamadour* was composed, a list of miracles that vastly increased the popularity of the shrine. Miracles were universally held to be revelations of God's will, and the medieval mind was certainly not given to questioning their reliability as evidence. Out of this deluge of miraculous events emerged the conviction that the carving of the Virgin and Child had actually been brought personally from the Holy Land by Zacchaeus himself.

Shrines could hardly get more sacred than this. Not only was Rocamadour seen to have been specially favoured by the mother of Christ, it now possessed a link directly to the place and time when Mary was still alive. It was a link achieved through the offices of this saint – Zaccheus who became Amadour – and who had actually known Jesus and whose wife had wiped his brow. As a result, the fame of Rocamadour became second to no other shrine in France. Soon monarchs and leading churchmen right cross Christendom were bending a knee before the altar of the 'Miraculous Chapel' above which the sacred statue was displayed.

But the story of Rocamadour grows even more complex. At some stage – it is unclear when – the legendary statue was described as the 'Black Madonna', and so became incorporated into that bizarre sub-culture centred on the veneration of 'black' images of the Virgin (described in Chapter 12). If the Rocamadour statue was ever black this is likely to have been largely due to centuries of exposure to altar candles: even so, its association with the Black Virgin which the French king, St Louis, had presented to the cathedral of Le Puy, would have been a compelling reason for Santiago pilgrims to have chosen to make the detour across the *causse* to pay homage to the saint.

Other pilgrims, perhaps in even larger numbers, would have made a detour from the opposite direction, travelling south across the mountains from Burgundy and the Vézelay road. And here, on the northern outskirts of Rocamadour, stands a settlement by the name of L'Hospitalet, so-called after the large hospice (the ruins of which survive) where pilgrims once sought accommodation before undertaking the climb – whether on their knees or not – up the south slope of the gorge to the famous Chapel of Miracles.

*

The story of Rocamadour is a tangled web of fantasy, fable and the most naïve credulity, all brought together by an overriding yearning to establish a direct link between the beleaguered world of medieval Christendom and that of Christ and his disciples – an urgent longing to drink from the spring where Christianity was born. Rocamadour itself was never on one of the primary pilgrim routes to Santiago, and is not even mentioned in *The Pilgrim's Guide*. For most Santiago pilgrims the place may have been hardly more than a sideshow: after all, they were pursuing their own link with the time of Christ far away in north-west Spain. Yet, from the broader perspective of our own times, Rocamadour succeeded in encapsulating much of what made the pilgrimage movement as a whole so powerful a social phenomenon in the Middle Ages, and so vibrant a creative force.

From the viewpoint of today's travellers it is this creative force which may engage the eye and the mind most strongly as we follow the pilgrim roads across France and into Spain. It is the experience of witnessing the astonishing richness of that legacy: there is always something new to surprise us – churches and abbeys, feats of engineering, masterpieces of sculpture and painting, entire towns and villages shaped by the needs of pilgrims over the centuries, all of them created in the service of this unending tidal wave of humanity on the move. It is this that makes a study of these pilgrim routes so rewarding to the historian and art-lover alike.

One such feat of engineering soon presented itself to pilgrims, both those who had made the detour to Rocamadour and those who had followed the principal route along the river valley and gorges from Figeac. It is a landmark which still exists: the remarkable Pont Valentré, a medieval bridge at Cahors with three lofty watchtowers which spans the Lot at the head of the long bend of the river that all but encloses the town in a narrow peninsula.

Cahors also offers a taste of what is to come further along the pilgrim road. The twelfth-century Cathedral of Saint-Etienne possesses a magnificent carved tympanum on the theme of the Ascension. This huge sculptural ensemble sits handsomely over the north door as though it has always been there. In fact it was originally set above the main entrance to the cathedral on the west front, and was then moved, stone by stone, when the west facade was rebuilt little more than a century later. In the fourteenth century Cahors was besieged by the English during the Hundred Years' War – but unsuccessfully: being protected by the River Lot on three sides kept the English army out and probably saved the cathedral from the customary pillage.

Further along the road to the south-west, one of the greatest abbeys in France was less fortunate: Moissac. And in view of its blighted history it seems little short of miraculous that the finest area of the abbey Church of Saint-Pierre should have survived virtually untouched: this is the incomparable south portal, which is a medieval masterpiece and one of the glories of the pilgrim roads.

Disasters haunted Moissac from the beginning. Founded as one of the earliest Benedictine abbeys in the seventh century it had scarcely begun to function when it was sacked successively by Saracen invaders from Spain, Vikings from the north and Magyars from the east. In 1030 the church roof fell in, and in 1042 a fire in the town spread to parts of the abbey. Such treasures as the abbey possessed continually went missing; a later chronicler described the place at this period as a 'robber's cave'.

Five years later a rescuer appeared. The Abbot of Cluny, Odilo (St Odilo), on one of his frequent missions to bring lapsed and failing monasteries into the Cluniac fold, was travelling from Burgundy and passing through this region on his way south. The authority of an Abbot of Cluny being close to that of a monarch, no opposition was raised to Odilo's proposal that Moissac become a dependency of Cluny, adopting the reforms in monastic life which the Burgundian abbey had instituted and was putting in place throughout its expanding 'empire'.

There were several remarkable features of the Cluniac takeover of Moissac. Odilo had by this time been Abbot of Cluny for fifty-three years, and must have been at least in his late seventies by this time: to be riding across France at such an advanced age, even with a retinue of attendants, was an astonishing feat even for a man of Odilo's redoubtable energy and sense of purpose. He was by now as powerful a figure in the Christian Church as the pope and the Holy Roman Emperor. He was also a dedicated champion of the cause of Reconquest in Spain, and accordingly of promoting and safeguarding the pilgrimage movement to Santiago. As we saw in Chapter 9, in the early days of his abbacy Santiago itself had been overrun and sacked by the celebrated Saracen warlord Al-Mansur, and for Odilo the wound had never healed. The fact that Moissac lay on one of the principal pilgrim routes to Spain would undoubtedly have contributed to his determination to annex the abbey and make it an important landmark and stopping-place for pilgrims on their way to the Pyrenees and Spain.

Odilo immediately appointed one of his most trusted monks at Cluny, Durand de Bredon, to become Abbot of Moissac. And so began a century of extraordinary fame and prosperity for the abbey, during which Moissac received lavish donations of land and property, acquiring in the process more than seventy daughter-houses of its own, and enjoying such prestige that in the Cluniac hierarchy the Abbot of Moissac ranked second in importance only to the Abbot of Cluny himself.

Odilo lived only two more years after the acquisition of Moissac, and it was left to his young successor, Hugh, to oversee its expansion during the second half of the eleventh century and into the twelfth. In fact Hugh managed to exceed his predecessor's period of office by five years, remaining Abbot of Cluny for sixty years until 1109. They were sixty of the most creative and influential years for Cluny, for Moissac and for the western Church in general.

In 1063, just sixteen years after the Cluniac takeover of Moissac, Abbot Durand had secured the finances and administration of the abbey sufficiently to begin the building of a new church and cloister. Over the next three-quarters of a century Durand and his successors were responsible for creating some of the finest works of sculpture and architecture of the entire Middle Ages.

But before looking more closely at the treasure which is Moissac it is worth recounting the bizarre sequence of events which followed this intense period of creativity. Combined with the centuries of insurrection which had preceded the Cluniac takeover they made these few intervening years an island of peace and prosperity in the midst of hurricanes and tidal waves. Troubles broke out little more than a hundred years after Durand became abbot. In the late twelfth century Moissac became a battlefield on which the disputes over boundaries between France and English-owned Aquitaine were fought. In the following century the town was seized and the abbey damaged by the heretical Cathars opposed to orthodox Catholicism. In the fourteenth and fifteenth centuries it was once again a battleground in the protracted Hundred Years' War between England and France. A century later still it was caught up in the French wars of religion, and again severely damaged. Then, in the early seventeenth century the abbey was officially secularised, and much of the abbey building and church allowed to fall into decay. What remained managed to escape the worst of the mob's fury during the French Revolution; but immediately afterwards the new National Assembly put both the Church of Saint-Pierre and cloister up for sale. The final insult came in the nineteenth century when the cloister was on the point of being demolished to make room for a new rail link between Bordeaux and the Mediterranean. Only last-minute intervention by the Beaux-Arts authorities in Paris forced the cancellation of the project, and the railway was diverted a short distance away.

Moissac – or at least the best of it – had just survived.

The cloister which was so nearly a railway track had been begun at the behest of Durand de Bredon in the last decades of the eleventh century. It was mostly built after his death in 1072, but he still presides over the place in the form of a full-length portrait carved in bas-relief on one of the marble columns standing amid the rows of arches on all four sides and at the four corners. He is in exalted company, the other full-size figures being Christ's apostles – a measure of the esteem in which Durand was held. Together they make up a remarkable group of carvings, executed with a simple gracefulness and delicacy, and a human touch, unlike the relatively crude sculpture we have seen on the Le Puy road so far. But then Abbot Durand came from Cluny, and would have been aware of the sculptures being produced in Burgundian workshops, far ahead of their time, and which were then beginning to enrich the churches of that region as well as the new abbey church of Cluny itself.

Whether Abbot Durand actually brought Burgundian stone-carvers to work here in Moissac is a matter of speculation and dispute. Cluny's empire by this time was expansive and far-flung, and the Cluniac love of rich decoration and fine workmanship was resulting in a high demand for men with the appropriate skills, particularly stonemasons and sculptors. Hence craftsmen and their workshops tended to travel to wherever those skills were most needed, creating temporary villages – families and livestock included – often set up along the pilgrim roads where so many new priories and abbeys, including Moissac, were being established.

Moissac's link with Burgundian workshops were matched by connections that were equally strong in quite the opposite direction, with northern Spain. This was once again through the agency of Cluny, which was in the process of establishing a chain of dependent abbeys along the pilgrim road to Santiago in lands newly secured from attack by Saracen armies. These links with Spain are particularly apparent in the Moissac cloister, where the capitals on all four sides are carved with figures combined with intricate geometrical patterns, the latter clearly the work of craftsmen operating in the Islamic tradition in which the representation of living forms was forbidden. What seems likely is that as the Reconquest of northern Spain progressed many Saracen craftsmen chose to pay lip-service to Christianity and found ready employment for their stone-carving skills in the decoration of new churches and abbeys, both in northern Spain and north of the Pyrenees, often working side by side with stonemasons from French workshops. Altogether the Moissac cloister is a supreme example of this cross-fertilisation of Christian and Islamic cultures.

Once the cloister was completed, about the year 1100, the monks turned their energies to creating a new church, including an elaborately sculpted main entrance, soon to be as massive and awe-inspiring as any church portal yet seen in France. Today, as we stand gazing at this extraordinary edifice we can see how the task unlocked the floodgates of the imagination as the sculptors drew on ideas and imagery that reflect the breadth and variety of the Cluniac empire itself. At the very centre – appropriately – is the debt to Burgundy and probably to the portal of the new abbey church of Cluny itself (which alas no longer exists). This is the monumental tympanum on the theme of the Vision of the Apocalypse, made up of twenty-eight blocks of stone, and with the grave figure of Christ in Majesty in the centre. Attending him on either side are the symbols of the four apostles, Matthew, Mark, Luke and John; while below him and on either side the twenty-four old men of the Apocalypse, familiar to many a pilgrim from so many portals throughout France, except that here the drama of this vision is intensified by the way they have involuntarily lowered their musical instruments to gaze up in wonder at the revelation of Christ. The entire semicircle of figures within the tympanum gives out an air of stunned silence.[27]

To the modern traveller the Moissac tympanum may be enjoyed as a monumental example of early Romanesque sculpture on a traditional theme more usually associated with the workshops of

27. See Plate 18.

Burgundy, where stonemasons were at that very time creating the majestic portals of Cluny, Vézelay, Autun, Souillac and so many others in the region. The medieval pilgrim, on the other hand, is likely to have viewed the tympanum with its dominant figure of Christ in a very different light, as a sign of reassurance from God, delivered by the hands of His representatives here on earth, that all might after all be well for troubled mankind at the end of the long road.

But if the great tympanum speaks of Burgundy, then the lower area of the portal echoes a place of origin altogether wilder and more violent. The twin doors of the entrance are flanked, left and right, by massive columns each carved with jagged shapes that give the impression of an open jaw set sideways, with teeth bared, waiting to close. The effect is dramatic and distinctly menacing, and one wonders what early pilgrims must have felt entering the abbey church through that portal. Then, in the centre of the double entrance is another image which must have surprised the medieval pilgrim: this is a huge marble pillar more than twelve feet in height, carved with three pairs of rampant lions, each pair crisscrossed one above the other like some acrobatic circus act.

Where did all this exotic imagery come from? Opinions abound. Scholars have been keen to point out the similarity between the pillar of lions and the sculpture on early Assyrian temples in the Middle East, long pre-Christian and even longer pre-Islam; though it is hard to understand how a twelfth-century stonemason in France could possibly have known about them. The probable answer is a good deal closer to home. The overriding theme of the Moissac portal is taken from the Book of Revelations, the apocalyptic vision of St John the Divine. The visionary account of events in the book made it a favourite source of material for medieval artists, and one work in particular tapped the further reaches of their imagination. This was a commentary on the Book of Revelations written by an eighth-century Spanish monk, St Beatus of Liébana, at exactly the time of the Saracen invasions of Spain (as described in Chapter 1). The immediacy of the Muslim threat gave Beatus' interpretation of the Apocalypse a vividness and an urgency which inspired artists to illustrate it with a wealth of exotic imagery in illuminated manuscripts produced in monasteries mostly in Spain during the early years of the Reconquest as if in a spirit of exorcism.

These richly imaginative illustrations, writhing with real and apocalyptic beasts of all descriptions, were widely circulated between monastery and monastery, where they became invaluable source material for sculptors and stonemasons throughout Europe whose job was to decorate the new churches with images designed to amaze and often terrify an innocent congregation; because images *were* the word – at least for most people in a largely illiterate world. Images possessed a hold on the mind more powerful and more lasting than any spoken words from the pulpit.

It was these exotic illustrations to the celebrated *Commentaries on the Apocalypse* which are the most likely source of the imagery on the Moissac south portal. Hence, in two quite different moods, the tympanum above and the carvings round the doors below both relate directly to the Book of Revelations, so becoming the theme of the entire portal – a vision of justice and order up above, and of wildness and disorder below. The two contrasting visions encapsulate the struggle which dominated the minds of medieval churchmen, and was a spur to the crusading movement as well as to the Santiago pilgrimage. It was no accident that the twin themes should have been chosen to decorate the entrance of a major church on one of the most popular pilgrim roads.

Then comes a surprise, and another revelation. On either side of the central column of lions are two full-size figures carved in low relief which become visible only as we pass under the lintel supporting the tympanum to enter the abbey church. On the left of the column is the figure of St Paul, while on the right is the prophet Jeremiah. Paul looks appropriately ascetic and stern, Jeremiah gentle and reflective. Both carvings are thought to be a little later in date than the figures on the tympanum above, and certainly they have a delicacy and sophistication which the former lack. Both figures are elongated, flattened into the stone as if with the lightest of touches. Jeremiah's body is twisted, his head turned slightly so that he looks away from us, lost in thought. He is the prophet who foresees only disaster, and can do nothing about it.

On these two figures at Moissac I wrote in my own book on the history of Cluny: 'This is sculpture that searches deep, laying bare something of the human soul. Only the greatest artists in any era have made inarticulate stone expresses the inner man, and the sculptor of these two Moissac figure is one of them. Few examples of European art express so eloquently the passionate and mystical nature of the mediaeval religious experience.'

No wonder a later abbot, gazing at the portal of his church, declared that the carvings before him were so beautiful that they must have been created 'miraculously rather than by a man'.

14. Crosses on a Mountain Top

At Moissac pilgrims crossed the broad River Garonne as it flows westwards towards Bordeaux and the Atlantic: then they entered the region of Gascony for which Aimery Picaud had already reserved some of his most bilious comments about the domestic habits of the locals. A short distance further, and the old pilgrim road crosses a tributary of the Garonne by means of a handsome five-arched bridge, the Pont d'Artigue, which still exists. This was essentially a Roman bridge, and the pilgrim road is now the original Roman road towards the Pyrenees and Spain. It is also specially marked out as the route taken by pilgrims bound for Santiago since it was now referred to in contemporary documents not simply as the *Via Podense,* the road from Le Puy, but as the *Via Publica Sancti Jacobi,* the public road of St James.

There may have been a special reason why at this particular point the road should have been identified in this way. Close to the bridge in medieval times was a hospice for the benefit of travellers, like so many on these roads, except that this one had been established and administered by a body of feudal barons in Spain known as the Knights of St. James, or Knights of Santiago. Nor was this the only establishment set up by them along the *Via Sancti Jacobi:* there would be others along the route between here and the Pyrenees.

The Spanish knights came together as a fighting force in support of the Reconquest; but their presence here in quite a different role is further evidence of the close connection between the military operations in Spain and the pilgrimage movement. Like the more celebrated religious orders of knighthood in the Middle Ages, the Templars and the Hospitallers, the Knights of Santiago were a product of the crusading spirit of the time. Half-monk, half-soldier, knights swore an oath of dedication to safeguard Christian shrines and to protect those who came to worship at them: hence the dual role.

It was in 1164 that a group of local barons in south-west Spain, a region still largely occupied by the Saracens, agreed to collaborate in assembling an armed force capable of recapturing towns and villages which were still in Muslim hands. In northern and central Spain the Reconquest was already at its height, the Spanish capital of Toledo having been recaptured more than seventy years earlier. Now the Christian armies were pushing further south. The barons formed themselves into an order of knighthood operating within monastic disciplines, which received papal recognition eleven years later, and they began their military operations in the two adjoining kingdoms of León and Castile.

The fervent religious spirit of the new order had a strongly symbolic flavour: it was said that the original group of knights numbered thirteen, this being a biblical echo of Christ and his twelve apostles. Membership of the order expanded greatly, as did the activities they undertook. Their pastoral role soon ran parallel to their military activity, and the order began to establish hospices, often attached to their own *commanderies*, and run by canons and canonesses whose task was to see to the needs of pilgrims and other travellers.

As the Reconquest pushed the Moors further and further south the order began to acquire ever-increasing quantities of territory and wealth, largely through endowments by landowners overflowing with gratitude towards the knights for having helped to drive out the Saracens and return them their property. After little more than a century since its foundation the order had established no fewer than eighty-three *commanderies* in Spain, and were in possession of nearly two hundred villages and small townships. And by the fifteenth century this number had more than doubled. In the meanwhile their activities and influence had spread far beyond Spain, particularly into France just across the Pyrenees where, as we have seen, they built hospices on the pilgrim roads. And so, like the Templars and the Hospitallers, and like the Cluniac and Augustinian monasteries, the Knights of St James played their part in aiding the flow of that powerful current of humanity which was the Santiago pilgrimage.

There was one significant difference between the Knights of Santiago and the other religious institutions championing the pilgrimage. Their full title was 'The Order of St James of the Sword'. The word 'sword' was pertinent. Their patron, the apostle James the Greater, was perceived not only as a saint revered as the cousin and disciple of Christ, and who had supposedly evangelised Spain: James was also held to have been the country's military saviour, personally responsible for leading Christian armies on the battlefield to expel the Saracens from Spain. Hence the sword which the knights took as the emblem of their order. It was designed as a cross, symbolising the order's dual religious and military role; and in case there should be any misunderstanding about the military aspect, the sword was coloured blood-red. The knights wore this insignia of a sword/cross as a badge on their white capes along with that of the pilgrims' scallop-shell.

The Knights of Santiago saw themselves as the heirs and avengers of their patron saint. Their chosen emblem of the bloodied sword held an extra significance: St James had himself had been beheaded by a Roman sword, but had now returned to the land where he had evangelised to lead the Reconquest. He had become *Santiago Matamoros*, St James the Moor-Slayer; and in doing so he became a hero in the eyes of every Spanish Christian, represented on churches and public buildings along the Spanish pilgrim road as a warrior on horseback, sword raised, the Infidel crushed beneath the stallion's hooves.

The dual role of St James as spiritual and military saviour of Spain was epitomised by the activities of the knights of Santiago, who were soldier-monks. They wore the mantle of their patron saint in both capacities, as evangelist and warrior. In addition, by establishing hospices along the pilgrim roads such as those here in Gascony they performed a third role, protecting pilgrims on their travels to the apostle's tomb.

The cult of St James came to acquire an irresistible mystique, which the knights helped to perpetuate. It was a mystique to which an extra touch of glamour was added when the legend of the saint became associated with the military deeds of the Emperor Charlemagne. Historically, there could have been no possible connection between Charlemagne and St James since the former's campaigns in Spain took place in the century before the discovery of the apostle's tomb. Folklore then came to the rescue. The Charlemagne story, centring on the heroic death of his nephew Roland in the Pyrenees near Roncesvalles, became a popular theme from the twelfth century onwards through the wide dissemination of the first French epic poem, *La Chanson de Roland*. Then, in the same century St James' own role in liberating Spain from the Infidel becomes intimately linked to the Charlemagne legend through an equally popular story which was included in the very manuscript containing *The Pilgrim's Guide*, the *Codex Calixtinus*. The *Guide* itself has little to say about Charlemagne, being more concerned with martyred saints to be venerated along the way. But elsewhere in the *Codex* (as described in Chapter Five) is the supposed chronicle of Archbishop Turpin, who had accompanied Charlemagne on his campaigns. And it is this chronicle, entirely fabricated though it is, which makes a direct connection between the Emperor Charlemagne and St James.

From now on pilgrims setting out for Santiago could follow the beckoning arm of the Milky Way confident that they were travelling under the divine protection of two warrior-heroes. And on this road, the *Via Publica Sancti Jacobi*, the medieval pilgrim would soon be in sight of the Pyrenees and anticipating the famous mountain pass where the dying Roland blew his ivory horn three times, and too late, to alert Charlemagne a few miles away to the north of an ambush. And on that same mountain pass, so the chronicle of Turpin maintains, St James appeared in a dream to the emperor, urging him to lead his army westwards towards the apostle's tomb under the guiding path of the Milky Way.

That place of legend, now only a few days away, was Roncesvalles.

*

As the landscape opens out and horizons expand journeys on foot become more easily flagged by landmarks. Places are more visible from afar. Today, as yesterday, it is often the village church which rises in the distance beyond the flat fields and the winding river. The stone tower and the tall spire are the welcome beacons that pilgrims and other travellers on the road have been following for centuries. They measure the progress of a journey at a pace that has never changed. Nothing unites the modern backpacker and the medieval pilgrim more closely than the experience of putting one foot after another, hour after hour, day after day, in all weathers. Walking is a great leveller.

In this part of the world they are united too by the places to be visited along the way – the churches and shrines that were newly built at the time of Aimery Picaud and *The Pilgrim's Guide*, and are now historic monuments carefully preserved and accompanied by postcard stalls and information leaflets, yet still giving out powerful echoes of their former role. Their names tell stories, like the twelfth-century collegiate church with a fine octagonal tower a short distance from the Pont d'Artigue, called Le Romieu. The word means literally 'of the Romans', and referred originally to pilgrims who had been to Rome, or were on their way there. Then, with the subsequent discovery of St James' tomb in Spain and the popularity of the Santiago pilgrimage, 'Romieu' became a generic term for all pilgrims no matter where their goal.

The old Roman road continues across Gascony, its progress punctuated every so often by landmark churches often visible half a day's journey away, just as they were in the Middle Ages: like the eleventh/twelfth-century church at Nogaro with its carved tympanum of Christ in Majesty that is worthy of Moissac; or Sensacq with its eleventh-century church of touching simplicity originally dedicated to St James; then Pimbo with its medieval church on the site of an abbey founded by Charlemagne; La Sauvelade and another monastery church dedicated to St James. And so on – village after village, church after church, with the far wall of the Pyrenees growing ever closer and higher.

By now we have left Gascony and the architecture of the region has changed. Whitewashed village houses are held together by solid oak timbers picked out in rich red, while local churches are simple and painted white with deep roofs and squat conical spires, like the appealing little country church at Olhaïby. And with this change in architecture comes a change in language. This is the Basque Country which we have met on the previous two pilgrim roads, and whose people speak what may be the oldest language in Europe, one that sounds and reads like no other. In *The Pilgrim's Guide* Aimery Picaud dismisses the language as 'barbaric', which, since it is long pre-Christian, is literally true.

A short distance further on and the pilgrim road descends through woods to a fast-flowing river and a long curve of stepping-stones that feel as ancient and well-worn as the Basque language.[28] And in this hidden place the sound of water rushing between rocks evokes the reality of everyday travel over countless centuries. These are stepping-stone we have visited in an earlier chapter, because it is at this point on the journey that the pilgrim road emerges from the woods and climbs towards the crest of a hill where it is seen to join up with two other roads, the one from Paris and the north, and the other from Vézelay and the north-east. Today they are no more than rough paths; yet this would have been a dramatic meeting-point in the Middle Ages. Here on the southern slope of Mont Saint-Sauveur our three of the 'four roads leading to Santiago' described in *The Pilgrim's Guide* finally join up to form 'a single road'.

And there, as we gaze down across the valley, is still that single road that Picaud wrote about nine hundred years ago, and which he would have taken on his own pilgrimage to Santiago just as millions before and after him have done. It is hardly more than a broad track cutting a swathe through the scrub and shale of the far hillside, until it disappears out of sight in the direction of the Pyrenees and Spain.

The tone of *The Pilgrim's Guide* grows more dramatic as we are led towards the high Pyrenees. We are entering a region of magical

28. See Plate 19.

appeal for pilgrims, because this is where the legends of Charlemagne, of Roland and Oliver, and of the Christian Reconquest of Spain, all joined together to attach themselves to the cult of St James. It was propaganda so powerful that much of the crusading energy driving the pilgrimage movement derives from it. Picaud's own account of this stretch of the road becomes almost euphoric as he describes what must have been his personal experience of the place from his own journey. 'In the Basque Country there is on the road of St. James a very high mountain which is called Port-de-Cize ... Its height is such that he who climbs it may feel he is about to touch the sky with his hand.'

Picaud goes on to recount the story of the Emperor Charlemagne's arrival here on his expedition to Spain in 778. 'On the summit of this mountain there is a place called the Cross of Charles, because it was here that Charles, setting out with his armies for Spain, opened up a passage by means of axes, hatches, pickaxes and other implements, and where he erected a sign of the cross of the Lord, and falling on his knees and turning towards Galicia he addressed a prayer to God and St James.' It is significant that Picaud's account of Charlemagne's prayer is not taken from the Song of Roland, which makes no mention of St James in this context, but from the version of the story in the so-called chronicle of Archbishop Turpin, a spurious account of events created – as we have seen – specifically to promote the Santiago pilgrimage, and which is contained in the *Codex Calixtinus*.

And so, by masterly sleight of hand the *Guide* has established the defining moment in the advocacy of Charlemagne as the first patron of the Santiago pilgrimage, awarding the emperor God-given prior knowledge of the whereabouts of the apostle's tomb, not as yet discovered.

Thereafter all pilgrims arriving here at the gateway to Spain would be following the emperor's example – as Picaud describes: 'Falling on their knees they would turn towards the land of St James and offer a prayer, each planting his own cross of the Lord like a standard. Indeed one can find there up to a thousand crosses; and that is why this place is the first station of prayer to St James.' In all, it was a promotional triumph. The message lit a fire in the heart of a million Christians.

This mountain route to Spain, so high that a traveller might feel he could 'touch the sky with his hand', was one of two ways across this stretch of the Pyrenees described by Picaud. In the earlier centuries it was the preferred route, perhaps because it was more arduous and more testing of a pilgrim's zeal; also because it was the old, well-trodden Roman road leading from Bordeaux to northern Spain. (Seven centuries later it also became the route Napoleon chose to lead his troops across the Pyrenees.) From the small town of Saint-Jean-le-Vieux the road led, as it does today, to the village of Saint-Michel and then into the foothills of the Pyrenees along a valley where the occasional outcrop of well-worn stone slabs bear witness to long use by travellers over the centuries. Finally the metalled road gives out and the traveller takes a stony track to the mountain pass at an altitude of almost 4,000 feet: and from this perch in the sky the meadows beyond and below are where Picaud's 'thousand crosses' once dotted the landscape. Further beyond still, and when the clouds lift, the eye can make out the broad roofs of another eagerly awaited landmark on a pilgrim's journey, the Augustinian monastery of Roncevaux – or, since we are now on Spanish soil – Roncesvalles.

The second road across the Pyrenees became the more popular route for pilgrims later in the Middle Ages, perhaps because it was easier, and the pilgrimage movement had by now lost its ascetic drive and become more of a passage from comfortable hospice to hospice. Already in Picaud's time it had become the alternative route: 'Many pilgrims who do not wish to climb the mountain go that way,' he wrote a little dismissively. Today it is an attractive route, beginning at the frontier town of Saint-Jean-Pied-de-Port (St John at the foot of the pass), with its cobbled street and Porte Saint-Jacques where pilgrims entered the town, and its elegant Roman bridge over the River Nive leading to the Porte d'Espagne where they departed.

This route, like the first, is signposted by historical landmarks that had already become legendary by Picaud's day. 'Near the mountain, towards the north,' he writes, 'there is a valley called Valcarlos where Charles himself encamped together with his armies after his warriors had been slain at Roncesvalles.' This was the celebrated incident on Charlemagne's return from his Spanish campaign when his rearguard was attacked and destroyed, and the emperor's nephew Roland blew his ivory horn with his dying breath. This was stirring stuff for pilgrims, who would mostly have known the story well from the Song of Roland and from other pilgrim songs recited and sung by minstrels accompanying them along the way. They would have been well primed for this journey.

Valcarlos, named after Charlemagne, is today the border village. The famous battle and slaughter on 15 August 778 took place a short distance further south along the road at the highest point of the pass. Here at Ibañeta the ground-plan of a church, San Salvador, is all that remains of the monastery the emperor is reputed to have established on the site of Roland's death. In Picaud's time there was a celebrated hospice on this historic site, where a bell would be rung to guide pilgrims when the pass lay under heavy cloud; because here was also where the two pilgrim roads met – the valley road up from Saint-Jean-Pied-de-Port, and the mountain path with its one thousand wayside crosses.[29]

We are over the pass now and heading south towards the great Augustinian monastery of Roncesvalles, built early in the twelfth century at about the time Aimery Picaud was preparing his text. He may even have witnessed it under construction. The Augustinians had spread their net widely: the roads leading to the Pyrenees were punctuated by small convents and priories owing allegiance to Roncesvalles, each with a hospice at the service of pilgrims. Today the old pilgrim track from Ibañeta keeps its distance from the modern road and picks its way through the dense beech woods that cloak the place.

Roncesvalles was the first major religious house since the junction of the three pilgrim roads in the French Basque Country; and accordingly the monastery might welcome up to three times the

29. See Plate 20.

number of pilgrims any of the French abbeys would expect to receive. Not surprisingly it is a huge complex of buildings. A monk would regularly stand outside the main gate offering bread to exhausted arrivals. There were separate houses for accommodating men and women, and inmates enjoyed the rare experience of sleeping on a real bed instead of the customary straw mattress on the floor. Two hospitals cared for the sick, and in the large refectory the food served was equally superior. Not surprisingly Roncesvalles was one of the highlights of a pilgrim's journey.

There was a more noble reason for the abbey's reputation and one which would have preceded it along the entire stretch of the pilgrim roads. More even than the site of the battle itself Roncesvalles was steeped in the Charlemagne legend; and any pilgrim arriving here would have identified the place with the emperor's campaign against the Saracens in Spain culminating in the heroic death of Roland. Roncesvalles had become the shrine to that legend. To this day the abbey's treasury displays what are claimed to be Roland's war clubs, while for many centuries the nearby Chapel of Saint-Esprit possessed tombs reputed to be of Roland's fellow-soldiers killed in the famous ambush on Charlemagne's rearguard. As for the 'enemy' that launched the attack from the hills, the *Chanson de Roland* describes them as Saracens, whereas historians are generally agreed that the attack was by local people of Navarre seeking revenge on Charlemagne for having pulled down the protective ramparts of their capital city of Pamplona.

Pilgrims arriving here had their own special chapel *de los peregriños* a little beyond the gate of the abbey. In contrast to the heavy grandeur of the monastery this is a modest building of elegant simplicity dating from a century after Picaud's time, though he would have recognised the sound of its bell because it was originally the celebrated bell that once guided pilgrims from the mountainside when it was rung from the long-vanished hospice of San Salvador at Ibañeta.

It was also the first chapel dedicated to St James that pilgrims would have encountered in Spain. They were now in what was then the Spanish kingdom of Navarre; and any pilgrims who had access to

Picaud's *Guide* might now have severe misgivings about the hospitality they were about to receive from the Navarrese. 'They dress most poorly and eat and drink disgustingly,' he begins. Then it gets worse. 'If you saw them eating you would take them for dogs or pigs ... This is a barbarous nation, distinct from all other nations in habits and ways of being, full of all kinds of malice, and black of colour. Their faces are ugly, and they are debauched, perverse, perfidious, disloyal and corrupt, libidinous drunkard, given to all kinds of violence, ferocious and savage...' and so on, in a floodtide of abuse. It was just as well that most twelfth-century pilgrims were illiterate.

From the high Pyrenees the pilgrim road makes a gradual descent to the Navarrese capital of Pamplona, a city whose reputation has been redeemed by a writer more widely read than Aimery Picaud, namely Ernest Hemingway, for whom Pamplona was the city of bullfighting and bull-running. The old pilgrim bridge over the River Arga still exists, over which medieval travellers approached the city, passing through the massive ramparts (rebuilt since Charlemagne's day) by means of the gate named in their honour: the Puerta de Francia, the Gate of France. Soon, next to the cathedral, they would find a hospice where the welcome and the accommodation were the very opposite of the *Guide*'s dire predictions. Here they enjoyed proper beds, and a meal a great deal more wholesome than the customary bread with a little wine, including fresh salad and – if they were lucky – meat.

So this was Spain. And the next day, after a modest hike of fifteen miles, there would be another reunion. To quote the opening words of *The Pilgrim's Guide*, 'There are four roads which, leading to Santiago, converge to form a single road at Puente La Reina, in Spanish territory.' And there, in that compact medieval town with its handsome bridge built specially for pilgrims as early as the eleventh century, travellers would find themselves mixing with others who had journeyed from Italy and from Provence, taking the most southerly of the four roads across France, the one leading from the ancient Roman city of Arles – which is where our next journey begins.

IV. Via Tolosana: The Road from Arles

15. Roman Footprints

ARLES WAS JULIUS CAESAR'S CITY, capital of his newly conquered 'province of Rome', hence the name Provence. Four centuries later it became the favourite city of the Emperor Constantine, who had converted the Roman Empire to Christianity.

Of the four roads listed in *The Pilgrim's Guide* the road from Arles seems to have been the most frequented by Santiago pilgrims. Many of them came from northern Italy and from Eastern Europe, either choosing the coast route or crossing the lower reaches of the Alps to Avignon or Aix-en-Provence. Climate, too, may have played its part in making the Arles route the most popular. Spring was always the favoured time of year for setting out on pilgrimage – returning in the autumn – and both seasons were a great deal more congenial for foot-travellers in Provence than in central and northern France. It is a reasonable assumption that pilgrims by and large found gratification of the flesh a lot more appealing than mortification, whatever the Church might preach.

Provence was especially rich in shrines to be visited along the way, mostly associated with the legends of early Christians arriving on these shores to proselytise the local 'heathens' who were living under Roman rule and required to worship a sequence of strutting emperors as deities. Also, Provence as the final home and resting-place of Mary Magdalene and her brother Lazarus, or so it was believed, had a particularly powerful appeal, endowing the whole region with a certain magical sanctity as though Provence itself was a natural extension of the Holy Land.

The entrance to Arles from the east was by way of the magnificent gate in the Roman ramparts built by the Emperor Augustus, Julius

Caesar's successor, in the first century AD. But this was not all: travellers first needed to pass between a long double-row of Roman tombs and monuments interspersed with Christian chapels, which lined the avenue on either side. To any visitor to the city it was like being welcomed by a guard of honour. It would certainly have been an impressive experience for any pilgrim arriving here tired and weary after a hot trek across the Provencal plains.

This long ceremonial approach to the city was the former Roman cemetery known as Les Alyscamps, meaning the Elysium Fields. In the Roman world Elysium was held to be the final resting-place of heroes; and here in the third city of the Empire was one of the most splendid of all Roman burial-grounds, famous throughout Europe. Families would vie for the privilege of being buried here, and one imagines that the waiting list was long. With the conversion to Christianity Les Alyscamps underwent a smooth transition to become a Christian cemetery – on an equally grand scale. Aimery Picaud had no reservations about the majesty of the place: 'In no cemetery anywhere except this one can you find so many and so large marble tombs set up on the ground.' Christian and Roman heroes lay side by side as if there had never been such a thing as religious persecution.

Les Alyscamps has a gracefully romantic air about it nowadays – a venue for picnics rather than for mourning. It is no longer any kind of entrance to the city, but a gated park inviting a gentle stroll among the monuments. The great avenue is presided over by the handsome bell-tower of the Church of Saint-Honorat, which in medieval times was especially appealing to pilgrims on account of the numerous relics of early Christian martyrs on display. Today Saint-Honorat, semi-ruined, is a solitary survivor: in Picaud's day there were no fewer than seven churches and chapels greeting pilgrims as they made their way towards the gate of Augustus and into the heart of the city.

There was one particular story relating to Arles which was a cause of great celebration among pilgrims arriving here; and it was one that created a direct link between the ancient Roman cemetery of Les Alyscamps and the medieval city itself. *The Pilgrim's Guide* makes it all clear. 'First of all pilgrims must visit in Arles the remains of the Blessed Trophime, the confessor. It was he whom the Blessed Paul, writing to Timothy, remembers, and it is he who was ordained bishop by the same Apostle and who was the first one to be directed to the said city to preach the gospel of Christ.'

Today the church dedicated to St Trophime remains one of the masterpieces of Romanesque architecture in France. It replaced a smaller Carolingian church of the ninth century, and immediately became an important shrine for pilgrims, especially those gathering in Arles before setting off for Spain. Here was where those who had chosen this route to Santiago received their final blessing before departure. The sheer size of the new church reflects the numbers expected. The cult of Trophime as a saint with supposed links to Christ's apostles would undoubtedly have cemented the association of the new cathedral with the Santiago pilgrimage, which was likewise linked to one of the apostles. So, in Arles the two cults would have merged. The immense carved portal on the west front was completed later in the twelfth century, and here the figure of St James is prominent on the right of the main door, while the portal itself is decorated with images of scallop-shells.[30] Then, behind the cathedral, hidden away behind high walls in the heart of the city, are the loveliest cloisters in Provence; and here on a panel depicting the Supper at Emmaus St James is depicted wearing a scallop-shell on his conical hat, as though he was a pilgrim to his own shrine.

The Saint-Trophime portal also bears a message to pilgrims which would have been all too familiar from the carvings and paintings on countless newly built churches throughout the land. Right over the entrance to the cathedral, in the centre of the tympanum, sits Christ as the Supreme Judge, while around him are arranged the symbols of the four evangelists whose gospels in the New Testament have spread his teaching far and wide. For the benefit of any remaining doubters the theme of Divine Judgment is

30. See Plate 21.

pressed home by threatening scenes of the Last Judgment, and these are complemented by further scenes illustrating the suffering of early Christian martyrs, all described with customary ghoulish relish.

Pilgrims would by now have grown accustomed to the punitive vision of human fate as preached by the medieval Church. To what extent that dark vision coloured their experience of pilgrimage is hard to gauge, except that illuminated manuscripts of the period generally depict pilgrims enjoying the pleasures of travel and the conviviality of each other's company rather than labouring under the burden of sin and dread as promulgated by official Church teaching and in the sculpture which illustrated it. Today, too, how often do we find ourselves admiring the joyous architecture of Raoul Glaber's 'white mantle of churches', yet recoiling from the relentlessly dark sermons in stone which decorate those same churches?

*

Dominating both the church and the cloisters of Saint-Trophime, and rising above the ancient city like a finger pointing triumphantly to heaven, is the majestic twelfth-century bell-tower, the finest in the whole of Provence, and a landmark visible for miles across the flat countryside of the Rhône valley and delta. For nearly nine hundred years travellers have mounted the stairway to the highest gallery of the tower and gazed southwards over that intricate expanse of marshland and waterways which was once the granary of Roman Gaul, the Camargue. Just visible in the distance, by the shores of the Mediterranean, rises another bell-tower, one that is quite different in shape, like a thin slab of golden stone set against the horizon. Beneath the tower is the hulk of a church jagged with battlements along the entire roofline, and clearly built for defence as much as for prayer.[31]

This is the medieval parish church of Les Saintes-Maries-de-la-Mer. Its very name – the Saint Maries of the Sea – identifies it as another special place of pilgrimage. It is not one that is listed in *The*

31. See Plate 22.

Pilgrim's Guide because it was not strictly speaking on the road to Santiago, and Aimery Picaud was not one to encourage diversions from the main track. Nonetheless a great many pilgrims would have known of it, and the story attached to it; and (like the detour to Rocamadour on the previous road from Le Puy) there would have been many keen to stretch their journey in order to visit the site of one of the most touching of all Christian legends of the Middle Ages.

The story of the Three Marys is as follows. After the Crucifixion the enemies of Christ continued their vendetta by placing members of his family and followers in an open boat, or raft, without sails or oars, and setting it adrift off the coast of Palestine. They consisted of Mary Salome, who was the mother of the apostles James and John, Mary Jacob who was the sister of the Virgin Mary, and Mary Magdalene. In addition to the three Marys the boat also contained the Magdalene's sister Martha and her brother Lazarus, Christ's friend whom he had brought back from the dead. Also on board the drifting vessel were two further disciples of Christ and saints, Maximin and Sidonius, along with a mysterious woman called Sara, who is believed to have been the Egyptian servant of Mary Jacob and Mary Salome. In all there was a complement of eight.

According to the legend, the only sign of habitation they found on this lonely stretch of coast was an abandoned Greek fortress, and here Mary Jacob and Mary Salome, together with their servant Sara, took refuge and established a small oratory, so creating the first Christian community in the western Mediterranean. Meanwhile the younger, more vigorous members of the party spread out to preach the gospel to the inhabitants of the nearby region. Lazarus headed eastwards for the Greek port of Massalia (Marseille), where he became its first bishop. Maximin and Sidonius travelled inland to what is now Aix-en-Provence, while Martha followed the River Rhône northwards to Tarascon, where she famously tamed a predatory dragon (whose sculpted effigy still decorates the town). As for Mary Magdalene, she was guided by an angel to a grotto where she remained in a state of continual prayer until her death thirty-five years later.

The appeal of the legend to Santiago pilgrims is clear enough. All the occupants of the magical craft, with the exception of the enigmatic Sara, were close associates of Jesus – which alone would have been a powerful magnet in a society yearning for close contact with events close to the life of Christ. Furthermore one of the Marys who stayed behind here to found the first Christian community was the mother of St James, whose shrine was the ultimate goal of their pilgrimage. Equally important, according to the legend, this was where Mary Magdalene first arrived on these shores. She had been witness to both the Crucifixion and the Resurrection, and it was this closeness to the two central events in the Christian story which accounts for her supreme importance in the eyes of the early Church. She was his messenger, that 'glorious Mary' whose shrine at the 'large and most beautiful basilica' at Vézelay was richly praised in *The Pilgrim's Guide*.

Mention of the great Burgundian abbey of Vézelay is particularly appropriate in the context of Les Saintes-Maries. The story of the three Marys cast adrift by their persecutors in Palestine before being miraculously carried here is a natural coda to the parallel legend described in Chapter Seven in which the body of Mary Magdalene was later stolen from this region and reburied at Vézelay, so enabling that abbey to become one of the leading shrines in Christian Europe as well as the starting-point of one of the four principal roads to Santiago.

The legend of Les Saintes-Maries is an invaluable preface to that fanciful and often disreputable saga which brought fame and wealth to one of the greatest of medieval abbeys, and led ultimately to its downfall.

Just how much of the story of the Three Marys would have been known to pilgrims in the twelfth century is open to dispute. The generally acknowledged source of the legend is that colourful account of the lives of the saints called *Legenda Aurea* (the Golden Legend), compiled in Italy by an eminent Dominican cleric and chronicler by the name of Jacobus (or Jacques) de Voragine in the thirteenth century. The work enjoyed immense popularity judging by the numerous copies made of it.

Jacobus de Voragine did not invent these 'lives': his achievement was to gather together material from a variety of sources, much of it consisting of folk-tales passed down orally over the centuries or gleaned from accounts by earlier churchmen. And here we begin to see that the Three Marys' legend may have its roots far deeper than is generally believed. We know that as early as the fourth century a church was founded on the coast of the Camargue on the site of a Roman temple, and that in the sixth century the Bishop of Arles described a church there as bearing a dedication to 'Sainte-Marie-de-Ratis' – St Mary of the Raft. Which particular Mary is unclear, but the dedication certainly suggests that the story of the arrival of a saint by that name by sea was already current, and perhaps had been so ever since Roman times during the reign of Constantine when the emperor was living in Arles only a short distance away. In other words, long before the *Legenda Aurea* was compiled pilgrims would have been making their way to Les Saintes-Maries-de-la-Mer fully aware of a special shrine related to the magical arrival of a vessel carrying biblical figures from the Holy Land.

By the twelfth century pilgrims bound for Santiago who were making a detour here would have been greeted by a gaunt fortress of a church that had recently been rebuilt after a long history of plunder and destruction by Saracen invaders from Spain. It was this edifice that survives today as the parish church of Les Saintes-Maries – a large and impressive hulk of a building that clearly would have served a more important function than that of a parish church serving a small fishing village. It had been built of sandstone quarried far inland, then shipped down the Rhône at no doubt considerable cost. What is more, the elegant band of blind arches running round the entire building is evidence of those highly skilled itinerant stonemasons from Lombardy whose work we have already seen gracing many of the early churches in Burgundy. In short, no expense seems to have been spared. It was a place of prestige, a church that must already have been well established as a popular centre of pilgrimage.

The story of the Three Marys did not end there. Three centuries later local curiosity led to another chapter being written. Hearsay and blind faith were no longer enough to satisfy a more sceptical society. Physical proof was required. In 1448 Count René of Provence (popularly known as 'Good King René since he was also the titular King of Naples) ordered an excavation beneath the church in the area of the high altar, its purpose being to put to the test the long-held belief that here was where Mary Salome and Mary Jacob would have founded their original oratory after their voyage from Palestine – and where they would ultimately have been buried. King René's conviction proved to be well-founded: bones were indeed discovered buried on either side of the present altar. Furthermore they were said to have given off a sweet odour as they were unearthed, considered to be conclusive proof that here were indeed the relics of the two Marys who had stayed behind here – one the sister of the Virgin Mary, the other the mother of the apostle St James.

Today the celebrations to mark these discoveries of five and a half centuries ago have shifted from pilgrimage to pageant. In a touching ceremony held every May effigies of the two Marys in a model boat, along with a statue of their servant Sara, are carried on a symbolic journey back to the sea, traditionally led by the Archbishop of Aix-en-Provence. As the procession nears the water riders mounted on white Camargue horses form a protective semi-circle facing the shore as the effigies are borne slowly into the shallows. Then, in an informal ceremony of baptism, sea-water is gently sprinkled over them. They have received the benediction of the sea which had brought them here.

The theme of the sea, and magical sea voyages, lies as close to the heart of the St James legend as it does the legend of the Marys. Every pilgrim setting out for Santiago de Compostela in the twelfth century would have been familiar with the story of how the body of their apostle was carried by sea from the eastern Mediterranean out into the Atlantic before finally reaching the shores of north-west Spain. A miracle of the oceans feeds both legends almost in parallel.

Pilgrims who had made a detour to Les Saintes-Maries in medieval times may have returned to Arles before heading west on the next leg of their journey. Alternatively they may have taken the old Roman road north-west across the wilderness of the Camargue, crossing one of the branches of the Rhône by ferry before making their way to the next stopping-place on the pilgrim road. Here was a place which carried a legend just as rich as those embracing Arles and Les Saintes-Maries. This was Saint-Gilles, with its historic abbey, and a wealth of miraculous events, about which *The Pilgrim's Guide* has a great deal to say.

*

The wild swamplands of the Camargue have always possessed a romantic mystique, quite apart from the touching legend of the Three Marys. There is a haunting magic about the place. Today, as yesterday, white horses roam freely among the reed-beds, the lagoons are speckled with scarlet flamingos in their thousands, and black bulls raise their heads imperiously as you pass, their lyre-shaped horns marking them out as a breed of great antiquity, once far more widespread. They date back at least as early as the third millennium BC, featuring in the Stone Age wall-paintings of the famous Hall of the Bulls in the Lascaux caves further north in central France.

Pilgrims setting out from Arles westwards by the direct route would have enjoyed at least a glimpse of the Camargue marshes before arriving at their next stopping-place, Saint-Gilles. Here was a town awarded a very special accolade by the *Guide* on account of the fame of the saint who gave his name to the town. He was 'the most Blessed Gilles' who was 'extraordinarily famous in all parts of the world'. The hagiography continues in full flow: 'After the prophets and the apostles nobody among the other saints is more worthy, nobody more holy, nobody more glorious, nobody more prompt to lend help … Oh, what a beautiful and valuable labour it is to visit his tomb.'

The author, presumably Aimery Picaud, is writing about Saint-Gilles as if this was a travel diary. He is actually there on the spot, which may account for the breathless tone of his account. Whereas accounts of other saints and their shrines are respectfully impersonal, here is an impassioned eye-witness description. 'I myself have verified what I am saying … I regret indeed having to die before being able to report all the saint's feats worthy of veneration, these being so many and so great.' Picaud's eulogy is accompanied by an account of some of the miracles attributed to Gilles, including one which apparently cured the Emperor Charlemagne of his (undisclosed) sins.

Picaud has introduced us to a shadowy figure who is nonetheless presented as special and remarkable; and it is intriguing to consider why. Gilles was by no means a 'super-saint': he had not been a disciple of Christ or part of his family circle. He had not even been martyred. A mixture of legend and flimsy historical evidence establishes St Gilles as having been born in Greece early in the seventh century. He received a divine calling to spread the gospel, leading him to set out on a raft which in due course brought him to the shores of Provence. (Similarities to the Three Marys legend are obvious, even with a gap of seven centuries, perhaps suggesting a long-held popular belief in this region that early Christianity was brought here miraculously by sea.) Why Gilles felt compelled to spread the gospel in southern France is puzzling since the area had already been converted to Christianity for three centuries. Gilles is then said to have lived the life of a Christian hermit befriended, so the story goes, by a deer he had saved by intercepting a huntsman's spear, and who proceeded to repay him by providing regular supplies of milk. The huntsman in question turned out to be the Visigoth (or Frankish) King Wamba. Amazed by what he had witnessed he undertook to found an abbey on the site, of which Gilles became the first abbot.

The cult of St Gilles spread steadily, stimulated by the usual accounts of miracles attributed to him. It reached its zenith in the late eleventh and twelfth centuries, attracting followers far beyond the boundaries of Provence. There was, for instance, a nobleman in Poland towards the end of the eleventh century who narrowly survived a hunting accident. As a result of his escape from death he offered a prayer promising to visit the shrine of St Gilles in thanksgiving – a promise he fulfilled. Clearly no saint closer to home would have been powerful enough to save him.

Such adulation from afar was no accident: rather, it was the natural outcome of an event which had taken place only a few years before the pilgrimage made by the grateful Polish nobleman. It was an event which in all probability also accounts for the effusiveness of *The Pilgrim's Guide*'s description of the place and its saint. What took place was this. In the year 1090 the abbey, which had been founded on modest lines four hundred years earlier, became one of a number of monasteries in this region to be placed under the reforming authority of the great Burgundian abbey of Cluny. This was a procedure we have witnessed many times before in earlier chapters as Cluny extended its empire of dependent abbeys and priories; except that the circumstances surrounding the take-over of Saint-Gilles were unusually propitious. The small town of Saint-Gilles was the principal seat of one of the most powerful and ambitious feudal lords in France, Count Raymond IV of Toulouse. Raymond would have recognised the huge benefit to his own position of becoming the patron of an abbey of international fame and prestige; and what more rewarding a step towards achieving such an ambition than to open negotiations with the most influential monastic house in the Christian world, Cluny? In addition, the Abbot of Cluny was a man who had held that position for forty years (and was to hold it for a further twenty years), and who already presided over many hundreds of monasteries right across Europe. Abbot Hugh, Hugh the Great, or St. Hugh as he became, besides being a pious churchman was a shrewd political animal, and would have seen the rewards of being supported by so powerful a figure as Raymond, particularly since Saint-Gilles was strategically placed on one of the main pilgrim routes to Spain. An important abbey here would greatly strengthen the pilgrimage movement leading to Spain, and in the process enhance the cause of Reconquest which lay close to the abbot's heart.

Altogether, an enduring agreement between the Counts of Toulouse and the Abbots of Cluny could become a formidable and lucrative partnership on both sides. And so it proved to be.

One further binding thread in the contract between Abbot Hugh and Count Raymond greatly boosted the prestige of their shared enterprise. Six years later, in 1096, as the enlarged Abbey of Saint-Gilles was beginning to take shape on an ambitious scale, the new high altar was consecrated by no less a figure than the pope. Again it was Hugh who played the key role in bringing the ceremony about. Pope Urban II was a Frenchman who had spent his early years as a monk at Cluny, eventually appointed by Hugh to be the abbey's Grand Prior before his election to the papacy. It was another political triumph for Hugh. Cluny now had their own man as head of the Church.

Pope Urban's arrival at Saint-Gilles took place in the wake of an extensive tour, largely organised by Cluny, which the pope had made in order to promote an undertaking that was to become one of the seminal events of the Middle Ages, the First Crusade, aimed at liberating Jerusalem and the Holy Land from the hands of the Muslims. The crusade was launched within months of Urban consecrating the high altar here. It could scarcely have been a more auspicious moment for the fortunes of Saint-Gilles, both the abbey and the town. To complete the picture Count Raymond himself became one of the leaders of the crusade, launching the triumphant assault on Jerusalem in 1098.

Furthermore the success of the First Crusade opened up a rich traffic in goods from Palestine and the Middle East which no longer needed to reach France by way of Venice. They could arrive directly here in Languedoc in Raymond's own seat of power, and this lucrative business was further aided by trading privileges in Palestine which the count had obtained. Until the construction of Aigues-Mortes closer to the sea more than a century later Saint-Gilles became the principal port in this region for receiving luxury items of all kinds – silks, ivory, metalwork – brought from the Holy Land and from further east. The annual trade fairs held here as a result brought together merchants from north and south, east and west, to the handsome benefit of all, including of course the new abbey beneath whose expansive walls these colourful events were regularly held.

With its fame now spread across Europe, rich trade from the East, gifts from returning crusaders and ever more lavish donations from wealthy pilgrims heading for Spain, Saint-Gilles became in a very short time one of the brightest jewels in Cluny's crown. And the abbey church itself soon took on a splendour to match. By the second half of the twelfth century the ghosts of Abbot Hugh and Count Raymond would have been wearing satisfied smiles.

The prestige of the Abbey of Saint-Gilles abbey at that time can be measured by the scale and grandeur of the new church, or at least those parts of it which have survived, above all the west front. Here is one of the most glorious church facades in France, and a masterpiece of Romanesque architectural sculpture. Aimery Picaud was here too early to be able to break into his customary eulogies. And, unlike the shrine of St Gilles in the crypt, the great west portal of the abbey church has mostly survived, even if somewhat battered by wars and religious conflict.

Set high above a flight of steps the facade consists of three elaborately carved portals which stretch majestically left and right across the entire width of the church. Within ranks of Corinthian columns each portal is decorated with wonderfully vigorous carvings on either side, accompanied by a frieze of further figures illustrating the life of Christ and his disciples. A tympanum characteristically crowns each portal, the central one devoted to the traditional theme of Christ in Glory. The whole facade bears strong similarities to the west front of Saint-Trophime in Arles, which pilgrims would have set eyes on only a short while before, and may well have been carved in the same stonemason's workshop. The entire mass of carvings is known to have been completed by the middle of the twelfth century, just a few decades after Picaud's visit. We even know the name of the principal sculptor involved, because inscribed on a statue of St Jude are the Latin words BRUNUS ME FECIT – 'Brunus made me'. This is all we know about him. We are reminded of that celebrated Latin 'signature', GISLEBERTUS HOC FECIT, which provides a shadowy identity to the authorship of an even finer masterpiece of medieval church carving, the great tympanum on the cathedral of Autun which was the subject of Chapter 10. In the overall anonymity of medieval artistry such glimpses of a living person are precious and rare. What kind of man, we would love to know, was Brunus, or Gislebertus –

21. The city of Arles in Provence, starting-point for the fourth road. Before setting off pilgrims would gather for mass in the cathedral of Saint-Trophime, with its rank of carved images of the evangelists on either side of the west door.
(Adam Woolfitt)

22. A major diversion for pilgrims: the fortified church at Les-Saintes-Maries-de-la-Mer in the Camargue, a shrine to the legendary miraculous raft said to have borne Mary Magdalene from the Holy Land.
(Wolfgang Staudt/ Wikimedia Commons)

23. Toulouse: the abbey church of Saint-Sernin had a special appeal for pilgrims heading for the Pyrenees. Its treasures included the so-called Horn of Roland, supposedly sounded to alert the Emperor Charlemagne of the pending attack on his army at Roncesvalles.
(Didier Descouens/ Wikimedia Commons)

24. A familiar musical theme greeting pilgrims on the carved portal of the church of Sainte-Marie at Oloron, near the Pyrenees: the Old Men of the Apocalypse, illustrating the Vision of St. John.
(Adam Woolfitt)

25. Across the Pyrenees into Spanish Navarre: the octagonal chapel of the Knights Templar, Santa Maria de Eunate.
(Adam Woolfitt)

26. The bridge constructed specially for pilgrims at Puente la Reina ('the Queen's bridge'), the Spanish town where all four roads finally become one – the *camino*. It was the construction of such bridges across northern Spain that made the Santiago pilgrimage possible.
(Adam Woolfitt)

27. At the junction of two rivers, the medieval bridge at Hospital de Órbigo – the longest, with twenty arches, in the 400-mile stretch of the Spanish camino. (Adam Woolfitt)

28. Sermons in stone on the cathedral at León. Pilgrims were rarely allowed to forget the punishments awaiting sinners at the Last Judgment. (Adam Woolfitt)

29. Inspired by the cathedrals of the Rhineland, and a major shrine for pilgrims heading for Santiago: the great cathedral at Burgos. (Adam Woolfitt)

30. Triumphant journey's end: the cathedral of Santiago de Compostela overlooking Praza do Obradoiro. The final bravura touch of twin Baroque towers was added in the eighteenth century. (arousa/Shutterstock)

31. St James looks down from his cathedral at dusk.
(Adam Woolfitt)

men who spent their lives creating some of the most noble works of Christian art to have come down to us?

The later history of the abbey would have saddened Picaud. The Hundred Years' War between France and England did Saint-Gilles no favours. Pilgrims dwindled in number. By the early fifteenth century donations to the abbey were so few that the monks were reduced to pleading to the Holy Roman Emperor that 'the devotion of Christians to St Gilles has altogether ceased and the faithful no longer come and visit his tomb. In former times the great affluence of pilgrims was a wonderful boon to the abbey and town of St Gilles, but now the place is deserted and impoverished.' Income was now so low that the monks claimed that they could no longer afford food and clothing.

The French religious wars in the following century led to a Protestant army occupying the town, slaughtering the local priests and choirboys. They used the abbey church itself as a fortress, and in their reforming zeal destroyed the celebrated tomb and reliquary of St Gilles which Picaud had described so lovingly. At least they left the great west portal of the church more or less intact, satisfying themselves with hacking off the stone heads of a number of Old Testament prophets to whom they took offence.

As a result, by sheer good luck, we are still able to admire some of the surviving masterpieces of medieval church carving. At the same time, those aware of the dark history of this now rundown town might feel relieved to take the next step along the pilgrim road towards the relative peace and tranquillity of 'the desert' which lay ahead.

16. Desert Songs

After Saint-Gilles the pilgrim road continues to skirt the Camargue marshlands before reaching what later became the important Protestant city of Montpellier. The medieval road then headed briefly northwards into the rugged hill-country known as the *garrigue*. This bleak and rocky landscape exerted an irresistible appeal to early Christian leaders in search of an ascetic life far from the madding crowd where they could contemplate their god in peace without the distraction of earthly pleasures. Two places close to one another came to prominence as early as the eighth century and exemplify this Christian yearning for solitude and self-deprivation. And as their fame became widespread and the pilgrimage movement gained momentum over the following centuries, both places became key shrines along the most southerly of the French pilgrim roads to Spain. Reaching them required a short meander into the wilds of the *garrigue*.

Both shrines have direct connections to the Emperor Charlemagne. The first of them, Aniane, only a short distance from Montpellier, subsequently fell victim to the fury of the French wars of religion between Protestants and Catholics in the late sixteenth century; and today there is nothing in Aniane to remind the traveller of how important a historical landmark this place once was. For medieval pilgrims Aniane may have been their first resting-place after Saint-Gilles; and if there were any among them with some knowledge of monastic history, then here was a place demanding the deepest respect.

The story of Aniane can be read as a parable of the early days of Christianity. The man who became known as St Benedict of Aniane (or 'the second St Benedict', the first being the founder of the order) spent his early years as a member of the court of Charlemagne, and subsequently rose to be one of the emperor's most successful field commanders during his campaigns against barbarian insurgents in northern Italy. Benedict then abandoned the military life and became a monk, and in about the year 780 he founded a small monastic community on his own estate here in the foothills, a location suitably remote from any town or village. The community was modelled on the isolated cells of Christian monks established during the third and fourth centuries in the Egyptian desert during the final decades of the Roman Empire.

Within a few years the Eastern model was replaced by a new, highly disciplined monastery at Aniane whose monks strictly followed the Rule set down by Benedict's illustrious namesake St Benedict of Nursia at Monte Cassino in southern Italy two hundred years earlier. The new monastery flourished, attracting donations from wealthy benefactors and ever-increasing numbers of pilgrims.

The success of Benedict's venture at Aniane rested on the widespread reforms in monastic life which he instigated, at first here in Languedoc and later in abbeys and priories throughout the Christian world. The significance of his work can only be fully grasped by understanding just how crucial monasteries were to the fragile structure of early Christian society. Monasteries were not only houses of God and guardians of the true faith, they were virtually the only seats of learning and literacy: they represented moral order, social stability and the rule of law and justice. Outside their secure walls lay disorder and disruption. Anarchy was forever threatening. Accordingly, when those monastic pillars of society were seen to be crumbling, social order itself was at risk. Benedict saw around him a monastic world in which rules of worship and moral codes were being widely flouted. Abbots, as well as the monks below them, were often living openly with their wives and mistresses, enjoying a life of comfort and privilege given them by their status as supposed men of God and by the lands and worldly goods the monasteries had acquired from bequests and donations. Many monks had become parasites rather than servants of God.

This was the common state of affairs which Benedict did much to rectify. Having been Charlemagne's ideal soldier Benedict became his ideal reformer. He helped create the orderly Christian institutions which the emperor believed to be vital in an unstable world. When Charlemagne was crowned in Rome on Christmas Day in 800 it was an event which perfectly symbolised the emperor's ambition to recreate a coherent Christian empire as it had been under the first Roman Christian emperor Constantine five hundred years earlier. Charlemagne's vision was to re-establish a Christian world in which the former Roman Empire was reborn within the embrace of the Frankish dynasty he had founded (a vision realised to this day in the name of the principal territory he ruled, France).

After Charlemagne's death fourteen years later it was left to his son and heir, Louis the Pious, to put into practice many of the monastic reforms he had urged. And it was under Emperor Louis that Benedict of Aniane was placed in charge of all the monasteries throughout the empire. Benedict proved to be a zealous and uncompromising reformer; yet his successes turned out to be largely short-lived. With the break-up of the Carolingian empire shortly afterwards and the resulting anarchy of the ninth century many of the religious houses whose practices and rituals Benedict had reformed slipped back into their old ways, while many others suffered irreparably from the Saracen, Magyar and Viking invasions which wrecked so much of France throughout that darkest of centuries.

There is no mention of St Benedict of Aniane in *The Pilgrim's Guide* even though the pioneer monastery he founded lay directly on the pilgrim road between Saint-Gilles and Toulouse, both of which are accorded much praise by the author, as is the celebrated shrine which pilgrims would soon be visiting barely a few miles beyond Aniane, Saint-Guilhem-le-Désert. We can only speculate on what would seem a surprising omission. Perhaps Aimery Picaud, whom we assume to have been the author, was unaware of the place, and indeed of its founder who also receives no mention in the text's catalogue of saints.

Or maybe the omission was quite deliberate, on the grounds that a fulsome tribute to St Benedict of Aniane and his monastic reforms would have detracted from the glory of Cluny, the abbey which had sponsored *The Pilgrim's Guide* and where, according to its final words, it was mainly written. As we have seen on so many occasions, the Santiago pilgrimage was Cluny's show, and not one to be easily shared.

Whatever the case, what remains true is that medieval travellers who benefitted from the charity of monks as they made their way from abbey to abbey, hospice to hospice, were welcomed into religious houses run on disciplined lines that owed much to the rigorous reforms first imposed by Benedict of Aniane. Weary after a long day on the open road they would have found themselves drawn into in atmosphere of calm and serenity, perhaps invited to participate in an elaborate church service that was rich in music and chanting: and this too was a debt to Benedict, who had laid such emphasis on liturgy and prayer in the daily life of a monk.

In many respects Benedict's reforms in monastic life foreshadowed those instituted by those indefatigable Abbots of Cluny several centuries later when the mood and resolve of Christian Europe was altogether more buoyant; at a time when, in the celebrated words of the Cluniac monk Raoul Glaber, 'it was as if the world itself was casting aside its old age and clothing itself anew in a white mantle of churches'.

*

From Aniane the pilgrim road heads for the 'desert', as the region is still described. The rough hills ahead are split by a gorge down which the River Hérault plunges towards the plains of Languedoc. The first intimation that here is a place of history is a bridge known as the Pont du Diable, the Devil's Bridge. It dates from the eleventh century, and was built by monks from the nearby Abbey of Saint-Guilhem, appropriately known as Saint-Guilhem-le-Désert.

We are again following in the footsteps of Charlemagne. Like St Benedict of Aniane, St Guilhem was one of the emperor's most successful generals, as *The Pilgrim's Guide* makes clear. 'The most saintly Guilhem was an eminent standard-bearer of King Charles the

Great, a most valiant soldier and a great expert in war. It was he who by his valour, as it is told, brought under Christian rule the cities of Nîmes, Orange and many others.' Guilhem was an aristocrat, a cousin and close friend of the emperor, and was brought up in the imperial court. As a soldier the victories enumerated in the *Guide* were against Saracen insurgents from Spain, whom he seems to have been responsible for expelling from much of Languedoc, temporarily at least.

On one of these campaigns his beloved wife died, and her death prompted him to abandon the life of a soldier in favour of the solitude of the barren hills to the north of Montpellier. Here, in 804 Guilhem built a monastery a short distance from where Benedict had established his monastic community at Aniane almost a quarter of a century earlier. And in recognition of Guilhem's services, and of his commitment to the monastic life, Charlemagne presented him with the most precious Christian relic in his possession, a fragment of the Holy Cross.

Unlike Benedict's community at Aniane, Guilhem's monastery survives today – at least part of it, namely the abbey church and fragments of the cloister. An enchanting village clusters round it, taking its name from the abbey's founder. Saint-Guilhem-le-Désert is a jewel in the desert.

The saint himself died in 812, just two years before the death of the emperor he had served. Processions and special services in the village still honour his saint's day (3 May) when the reliquary containing the fragment of the Holy Cross presented to him by Charlemagne is solemnly carried through the village to the church, those taking part in the procession traditionally carrying snails' shells as oil lamps through the narrow streets. Folklore has preserved touches of the Middle Ages in Saint-Guilhem, and everything about the immediate setting and the embracing hills around contribute to making a visit here a journey into a past era re-enacted before our eyes.

The church itself dates from the eleventh century, two and a half centuries after Guilhem's death. As so often with early Church leaders their fame, and the cults that grew up around them, blossomed long after their lifetime in response to a radically different social and political climate. St Guilhem's fame became widespread throughout

Europe largely due to a new spirit of religious fervour in the eleventh and twelfth centuries which expressed itself as a cult of the saints and their shrines, and in the resulting popular urge to go on pilgrimages to visit those shrines.

A further accompaniment and stimulus to the pilgrimage movement onwards was the emergence of stories and songs – the *chansons de geste* – which dramatised the feats of Christian heroes of the past, and filled the ears and imaginations of pilgrims as they made their way to some chosen shrine. Again we have the example of Chaucer's band of pilgrims setting out for Canterbury and entertaining each other with tales and music to while away the time on the lonely road. They were making their way through the fertile garden of England rather than the 'desert' of Languedoc; yet there is no reason to suppose they would have entertained each other in a different way.

The song recounting the exploits of Guilhem was among the most popular of these *chansons de geste*, largely on account of its bloodcurdling account of the hero's slaughter of Saracens invaders. Its bellicose theme would have found particular favour with the sponsors of the Santiago pilgrimage (notably Cluny) for whom the cult of St James and the Christian Reconquest of Spain were inextricably linked. Notoriety brought wealth to Saint-Guilhem chiefly through donations by well-to-do pilgrims. As a result a new and much enlarged abbey church was built in the late eleventh and twelfth centuries, and which today stands handsomely in the heart of the village. A finely carved west door opens out on to a gracious square where a tangle of narrow alleys converge.

The abbey church survived the desecrations of the religious wars and the French Revolution by becoming the local parish church, which it still is. The abbey itself was less fortunate, and nothing of it remains. The cloister suffered only marginally less. In the twelfth century it was rebuilt as a two-storey cloister, which only the wealthiest religious houses tended to permit themselves, with Corinthian columns bearing traditional acanthus-leaf capitals combined with medieval imagery of flowers and vines. Here at Saint-Guilhem sadly little remains of what would have been one of the glories of Romanesque church architecture, though much of it has recently been recreated. After the French Revolution the cloister was transformed into a veritable shopping precinct, including a tannery. The entire abbey complex was then sold off as a stonemason's yard (a fate shared by the abbey church of Cluny). Much of the present village of Saint-Guilhem is built of it, and there is scarcely a farmhouse or inn within an hour's journey of the place that does not owe its limestone walls to the abbey founded by Charlemagne's legendary standard-bearer.

Late in the nineteenth century many of the carved columns from the cloister were discovered supporting a vine arbour belonging to a lawyer in nearby Aniane. A far-sighted American benefactor acquired the columns, and today the finest record of Saint-Guilham's majestic cloister graces the Cloisters Museum in New York.

*

It may seem a curious coincidence that two monasteries within a very short distance of one another, at Aniane and Saint-Guilhem, should each have been founded by a leading soldier serving under the Emperor Charlemagne, both of whom then abandoned a military career in favour of the solitary life of a hermit in the wilderness. Yet a closer look reveals a certain shared significance – in when the two monasteries were founded, and in the locations chosen. Wars and revolution have subsequently taken a heavy toll on both places, and today a great deal of reconstruction in the mind's eye is required to bring them to life; yet pilgrims arriving here in the twelfth century on this the most southerly road to Spain would have found themselves in a setting rich with echoes of the very beginnings of Christian monastic life. And the strongest of those echoes was the call of the wild – a belief in the healing power of the wilderness.

The appeal of the desert originated in the example of Christ himself, who had spent forty days and forty nights in the wilderness battling with Satan and overcoming him. For fervent believers here lay the only route to spiritual maturity, removing themselves from the marketplace of the world to live as hermits. Where Christ had led, others must follow. Hence, when persecution and social alienation contributed to driving early Christianity underground, it surfaced in places as far removed as possible from that busy world, in remote place reminiscent of Christ's wilderness, the chief of them being the Egyptian desert. It was here that the most uncompromising believers chose to remove themselves, convinced that only a life of solitude and the harshest asceticism could permit a profound understanding of God. The Ancient Greek philosophers had taken quite the opposite view, that civilisation could only be found within the city walls: life outside the city gates was a Bacchanalian chaos, and if you lived there you were an outcast. But for the desert fathers towns and cities were 'Babylon', the natural consequence of mankind after the Fall.

One of the most eminent of modern medievalists, Christopher Brooke, has aptly put the question: 'How can one begin to characterise a movement of the human spirit so distant and so strange?' Yet, however distant it may seem, the hermitage ethic, and the extreme asceticism that accompanied it, lie at the very roots of western monasticism, and therefore inevitably part of the bloodstream of the medieval pilgrimage movement which sprang from it.

Solitary though these 'desert fathers' initially were, many of them began to attract followers, so that soon small communities were established in the desert. Hence Christian monasticism was born. The man generally acknowledged to have been the founding father of these desert cells was St Anthony, who was born about 251 AD, and who spent some twenty years in the Egyptian desert until his death in 356 at the age of over a hundred (which, if true, says a great deal for the rewards of an ascetic life). His was a lifespan which took in several of the most historic events in the early history of Christianity, two in particular: the final and most severe persecutions of the Christians under the Roman Emperor Diocletion at the very beginning of the fourth century, and – secondly – the sudden Roman conversion to Christianity under his successor, the Emperor Constantine, barely ten years later.

To have experienced two of the most cataclysmic events in Christian history clearly had a volcanic effect of St Anthony's life and outlook: he became a passionate believer in the holy nature of martyrdom, allied with a corresponding horror of all emotions of joy and celebration, especially pleasures of the flesh. In doing so, he and those who followed him (such as St Jerome) supplied the early Church with an ideal of extreme asceticism as the perfect way of serving and understanding God.

This combination of a cult of suffering with a loathing of all physical pleasures, born of these remote communities in the Egyptian desert, set the tone for much of the religious thought and teaching of the early Church, as well as providing a field-day for painters and sculptors required to illustrate the most lurid scene of carnal temptation. And though the extreme asceticism preached by St Anthony became softened in the writings of St Augustine and in particular St Benedict, founder of the Benedictine order, it was nonetheless never far away from the ambitions of those zealots who gave up their worldly careers in order to found the earliest monasteries in Europe – men such as St Guilhem who chose as his ideal setting a 'desert' as close in spirit to the Egyptian desert as France could offer, as well as being safely removed from all distractions and temptations of human society. The spirit of St Anthony was never far away from the Languedoc hills.

The dark legacy of the desert fathers led to a host of contradictions for the monasteries of Western Europe which grew out of that Eastern tradition, principally because medieval monasteries flourished in a very different world. And inevitably these contradictions were shared by the pilgrimage movement which depended to a large extent on those monasteries, without which there would have been no pilgrimages. So, we may wonder, was the medieval pilgrim making his way to a shrine in 'the desert' here in Languedoc imagining that he was shunning the corrupt world of 'Babylon'? Probably not; yet the monastery he was visiting had been founded in precisely that spirit.

This conflict of purpose illuminates a key question which has been asked ever since the beginning of Christianity: is the good Christian life compatible with earthly joys and pleasures? Or does that life in its truest form demand asceticism and a renunciation of such earthly pleasures? St Anthony would have had no problem answering the second question in the affirmative, even though Christ himself would probably not have agreed, having been happy to turn water into wine to aid festivities at the wedding in Canaan. It would seem to be in the nature of human zeal that those who most vigorously point the way to God tend to be more disapproving of earthly pleasures than God's own son would have been. If we read Chaucer's *Canterbury Tales,* or look at mediaeval manuscripts illustrating scenes of pilgrims singing and dancing on their way to Santiago, we see little of St Anthony's bleak certainty. The spirit of pilgrimage was a rare fusion of a renunciation of worldly comforts with a joyful embrace of the physical world through which the pilgrim boldly made his way.

At the same time the world the pilgrim encountered on his long journey through Western Europe was never free of that long-standing Christian conflict between body and spirit. Both in France and Spain the pilgrim roads led to hermitage after hermitage, many of them established by men who had built roads and bridges to aid travellers, and who were bravely dedicated to safeguarding their region against bandits, thieves and of course Saracens. As hermits they may have shunned the busy world, yet by their tireless exertions they still contrived to make it a better place. The hermit's life exemplifies one of the major contradictions that coloured medieval Christianity – between the ideal of renunciation of the material world, and the equally powerful determination to improve it.

In short, one of the most compelling aspects of the medieval pilgrimage movement is how the long and winding road that pilgrims were compelled to take manages to draw together so many of the diverse religious impulses that drove Christians of the age to lead the life they chose. The pilgrim roads, today as yesterday, lead the traveller through an illustrated history of Christianity, from its darkest moments to its triumphant hours, from martyrs to heroes, masterpieces of art and architecture to personal messages scratched on the door of an inn. All life is there – even in the 'desert' of Languedoc from where the next stage of this road takes the traveller westwards to the great city which gave this road its name, the *Via Tolosana*. That city is Toulouse.

17. A Cargo of Relics

FROM ST. GUILHEM-LE-DÉSERT PILGRIMS CONTINUED to be led from one local saint to another. The road was a narrow thread linking shrine to shrine through the rough countryside of the *garrigue*. Today's traveller, following in their footsteps across this primordial landscape, wanders from village to stone village, each of them having grown up over the centuries like a dependent family round one or other of these local shrines.

A recurring feature of early Christian saints is that reliable information about them is often thin on the ground. There are usually no more than a few bare facts, and the rest is folklore, changing colour and content over the succeeding centuries. Then, with the pilgrimage movement under way there grew up a cult of these early saints whose shrines could now be venerated. In response disingenuous churchmen began to create fanciful biographies of these shadow figures from the past, making imaginative use of the few fragments of available material and thereby greatly enhancing the appeal of the saint's shrine to passing pilgrims and potential benefactors. The biography industry within the medieval church became a flourishing affair. History was widely re-written, or more often simply invented. Hagiography became a fine art, contributing much to the aura surrounding these early Christian heroes and martyrs, upon which much of the popular appeal of pilgrimages depended.

An example of just such an embroidered image confronted the medieval pilgrim a short distance after leaving Saint-Guilhem-le-Désert, at Lodève. Travellers today arriving here in May can still find themselves participating in a week-long celebration which has been conducted ever since pilgrims bound for Santiago came here in the Middle Ages. The occasion is the annual feast of the local saint, St Fulcran, who was bishop here in the mid-tenth century, and was responsible for building Lodève's first cathedral, long since replaced by the present Gothic pile dedicated to him.

The only written source of information about Fulcran is a pious biography by a successor as Lodève's bishop four centuries later. From this account we learn that Fulcran led a pure and holy life dedicated to aiding the poor and sick; that he founded and endowed hospices, was canonised for his good works and had undertaken the pilgrimage to Santiago. In this instance history may well have been re-written in the interests of the pilgrimage movement. If Fulcran had indeed made the journey to Santiago he must have been among the very first leading churchmen to do so, rivalling the claim generally made for the Bishop of Le Puy who is known to have made the pilgrimage in 950 (see Chapter 12). Perhaps the more likely scenario is that the saint's biographer, writing soon after the high noon of the pilgrimage movement when Fulcran's tomb had by now been venerated by millions of Santiago pilgrims over the past three centuries, concluded that the legendary bishop must surely have undertaken the pilgrimage himself, so making the saint an honorary recruit to the Santiago cause.

In reporting the lives of early saints any possible connection with Spain was welcomed, particularly as the pilgrim roads were now drawing closer to the Pyrenees. The goal of St James' own city combined with the mission of the Reconquest gave the Spanish peninsula an air of the Promised Land. With the Pyrenees now on the southern skyline, pilgrims continued deeper into Languedoc, reaching the town of Castres which had grown up round one of the early abbeys reformed at the beginning of the ninth century by St Benedict of Aniane. Castres had been a prominent Roman town, as its name suggests (*castrum*, a fortified place). To the medieval pilgrim, however, the Roman association had a very different significance. Later in the ninth century the abbey had been presented with the relics of one of the most celebrated of Christian martyrs in Spain during the final savage persecutions under the Roman Emperor Diocletian. The martyr was St Vincent of Saragossa. And over the following centuries his relics brought fame and wealth to the town and abbey of Castres to an extent which might seem out of proportion to St Vincent's importance historically. Yet in a religious climate which held relics of the saints to be a spiritual link between humans and God a shrine such as this possessed much that a worshipper would travel far to venerate. Here was an early martyr who had been horribly tortured, whose body was subsequently protected by ravens from vultures, and finally spirited away from Saracen lands to a Christian country where pilgrims could pause to offer up their prayers and hopes for a reconquered Spain now only a few days ahead. It was a powerful and appealing narrative.

Castres flourished on the fame of St Vincent until the fates turned against the town. It became a stronghold of the heretical Cathars only to be crushed in the Albigensian Crusade of the thirteenth century. Worse followed. The Black Death devastated the town in the following century, and it was then sacked by the English army under Edward the Black Prince during the Hundred Years' War. The sixteenth-century religious wars were no kinder to Castres either: as a predominantly Protestant town it was brought to heel, and its fortifications formally demolished. Even the relics of St Vincent, revered by many centuries of pilgrims, perished in the course of the town's turbulent history. In the absence of surviving monuments to its gilded past the modern traveller may feel that the most appropriate comment lies with yet another, more recent connection to Spain. Here in the local museum devoted to the eighteenth-century Spanish artist Francisco Goya, his incomparable series of etchings, *The Disasters of War*, are displayed across its walls as a most telling *memento mori*. Goya's horrific images of human cruelty feel like a match for those gruesome depictions of early Christian martyrs on the face of so many churches lining the pilgrim roads to Santiago.

Castres suffered humiliatingly from the ruthless suppression of the heretical Cathars in the thirteenth century. Yet one outcome of that heartless campaign was a policy of vigorous propaganda by the triumphant Church authorities to 'sell' those aspects of the orthodox faith which had been rejected or ignored by the Cathars. Prominent among the beneficiaries of this propaganda was the pilgrimage movement itself. Suddenly funds were made available for sophisticated artists to decorate churches with appropriate narratives of the saints, in particular St James.

To the west of Castres, close to Toulouse, lies the village of Rabastens; and here the local parish church, formerly attached to a Benedictine priory, is covered wall to wall in frescoes illustrating the life of St James. These robust and colourful paintings were executed soon after the suppression of the Cathars, and were later concealed behind layers of whitewash (which at least preserved them) not removed until the late nineteenth century. Here is a new world of official imagery from the thirteenth and early fourteenth centuries. Time has moved on from the early days when St James was depicted simply as one of the twelve apostles. Now he is his own champion, promoting his own pilgrimage. He is a pilgrim to his own shrine. And he wears the full pilgrim's gear – scallop-shell on the brim of his hat, staff grasped in his hand, gourd for carrying water at his waist. Present-day pilgrims could even recognise him as one of their own. The identity is complete. At Rebastens the tourist industry of the present century can feel not so far away.

*

From here it is only a short distance to Toulouse, the city that gave this pilgrim road its name. Toulouse had long been one of the most important cities in France, politically and spiritually. It was the capital established by the Visigoths after the collapse of the Roman Empire in the fifth century. Then, from the mid-ninth century successive Counts of Toulouse ruled a virtually independent Languedoc with buccaneering panache for the next 350 years until losing most of their powers to the French crown as a result of the Albigensian Crusade against the Cathars, whom the Counts of Toulouse stubbornly refused to denounce, so bringing about their own downfall. By the thirteenth century pilgrims setting out on the *Via Tolosana* some days earlier would have prayed in the great abbey church of Saint-Gilles where Raymond VI, Count of Toulouse, had been stripped naked and publicly whipped in the presence of twenty bishops and a representative of the pope.

For pilgrims earlier in the Middle Ages these dramatic events were still to come. To them the pervasive Cathar cult would have been merely an unorthodox local variant of the Christian faith, one to which some Church authorities were apparently content to turn a blind eye. Pilgrims came to Toulouse for quite other reasons. Here was a shrine with a special appeal since it contained the remains of the first Bishop of Toulouse from the third century who was martyred at the hands of the Romans in a spectacularly gruesome fashion even by the standards of the day, as *The Pilgrim's Guide* recounts with some relish. 'On this route,' the author insists, 'one should visit the most worthy remains of the Blessed Saturninus, bishop and martyr who, when arrested by the pagans on the capital of the city of Toulouse, was tied to some furious and wild bull, and then dragged from the heights of the citadel down a flight of stone steps for a mile. His head crushed, his brains knocked out, his whole body torn to pieces, he rendered his worthy soul to Christ. He is buried in an excellent location close to the city of Toulouse where a large basilica was erected by the faithful in his honour.'

St Saturninus became abbreviated to St Sernin (perhaps because this sounded less pagan), and the 'excellent' basilica mentioned in *The Pilgrim's Guide* would have been the predecessor of the abbey church of Saint-Sernin which the author would have known soon after it was constructed, and which still stands today. It is one of the five huge 'pilgrim churches' built to a similar pattern during the eleventh and twelfth centuries (as described in Chapter 3), all of them designed specifically to accommodate large numbers of pilgrims. As Kenneth Conant has stated, 'the pilgrimage formula was brought to a climax at Saint-Sernin',[32] the only other surviving church of comparable size

32. Kenneth J. Conant, *Carolingian and Romanesque Architecture, 800-1200* (London: 1959)

in the group being the cathedral of Santiago de Compostela itself. It has even been claimed by scholars that the architect of Saint-Sernin, or at least a pupil, may have been responsible for the design of the great Galician cathedral, built at much the same time.

Surprisingly, up until the tenth and early eleventh century the tomb of St Sernin had been a more respected place of pilgrimage for Frenchmen than Santiago. This may partly have been due to geographical convenience, as well as to the relative safety of travelling to Languedoc; but it was also because of a bewildering quantity of holy relics which the abbey had come to possess. These included – so the abbey proudly claimed – no fewer than twenty-seven entire bodies of Christian martyrs. The most important of the relics were the contents of a veritable cargo of holy artefacts donated by the Emperor Charlemagne. Among the most popular of these was the celebrated Horn of Roland, which the emperor's nephew had blown with his dying breath at Roncesvalles (see Chapter 15). Many of the abbey's treasures met the fate of so much church property, looted or destroyed in the fury of the French Revolution. Among the survivors is the magnificent thirteenth-century reliquary containing the remains of St Sernin to whom the abbey was dedicated, and which was its most venerated treasure.

Inventories show that in addition to the customary fragment claimed to be of the Holy Cross Saint-Sernin possessed a vast store of gold and silver reliquaries, caskets and statues, as well as fragments of the bodies of six of Christ's apostles. All these assorted relics were publicly displayed in the various radial chapels which worshippers could approach by means of the broad ambulatory beyond the high altar characteristic of these huge pilgrim churches.

One richly decorated reliquary no longer in existence must have created some confusion among pilgrims about to head for Santiago. We know from the abbey's medieval inventory that it was a casket displaying an image of St James portrayed as a pilgrim to his own shrine, wearing a pilgrim's brimmed hat complete with scallop-shell. Since this was a reliquary it must have contained human remains, presumably believed to be those of St James himself. In all probability this was one of the fragments of the six apostles known to have been donated to the abbey by Charlemagne. This had taken place around the year 800, several decades before the discovery of the supposed tomb of St James in north-west Spain. So, at this point there were suddenly two bodies of the saint to be venerated on the same pilgrim road. Santiago had a rival. We may be reminded of the pilgrim in France a few centuries later who was proudly shown the head of John the Baptist at two successive shrines, only to be reassured by the priest at the second shrine that the first head must have been that of St John as a young man.

It is generally believed that the discovery of the apostle's tomb in Spain barely a quarter of a century later cast a serious doubt over the authenticity of the Toulouse relics. (After all, the abbey still had the remains of five apostles to display.) It would also have been in the interest of those promoting the pilgrimage to Santiago to ignore the Saint-Sernin relic. Not surprisingly, *The Pilgrim's Guide* makes no mention of it. The abbey, on the other hand, clearly decided to have it both ways by commissioning a handsome new reliquary for the now-discredited relics, proudly decorated with the image of the apostle dressed as a pilgrim making the journey to his own 'real' tomb in far-distant Spain. Were pilgrims to Saint-Sernin perplexed when they set eyes on the reliquary? We have no record.

*

The Pilgrim's Guide makes it clear that the abbey and Church of Saint-Sernin lay outside the city walls. With its enormous size it must have been an astonishing sight for pilgrims approaching Toulouse across the Languedoc plain. And it would have become an even more dominant landmark from the fourteenth century when the handsome octagonal bell-tower was raised higher still, then even higher a century later with the addition of a tall spire.[33]

Saint-Sernin has hardly changed, and the magnificent bell-tower still dominates the surroundings, except that the great pilgrim church no longer stands commandingly in the open countryside.

33. See Plate 23.

Toulouse has grown round and beyond it. The church was begun in about 1070. While it conforms to the 'formula' for pilgrim churches, one unusual feature is that a large part of it is constructed of brick, this being the most readily available building material in the alluvial plain in which the city is set. The proportions are huge, the nave being more than 350 feet in length, barrel-vaulted at a great height. From the beginning it was always an Augustinian house, as were so many abbeys and priories on the approaches to the Pyrenees, in many cases dependences, or 'out-stations', of the great Augustinian monastery of Roncesvalles. Saint-Sernin, on the other hand, was always its own master, and being on the *Via Tolosana* it prepared pilgrims for a more demanding crossing of the High Pyrenees than the Pass of Roncesvalles, as *The Pilgrim's Guide* explains (see the following chapter).

As the Santiago pilgrimage grew in strength and numbers in the latter part of the eleventh century the role of Saint-Sernin as a key stopping-place on one of the principal routes to Spain became increasingly important: hence the decision to build an enormous church. Accordingly it is no surprise that the Burgundian monastery of Cluny, sponsors of the pilgrimage in so many of its aspects, should have made a move to add it to the growing list of religious houses already under its authority. In the year 1082, at the height of Cluny's empire-building at the hands of the formidable Abbot Hugh, the Bishop of Toulouse, himself a Cluniac, took the bold step of dismissing the Augustinian canons of Saint-Sernin and replacing them with monks from Cluny. For a brief period the abbey, with its famous treasury of relics and its vast new pilgrim church in the process of construction, became the most valuable of all Cluny's possessions along the pilgrim roads. But for once Abbot Hugh's ambitions were thwarted. At first the papacy turned a blind eye – not surprisingly since Pope Urban II had himself been a monk at Cluny and been appointed by Hugh as the abbey's Grand Prior. But subsequently the papacy felt compelled to rule that the behaviour of the Bishop of Toulouse was unacceptable, and Augustinian canons were restored.

Even so, relationships with Rome seem to have remained cordial since in 1096 Pope Urban made the journey to Toulouse in order to consecrate the new high altar; while a quarter of a century later his successor Calixtus II (the very pope whose name is quoted as part-author of *The Pilgrim's Guide*) presided over a ceremony dedicating an area of the new abbey church.

The main part of the high altar consecrated by Pope Urban survives. It is a magnificent slab of carved marble, and we even know who carved it since his name is engraved discreetly on the side, which is an indication of the esteem in which he was held. The craftsman was Bernard Gelduin, about whom we know very little except that he was a specialist in marble sculpture and a master of his art. Saint-Sernin contains some of the most refined and sophisticated carvings of this period anywhere in Europe, and since Gelduin was permitted to inscribe his own name on the most important object in the church it seems more than likely that he and his workshop were responsible for the other carvings, made at the same period, for the eastern end and crypt of the church. The finest of these is a series of seven marble plaques in low relief: they are of a feathery delicacy which makes us wish that a larger body of Gelduin's work had survived for us to admire. The theme of the seven plaques is the familiar one of Christ in Majesty accompanied by the customary symbols of the six evangelists – perhaps in this case a tacit reminder to pilgrims that the abbey claimed to possess remains of all six!

The plaques are among the glories of this abbey church. But there are other outstanding works of sculpture at Saint-Sernin, notably the carved figures round the south door of the church, known as the Porte Miègeville. And there on one side of the door is the figure of St James, as if to remind us that this is one of the principal churches built specifically for pilgrims, many of whom would be heading off to the apostle's shrine in Spain. The Porte Miègeville carvings are a little later than the Gelduin plaques and high altar: we have now moved into the early years of the twelfth century. Together these works point to the existence of a major school of sculpture in south-west France, as we have also come across in Moissac, Conques and Saint-Gilles.

Significantly this was the very period when many of the new abbeys and priories were being established in northern Spain safeguarding the main pilgrim route to Santiago, the *camino*. It was also when Santiago's cathedral – a match for Saint-Sernin – was also being built. As we shall see in later chapters, it was these talented and successful workshops in France which came to play a key role in building and embellishing the new religious houses in northern Spain, both humble and grand. The skills of these architects, stonemasons and sculptors were taken across the Pyrenees to help create a new Christian Spain, often combining with the very different skills of Moorish craftsmen now working for their new Christian masters; the result was a compelling hybrid of creative achievements in northern Spain as if the Holy War had never existed.

Before long there were darker days for Toulouse and Saint-Sernin. When the Albigensian Crusade crushed the Cathars early in the thirteenth century Toulouse was besieged by the French armies of the north acting in the interest of religious orthodoxy combined with the acquisitive ambitions of the French crown. One incident which took place here at the pilgrim church during that siege may be seen as an appropriate act of retribution. The leader of the crusade, Simon de Montfort, had turned the campaign into a personal vendetta against the ruler of Languedoc, Count Raymond VI of Toulouse. It was Raymond who had been held responsible for the assassination of the papal legate near Saint-Gilles in 1208, an event which had sparked off the brutal campaign against the Cathars. Now, ten years after the murder, and with the Cathars all but destroyed, Raymond fled to Spain to avoid capture. Then, as de Montfort and his army were besieging Raymond's capital from outside the walls of the city Cathar supporters had taken refuge on the high roof of the new pilgrim church. One of them hurled a stone at the soldiers gathered below. The stone struck Simon de Montfort, killing him instantly.

A decade separated the two violent deaths. It was a decade which also saw the death of Count Raymond's political ambitions for the independence of Languedoc. As so often medieval pilgrims passed through territories fraught with dangers and disruption, protected only by their staff and recognisable clothing, and by the blessing (they hoped) of God.

Today's traveller walking the same road may be spared those hazards. Instead what the pilgrim roads offer is a journey through history – political history, religious, artistic, architectural, as well as the history of peoples and of social change. This road, the *Via Tolosana,* presents the traveller with an especially rich variety of these historical landmarks. It begins in Arles with the first flowering of Christianity in Roman Gaul, and the touching legend of the Three Marys arriving on the nearby shores of the Camargue. Then Saint-Gilles and one of the finest abbeys of Cluny's vast empire. Next, Saint-Guilhem-le-Désert and the legacy of Charlemagne's generals with their nostalgia for the wilderness and the life of the early desert fathers. Finally Toulouse and the death-knell of the Cathar heresy and all hopes of an independent Languedoc.

And tomorrow – the last trek southwards, towards the High Pyrenees, and into Spain at last.

18. Into Spain

THE FOUR PILGRIM ROADS ARE DRAWING CLOSER TOGETHER NOW as we approach the Pyrenees. The fourth road, the *Via Tolosana*, keeps a certain distance from the other three as it heads south, and before long will make its own crossing of the mountains before joining up with the others on the farther side, in Spain, or – more precisely – the region of Spain which was then the kingdoms of Aragon and Navarre.

At first the road from Toulouse continues westwards, keeping away from the mountains. There are frequent reminders that this has long been a route for Santiago pilgrims. The small town of L'Isle-Jourdain was the first halt after leaving Toulouse. Here the former hospice of Saint-Jacques is plentifully engraved with scallop-shells, while it also boasts a polychrome wooden statue of the saint in full pilgrim's outfit including multiple scallop-shells. The figure dates from many centuries later than the foundation of the hospice, after the French wars of religion at a time when the Catholic Church was reasserting its authority, keen to promote its long links with history including the heroic years of the Santiago pilgrimage and its contribution to the Reconquest of Spain. Soon the road leads to the city of Auch, the capital of Gascony, and here too there is a late tribute to the pilgrimage in the form of a window in the sixteenth-century cathedral with a colourful depiction of St James dressed as a pilgrim *en route* to his own shrine. Again we are reminded that as the era of pilgrimage fervour passed, and lost its sense of mission, so the cult of St James came to be celebrated almost sentimentally, with images that stressed the glamour of the pilgrimage movement rather than its spirit.

Only one major staging-post remained before the Pyrenees. And here at Oloron-Sainte-Marie the medieval church survives where pilgrims would have attended their last mass before heading for the mountains; and it possesses one of the finest carved portals in the whole of south-west France. Formerly the city's cathedral, the Church of Saint-Marie possesses a main doorway comparable to that of Moissac. It has classic Romanesque proportions, with its central column supporting a magnificent tympanum in marble framed by bands of figures above and on either side. The carvings include the customary twenty-four old men of the Apocalypse with their musical instruments and jars of perfume; yet unlike the usual stereotypes these are a humorous and joyful bunch, suggesting that the sculptor took pleasure in presenting them as local people of the town.[34] And this impression is reinforced by an accompanying frieze of carvings illustrating lively scenes of local peasant life – boar hunting, salmon fishing and filleting, cheese making, barrel making, preparing hams, plucking geese, and so on. Such glimpses of simple daily life are a refreshing rarity after so many didactic sermons in stone.

From Oloron the climb begins. The Somport Pass is at an altitude of almost six thousand feet. The Romans had used it to move their legions to and from northern Spain. The Carthaginian general Hannibal had crossed the Pyrenees here with his elephants on his way to attacking Italy. It was a popular trade route for merchants bringing goods northwards from Spain; and now it had become one of the two main crossing-points for pilgrims making for Santiago. They would normally be taking the pass in late spring, returning in late summer, so snow would not pose a problem. On the other hand, there were always winter travellers, and it was apparently customary for local mountain people to keep the pass clear of snow, and in return for such service they would be excused the customary border controls and taxes.

In the tenth and early eleventh centuries the Somport Pass seems to have been the favoured crossing for pilgrims on this southern

34 See Plate 24.

route from Languedoc, Provence and northern Italy. But with the glamour of the Charlemagne legend cultivated by the popularity of the *Chanson de Roland*, by the late eleventh century the Pass of Roncesvalles was becoming more widely used, and many pilgrims reaching Oloron would then head westwards a mere day's journey to Saint-Michel-le-Vieux from where they would take the Col de Cize over the mountains to Roncesvalles, their imaginations fired by the sound of Roland's celebrated horn drifting on the wind.

The fame of the Somport Pass rested on the reputation of its hospice which welcomed travellers who had made the long climb from the plains of Gascony, or from the valleys of Aragon and Navarre to the south. This was the hospice of Santa Cristina de Somport; and the fourth chapter of *The Pilgrim's Guide* proudly nominates it as one of the 'Three Hospices of the World', the other two being in Rome and Jerusalem. All three had been established 'in places where they were very much needed ... for the restoring of saintly pilgrims, the resting of the weary, the consolation of the sick, the salvation of the dead, and assistance to the living'. The exact circumstances of its foundation are obscure, but Santa Cristina seems to have been founded early in the eleventh century, and to have expanded greatly over the next hundred years as the numbers of pilgrims heading for Santiago hugely increased. The hospice was attached to a priory, and like Roncesvalles it was administered by Augustinian canons. Vulnerably isolated as it was, it enjoyed invaluable protection from the local Viscounts of Béarn on the French side of the Pyrenees and from the rulers of Aragon and Navarre on the Spanish side.

By the twelfth century Santa Cristina had become a major link in the long chain of hospices which were established across France and Spain for the benefit of pilgrims – in itself a measure of their numbers. Each hospice tended to be within a day's journey on foot from the next. The quality of the services on offer obviously varied considerable, but in those attached to richly endowed priories the spirit of Christian charity sometimes led to a fierce pride in being able to provide food and accommodation superior to those of rival establishments. Santa Cristina was certainly one of these, and developed a competitive rivalry with Roncesvalles even though they were both Augustinian houses. Lacking the glamorous appeal of the Charlemagne legend, Santa Cristina seems to have been keen to compensate in other ways. Endowments made it possible to provide hospitality on a relatively lavish scale: instead of the customary single crowded dormitory there were at least eight separate rooms for smaller numbers where pilgrims might actually enjoy a night's sleep. Not surprisingly, Santa Cristina earned a reputation for being among the most welcoming of hospices along the road to Santiago. Under the patronage of the Kings of Aragon and Navarre it provided a royal introduction to Spain.

The more normal experience of pilgrims seeking food and a bed for the night was a great deal less salubrious, unless they were able to pay for an inn, which few were in a position to afford. Many hospices offered no more than the basics, which might consist of a large straw mattress on the floor of a single dormitory; and this mattress would be shared by any number of travellers, often as many as twenty, together with an even larger host of fleas, lice, cockroaches, mosquitoes and other predatory creatures of the dark. There would have been plenty of pilgrims in the depths of the night nursing severe doubts about the sacredness of their mission.

More fortunate were travellers who found themselves welcomed by monasteries, or by hospices that were attached to monasteries and administered by monks, nuns or lay brothers, Here, as at Santa Cristina, the principle of free hospitality for pilgrims would generally prevail. This was a fundamental tenet of Christian charity in the medieval Church, and monasteries were even required to set aside a proportion of their revenues to provide it. Sometimes the abbot himself would undertake to wash the feet of pilgrims, a humble echo of the Last Supper and Christ washing the feet of his disciples. As *The Pilgrim's Guide* urged its readers to understand. 'It should be known that the pilgrims of St James, whether poor or rich, have the right to hospitality and to diligent respect'. This is the final sentence of the *Guide* before the concluding words explaining that the book was written 'mainly in Cluny'.

Santa Cristina was not a Cluniac outpost unlike so many of the religious houses along the pilgrim roads. Nonetheless, in the context of the vast enterprise of the pilgrimage movement to which successive Abbots of Cluny were dedicated, Cluniacs and Augustinians were a single brotherhood, and according to the *Guide*, Santa Cristina's founders, whoever they were, 'will partake without any doubt of the kingdom of God'.

Today Santa Cristina, unlike Roncesvalles, is nothing but an archaeological site. Amid the turmoil of the French religious wars in the sixteenth century the Augustinian canons abandoned the place and sought refuge south of the Pyrenees safely away from France, in Aragon. They settled at the foot of the valley in the city of Jaca which – ironically – had in any case been the next stopping-place for Santiago pilgrims leaving Santa Cristina and the Somport Pass.

The track they would have taken survives, as old roads often do, being too narrow and winding to be transformed into modern highways. Instead, they become the favoured paths for the modern traveller and pilgrim following in the footsteps of history. Here the old pilgrim road southwards from the ruins of Santa Cristina hugs the valley of the fast-flowing Rio Aragón as it flows towards Jaca. Pilgrims were now deep into the kingdom of Aragon, the neighbouring kingdom to that of Navarre, where the road from Roncesvalles a short distance to the west was the combined route bringing pilgrims from Paris, Vézelay and Le Puy. Soon the fourth road would join them and become a single pilgrim road across northern Spain all the way to Santiago – the *camino*.

Meanwhile pilgrims who had crossed the Pyrenees by the Somport Pass made for Jaca, then the capital of the kingdom of Aragon. Strangely *The Pilgrim's Guide* has nothing to say about Jaca, or about the people of Aragon. This silence is in striking contrast to the author's salacious comments of the domestic and sexual habits of the neighbouring Navarrese (alluded to in Chapter 15). All he writes, dispassionately, is that 'having cleared the Pass of Somport, one finds the country of Aragon'.

Gateway to Spain at the foot of the Pyrenees, Jaca was the first major stopping-place for pilgrims after crossing the mountains.

Today it remains a gem of a city, small and compact, and possessing one of the earliest cathedrals in Spain. In the late eleventh and twelfth centuries Jaca was not only the capital of the newly established kingdom of Aragon, but was also a bright symbol of a new Christian Spain that was at last rebuilding itself, materially and spiritually, after the long centuries of Saracen incursions from the south. The banner of the Reconquest was now flying proudly. With the aid of Burgundian knights Toledo had fallen to the Christians in 1085, soon to become the seat of the Spanish Church with a Cluniac monk from Languedoc as its first archbishop.

Jaca's Romanesque cathedral was begun at about this time in the new spirit of resurgent Christianity; and pilgrims arriving at the city from the Somport Pass would soon have found themselves in the company of those who were building it. By the entrance to Jaca, outside the city walls, a rapidly expanding community of foreigners was establishing itself. Some would have been former pilgrims who decided to stay: but mostly they were builders and craftsmen of all kinds, together with merchants and tradesmen, administrators, clerics and churchmen, the majority immigrants from southern France, Poitou and Burgundy, all of them welcomed here with special privileges by the rulers of Aragon, and all of them putting their shoulders to building a new and flourishing city and region free at last from the Saracen threat. They were people with all manner of skills that were urgently needed in the newly liberated kingdom of northern Spain. The passes over the Pyrenees, which since Roman times had seen the passages of armies, were now pilgrim roads, trade routes and channels for artisans, architects and craftsmen, as well as monks and ecclesiastics fired with a missionary zeal. Pilgrims had become so many Pied Pipers leading the way south. And as the area of the new Christian kingdoms expanded dramatically with the Reconquest, so this diverse migration from across the mountains helped fill the vacuum left by the departing Saracens. In the wake of the conquering Christian armies huge opportunities were suddenly opening up for churchmen and craftsmen alike.

When it came to creating the new churches and priories of northern Spain the inspiration and creative ideas came principally from north of the Pyrenees – from Languedoc, Poitou and of course from Cluny and Burgundy in general – with the grateful support of the Spanish rulers. But there were also local traditions and local skills on hand, and these were readily incorporated in the new building programme. There was a long tradition of church building in Spain pre-dating the Saracen invasions. In addition there was the influence of Islamic building, in particular the Great Mosque at Córdoba completed in the tenth century. In fact in some respects Islamic building skills exceeded those of the Christian Church, particularly in areas involving geometrical design, including the construction of domes. Muslim craftsmen were forbidden by the Koran to represent living forms: hence the carved figures round the portals of the new Spanish churches tended to be the work of sculptors from north of the Pyrenees, whereas much of the architectural detailing is more likely to have been the work of Muslim craftsmen.

Jaca's cathedral displays precisely this hybrid character – a harmonious blend of several cultures. The tunnel-vaulted porch and carved portal carry strong echoes of Burgundy; the intricate capitals in the interior feel closer to south-west France, while the nave itself suggests the early Romanesque churches of the Loire, Saint-Benoît in particular. In all, pilgrims who had travelled from Paris, Vézelay or Le Puy may have felt they had brought their own world with them – at least until the architectural detailing told them that here were touches of Muslim Spain.

Suddenly, when it came to building a new Christian world in northern Spain, military Reconquest had succeeded in opening the way to a creative partnership. There would be a great many churches and priories along the *camino* all the way from here to Santiago which would remind the medieval pilgrim, as they do today's traveller, of that partnership between the Christian vision of worship and that of Islam.

*

From Jaca the fourth pilgrim road strikes westwards across the hilly countryside into Navarre. Everywhere they stopped for a night's rest, or to pray, travellers were made aware of those same links with places they had come from north of the Pyrenees. At Sangüesa the new rulers of Navarre founded a royal chapel here, Santa Maria la Real, celebrating the departure of the Saracens by erecting the most majestic of towers rising triumphantly above the town. They also commissioned a massive carved south portal packed with figures on the theme of the Last Judgment strongly reminiscent of so many churches in Burgundy under the shadow of Cluny. Those travelling workshops of skilled stonemasons and sculptors we detected at Jaca had moved westwards along the pilgrim road.

In the context of the pilgrimage a more important link with Burgundy lies a short distance away in the foothills nearby. The abbey of San Salvador de Leyre was established early in the eleventh century only to be largely destroyed by the Saracens. Early in the following century the abbey was re-settled by monks from Cluny who substantially rebuilt and enlarged it, making it one of the key monasteries and hospices on the pilgrim road to Santiago. A further rebuilding of the abbey church took place in the thirteenth century at the hands of the Cistercians; but parts of the Cluniac church survive, in particular a superb west portal with its central column and bands of richly carved figures and writhing beasts crowded into the arches above. Here the Cluniac monks seem likely to have employed another of those travelling workshops, this one from western France. Aimery Picaud, had he come here, would have been happily reminded of those numerous jewel-box churches of the Saintonge in his native Poitou.

Further west, and another striking church catches the eye. It is a curious octagonal chapel set within an arcade of columns in the middle of open fields. This is Santa Maria de Eunate. Its connection with the pilgrim road has long been a matter of disagreement. It has sometimes been claimed that the Knights Templar built it, copying the shape of the church of the Holy Sepulchre in Jerusalem. But why would the Templars have chosen to build it right on the pilgrim road? A more likely explanation is that whoever built it intended it to be a funerary chapel for pilgrims who died along the way, and whose bones have been found buried here.[35] The chapel becomes a salutary

35. See Plate 25.

reminder that pilgrimages were not always the jovial outings evoked by Chaucer.

The Eunate chapel is also a reminder of why one of the longer chapters of *The Pilgrim's Guide* is devoted to 'The Bitter and Sweet Waters to be found along the Road'. The chapter is Aimery Picaud at his most personal and graphic. In the same chapter we have already heard his account of murderous boatmen in Gascony: now he offers a salutary warning of the fate which can befall pilgrims attempting to cross rivers here in Navarre. 'There runs a river called the Rio Salado. Beware of drinking its waters, or watering your horse, for this river is deadly. While we were proceeding towards Santiago we came across two Navarrese seated on its banks and sharpening their knives. They make a habit of skinning the mounts of the pilgrims that drink from that water and die. To our question they answered with lies, saying that the water was indeed healthy and drinkable. Accordingly we watered our horses in the stream, and had no sooner done so than two of them died: these men then skinned them on the spot.'

True or not, this is one of the few passages in the *Guide* which offers a glimpse of the author's personal journey to Santiago – which we know from a surviving letter he is reputed to have made with two companions (see Chapter 3). Unlike the great majority of pilgrims he travelled on horseback, not on foot, which as a privileged member of the Cluniac operation he was clearly entitled to do, even if his horse did end up skinned by the hated Navarrese before his eyes.

After the rural chapel of Eunate there was one short stretch of the *Via Tolosana* remaining. 'Finally,' the *Guide* states, 'you arrive at Puente la Reina.' Today, at the eastern edge of the town a statue representing the eternal pilgrim stands by the roadside at the point where the fourth pilgrim road joins the one from Roncesvalles which had combined the other three on the far side of the Pyrenees.

Here was the meeting-place for all those pilgrims from every corner of Europe. The giant spider's-web which had spread across an entire continent had become a single thread. From now onwards there would be one principal road, the Spanish *camino*, known generally – since the majority of pilgrims using it were from north of the Pyrenees – as the *camino francés,* the Way of the French.

At that meeting-point stand the medieval Church of the Crucifix. And here those pilgrims from all over Europe would celebrate their first mass together, as suddenly every language known to the Christian was subsumed by the unifying sound of Latin. Between the church and the former hospice where they had rested rises an arch over the porch, and here pilgrims would pass as they made their way into the first town of the *camino,* Puente la Reina. They made their way, as we do today, down the long corridor of a central street, the Calle Mayor. The Church of Santiago, St James, still stands, and as an enduring echo of when pilgrims on the open road needed to be warned that town gates would soon close the church bell still rings out forty times at nightfall.

At the far end of town the Calle Mayor opens up to a sweep of the River Arga, and rising high over it the most famous bridge on the entire Spanish stretch of the pilgrim road. The magnificent hump-backed bridge of six Romanesque arches which gives its name to the town was built early in the eleventh century on the orders of the consort of King Sancho III of Navarre, Doña Mayor (although Doña Estefanía, the wife of his successor Garcia el de Nájera, has also been credited). And it was constructed principally for the benefit of pilgrims.[36]

There is a resonance, an aura, about this great medieval bridge carrying the pilgrim road westwards which makes it a symbol of the pilgrimage itself. It seems to tell a story of how it all became possible. It was built at a time when the Saracens still controlled most of the Iberian Peninsula. Nowhere was safe from their marauding bands. Roads were hazardous, if they existed at all, and bridges were even fewer. The Christian rulers of northern Spain clung to their fragile kingdoms hoping that the tide might soon turn in their favour. Even Pamplona, the capital of Navarre, had been briefly overrun by the Saracens; and only a little earlier Santiago itself has been sacked.

36. See Plate 26.

This was King Sancho's inheritance.

One thread of hope lay in the growing appeal of the Santiago legend and the crescendo of fervour within the pilgrimage movement it inspired. Since the discovery of the tomb St James had been seen as the champion of the Reconquest, and the pilgrims undertaking the long trek to reach his shrine were his resolute standard-bearers. Hence creating a safe path for pilgrims through this hostile terrain became a vital weapon in the fight against the Infidel; and the great bridge of Puente la Reina was a mark of the Christian will to make that journey possible.

At the heart of this resurgence lay the relationship between the beleaguered ruler of Navarre, King Sancho III, and Christian leaders across the Pyrenees in France, above all Cluny. It is an intriguing anomaly that in the century following the building of the great bridge at Puente la Reina the Santiago pilgrimage should have flourished on this unlikely partnership – between a Burgundian abbey and a dynasty of Spanish monarchs. The Abbots of Cluny were men of God dedicated to the role of moral leadership and unwavering monastic discipline. The Christian monarchs of northern Spain, on the other hand, were for the most part unscrupulous political operators bent on the acquisition of territory and power by any available means, and who thought nothing of killing or robbing each other if necessary. Yet over a period of more than a century the two institutions formed a liaison that proved to be of enormous material benefit to both.

What made such a partnership workable was a shared ambition to reclaim the territories in northern Spain that had long been in Saracen hands. For Cluny this meant re-establishing the power of the Church in Spain. For the Spanish rulers it meant re-establishing their own dynastic power in those same lands. Their twin ambitions matched perfectly.

Queen Doña Mayor's great bridge which opened the way to Santiago stands as a monument to that partnership. It had begun early in the eleventh century when the young Sancho sought to establish a cordial relationship with Cluny's Abbot Odilo. Cluny was then beginning an extraordinary expansion of its monastic empire and influence throughout Europe. Lavish gifts of property and land were also making the abbey exceedingly wealthy. It was known to King Sancho that the reclaiming of Spain for Christendom was Odilo's most burning ambition. Contact between Navarre and Cluny became established, maintained by a regular exchange of letters and by visiting ambassadors. As a result Cluny began to employ its prestige, wealth and powerful connections (especially with the papacy) to sponsor military campaigns against the Saracens in collaboration with the Spanish kings.

It is unclear what direct support Cluny may have given to these campaigns, though the vital role played in the Reconquest by Burgundian knights suggests that the abbey's powerful feudal connections in Burgundy played an important part. The immediate result was a large expansion of Sancho's territories. In gratitude the Spanish monarch showered the abbey with gifts, many of them plundered from former Saracen lands. He also sent monks to be trained at Cluny, and invited Cluniac monks to Spain where they were soon installed in priories providing facilities for the ever-increasing flow of pilgrims. Military success, plunder, servicing the pilgrim road, the growth of monastic power in Spain: all these disparate elements came together.

So the pilgrim bridge at Puente la Reina pointed not only to Santiago, but to the continued success of that collaboration between monarchy and monastery in the decades to come. King Sancho maintained his relationship with Cluny right up to his death in 1035. It was then continued with increasing benefit to both sides by his son Ferdinand I, and finally by his grandson Alfonso VI, a relationship which culminated in the ultimate triumph of the capture of Toledo from the Saracens in 1085. The back of Saracen power in Spain had now been broken.

Three generations of Spanish kings had been the instruments of that success; while several hundred miles to the north, at Cluny, two generations of abbots had made that success possible. Odilo died in 1048 having been abbot for almost fifty-five years. He was succeeded by Hugh the Great, who remained abbot for a further sixty years.

Their combined period of office overlapped three centuries, from the end of the tenth century to the beginning of the twelfth. In the story of the Santiago pilgrimage this extraordinary chapter is far and away the most important.

*

Travellers today who stand on that Bridge of the Queen, where the four roads have become one, can follow the line of the old pilgrim road westwards as it climbs the far hill. Soon they will be enjoying the rich legacy of that partnership between France and Spain which has made the *camino* – the Way of St James – one of the historic journeys of the world.

There are just four hundred miles to go.

V. Camino Francés: The Spanish Road

19. The Way of St James... and Crowning Glory

As its name suggests, the Way was created specifically for pilgrims, together with a host of stonemasons, craftsmen, administrators, churchmen, engineers, merchants, peddlers, hangers-on and functionaries of every kind. All these diverse bands of travellers on the road contributed in one way or another to building and servicing what was in effect a new city, Santiago de Compostela, St James' city. It had a new population drawn from all over northern Spain and beyond, new housing, new urban facilities and a vast and ambitious new cathedral set at its very heart. Without the shrine of the apostle the city would never have existed.

In Spain the Way is known as the *camino*; and today's pilgrims trekking towards Santiago may justifiably feel it to be their Way of St James. By contrast, the pilgrim roads north of the Pyrenees were mostly former Roman roads long used for transporting armies to and from Spain, and later as busy trade routes. Building the new road, then servicing it for the benefit of pilgrims in their thousands, was always going to be a Herculean task for those on whose shoulders it fell. Until the late tenth century, much of this 400-mile stretch of northern Spain was intermittently under Saracen rule; and even when the beleaguered Christian rulers of the region managed to regain a degree of control of their lands it still remained a lawless area. Besides, there were numerous rivers to cross, and few bridges over them – which is why the Queen's Bridge at Puente la Reina was such a heroic achievement in the early days of the *camino*.

In the late eleventh century a great transformation took place. A distinctive road was established, hospices and inns set up, churches and priories founded. Cart tracks became roads. Bridges replaced fords, as at Hospital de Órbigo, where the thirteenth-century bridge is the longest on the *camino*.[37] Villages grew into towns. By the end of that era there would be a place for pilgrims to rest and be fed within a day's walk along the entire length of the *camino*, with lodgings of some description no more than twenty miles apart, most provided by the new monasteries.

In such an unsafe and unstable world, the monasteries were crucial for all travellers. They were havens of safety, and of physical and spiritual comfort. And at this time when a nation was being rebuilt after centuries of Saracen dominance, it was the monastic orders north of the Pyrenees that made the largest contribution to that rebuilding. Here lay the building skills, the craftsmanship, the organisation and the wealth needed to undertake so massive a task.

Successive rulers in northern Spain gave every encouragement to these foreigners. French masons and stone-carvers brought invaluable skills south of the Pyrenees. To a lesser extent this traffic in skills also worked the other way round, with Saracen craftsmen invited to employ their special carving skills on abbey portals and cloisters in southern France, such as Moissac. But in Spain the influx of skilled artisans from the north amounted to immigration on a widespread scale, encouraged by tempting offers of tax exemptions and other privileges if foreign craftsmen agreed to settle there. In the Navarre capital of Pamplona in the eleventh century it was reckoned that there were more French settlers than natives.

It was a similar story at Estella (Lizarra in Basque), the first town of any size along the *camino* after Puente la Reina. The Saracens had wrecked much of it in the tenth century, but now its reconstruction was to a large extent the work of French settlers – builders, craftsmen, merchants and traders – who enjoyed the same privileges as those given to foreigners in Pamplona, in addition to the unlimited opportunity for practising their skills (which the

37. See Plate 27.

burgeoning city welcomed). The area round what is today the Plaza San Martín was virtually a French colony, and it was here that pilgrims naturally gravitated. The local church was even dedicated to a French saint, St Martin of Tours.

Estella retains the look of a pilgrimage town. It bristles with Romanesque churches, and these bear evidence of immigrant craftsmen from north of the Pyrenees as well as from the Muslim south. From the Plaza San Martín a long flight of steps leads to San Pedro de la Rúa, one of the finest pilgrim churches on the *camino*. The magnificent portal is clearly to a large extent the work of Saracen stone-carvers, while the most elegant of cloisters possesses carvings whose spiritual home is western France, Poitou and the land of those jewel-box churches of the Saintonge.

Echoes of pilgrimage are everywhere in Estella. In the Church of the Holy Sepulchre there is an exceptionally fine carving of St James dressed as a pilgrim to his own shrine. The Church of San Miguel Archangel possesses a carved portal whose sculpted figures would have reminded any traveller from Burgundy of those powerful, elongated figures on the abbey churches of Vézelay, Cluny and Autun: evidence of yet another travelling workshop. And on the side of the twelfth-century palace of the Kings of Navarre, in the heart of the pilgrims' quarter, stands a carved stone capital depicting Roland killing a giant Saracen with his lance – one more instance of the Charlemagne legend being hitched to the Santiago cult.

Towns like Estella were key places for pilgrims to assemble after days on the road, and to feel at home in what was in effect a French colony. Yet on the bare stretches of road between such towns it was very different; and here it was the monasteries that came into their own. For the traveller they were oases in the desert – a desert, what is more, that all too recently had been patrolled by Saracen armies, and were still a hunting ground for bandits taking advantage of the vacuum left by the departing Muslim soldiers. A short distance to the south-east stands the monastery of San Juan de la Peña, built in the ninth century at the base of a protective cliff – which proved to be no protection at all, as the monastery was plundered by the

Saracens soon afterwards. The monastery limped on for a further century until, early in the eleventh century, it was colonised and rebuilt by monks from Cluny at the invitation of King Sancho, ruler of Navarre. This was about the time when the king's consort, Queen Doña Mayor, was apparently sponsoring the construction of the great bridge at Puente la Reina. These twin ventures – the pilgrim's bridge and the rebuilt monastery a short distance away – are among the first tangible achievements of that remarkable partnership between successive Abbots of Cluny and the rulers of northern Spain. Bridge and abbey: they were the foundation stones upon which the great enterprise of the Santiago pilgrim road came to be built.

It was the most powerful of the Christian rulers of northern Spain who made the most valuable contribution to the *camino*. He was King Alfonso VI, ruler of Aragon, Navarre, Castile, León and Galicia. His relationship with Abbot Hugh of Cluny led to lavish gifts to the abbey, including a chain of monasteries and priories in his own kingdom, most of them on the Spanish pilgrim road. These religious houses acted as service stations for pilgrims heading for Santiago as well as greatly strengthening the Church's grip on territories only recently in Saracen hands.

By far the most important of these monasteries was the abbey of Sahagún, midway between two of the major cities along the pilgrim road, Burgos and León. Today Sahagún is a hollow shell: little remains of the former abbey complex except a semi-ruined chapel that was once attached to the monastery. Yet in the eleventh and twelfth centuries at least fifty dependent priories were under the authority of its abbot. To have acquired Sahagún represented a huge expansion of the Cluniac monastic empire.

Today the impact of Cluny on the region is greatly reduced, since so many of its most important monasteries have long been destroyed: Sahagún, Nájera and Carrión de los Condes among them. The network of smaller religious houses along the pilgrim road remains the brightest legacy of Cluny. The modern traveller frequently comes face to face with small, elegant Romanesque churches that look as if they had been transplanted from north of the Pyrenees.

These echoes of Burgundy, and of Poitou and Languedoc, are among the small gems of the *camino*. They feel particularly precious because they date from the earliest days of the Santiago pilgrimage, a time when travelling the pilgrim road was still a hazardous undertaking. The Church of San Martín at Frómista, to the west of León, was one of the very first to be built along the *camino*, later drawn into the Cluniac empire. Its carvings tell of those travelling workshops from western France – Aimery Picaud's beloved Poitou. Even more French, with another portal indebted to Poitou, is the little pilgrim's chapel dedicated to St James at Villafranca on the edge of the El Bierzo mountains, which form the final land barrier before Galicia and Santiago itself.

In Spain as in most of Western Europe, by the thirteenth century the Gothic style of church building had superseded Romanesque; this included the regions spanned by the *camino*. Accordingly the story of the Santiago pilgrimage, and what was created around it, is multi-layered, its early chapters often concealed beneath the grandeur that followed. The two key cities of Burgos and León exemplify this transformation from humble beginnings to splendour. Both cities are dominated by magnificent Gothic cathedrals which are among the glories of the Spanish pilgrim road. The great Gothic cathedral of Burgos has a mixed inheritance. The basic design was modelled on that of the French cathedral at Bourges. Its present spectacular appearance, bristling with spires and pinnacles, is more Germanic, derived from the Gothic cathedrals of the Rhineland, especially that of Cologne, where its architect, known as Juan de Colonia, came from.

León, too, possesses one of the loveliest cathedrals in Spain, but also with some of the most terrifying iconography of damnation.[38] Purely Gallic in style, it has the look of having been transported from northern France where it would have kept company with the early Gothic cathedrals of Reims and Amiens. Once inside, however, the colours of Spain and the burnished sierras take over. León cathedral

38. See Plate 28.

possesses the finest stained glass south of the Pyrenees. Generations of pilgrims on their way to Santiago have stood in the gloom of this nave, gazing up to marvel at how the sunlight seems to strike these windows with a burst of fire, transforming the expanse of glass into a revelation of light.[39]

The symbolism is timeless. At heart all pilgrimages are about travelling from a place of darkness in search of light. At the end of the *camino*, as legend has it, that point of light had been a star – Compostela, the Place of the Star. And the road leading to it has been under a canopy of stars, the Milky Way, La Voie Lactée, as French-speaking pilgrims have known it. What was created there, in that Place of the Star, is the subject of the final section of this book.

*

'Finally Compostela, the most excellent city of the Apostle ... the happiest and most spiritual of all the cities of Spain.' Thus ends Chapter 3 of *The Pilgrim's Guide*.

The first Santiago cathedral had been a modest affair, built in the ninth century only decades after the apostle's tomb was claimed to have been found. This early building was severely damaged in 997 by the notorious Saracen warlord Al-Mansur. A century later the experience of seeing that church, still bearing the scars of Saracen assault, would have been deeply etched in the mind of a young man who was soon to become responsible for much of the cathedral that replaced it. He was Diego Gelmírez (c. 1069-1149), a key figure in the story of Santiago and the pilgrimage, and later the city's first archbishop. It was during his lengthy period in charge of operations – almost forty years – that a glorious phoenix rose from the ashes.

Work on the new cathedral began sometime between 1075 and 1078. According to *The Pilgrim's Guide*, 'From the year the first stone was laid until the final one was in place 44 years passed.' The claim that the entire cathedral was constructed in under half a century is only partly true: much work remained to be done, particularly at the west

39. See Plate 29.

end, which was not completed until late in the twelfth century. And the ultimate bravura touch of the twin Baroque towers overlooking the Praza do Obradoiro[40] was not added until the eighteenth. Nonetheless the main body of the basilica – the nave, the north and south portals, the choir and apsidal chapels were indeed finished, or nearly finished, in those 44 years – a truly remarkable achievement.

While Diego Gelmírez deservedly receives the credit for overseeing the bulk of the work, it was one of his predecessors who was responsible for commissioning the original design of the cathedral in the 1070s and supervising the earliest building work. He was Diego Peláez, Bishop of nearby Iria Flavia (today Padrón), Santiago not yet being a bishopric. Bishop Paláez recognised the need for a cathedral able to accommodate the ever-growing numbers of pilgrims who were arriving here now that the *camino* was relatively safe, with new bridges to facilitate travel and new monasteries and hospices to provide food and accommodation along the way.

By the year 1088 a great deal of the basic work on the east end of Santiago cathedral was completed. It would have been an extraordinary sight – this huge stone edifice towering high above the clusters of timber-built houses and shacks that are all that the city would have been at this time.

Then, in that year, a power struggle led to the deposition of Bishop Peláez. A long period of political unrest and insurrection overtook Santiago and Galicia as a whole, bringing building work on the cathedral to a halt for a number of years. The partly built cathedral remained an empty shell.

The deadlock was eventually broken in 1094 by the appointment of a monk from Cluny by the name of Dalmatius as the first Bishop of Santiago, now replacing Iria Flavia as the seat of the local bishop. The authoritative hand of Cluny was once again controlling events at the very heart of the Santiago pilgrimage.

At much the same time, and probably with the connivance of Cluny, Count Raymond of Burgundy came to Spain to marry the

40. Workshop Square, an allusion to the stonemasons' workshops located here during construction.

daughter and heir of King Alfonso VI, the eight-year-old Urraca, whose mother, Queen Constance, was Abbot Hugh's niece. On marrying Urraca Raymond received the title of Count of Galicia from King Alfonso, so becoming the administrator of the entire region, which included Santiago. Altogether it had been a multiple Burgundian triumph.

It was also a turning point in the fortunes of Santiago and its empty shell of a cathedral. In about the year 1092 the new man in charge of Galicia, Raymond, appointed Diego Gelmírez to be his secretary responsible for all building operations relating to the cathedral. An ambitious young man, able and industrious, Gelmírez immediately saw to it that construction work was resumed, now under the supervision of a new master mason known to us only as Stephen.

Before long Gelmírez was doubly in charge since Bishop Dalmatius had died only a year after taking office. There followed a hiatus of several years until 1100, when Gelmírez was elected Santiago's second bishop. Over the next quarter of a century, under his sharp eye, the bulk of the new cathedral was completed. And it was during this period, probably during the 1120s, that the description of the cathedral incorporated into *The Pilgrim's Guide* would have been recorded. 'It is true to say,' the author claims, that 'you cannot find one single crack or defect in it. The basilica is wonderfully built, spacious, bathed in light, of excellent dimensions and proportions in width, length and height, and altogether of the most marvellous workmanship.' The account, which goes on at great length, was evidently designed to be a tribute to Bishop Gelmírez, who in all probability commissioned it.

From the time of his election as bishop, Gelmírez' greatest ambition was to expand both the importance of his own office and the prestige of his city as the principal focus of pilgrimage in Christian Europe. Essential to these twin ambitions was the need to cement relationships with both the papacy and with Cluny.

Accordingly, early in his time as bishop he visited Rome twice (in 1100 and 1106), on both occasions travelling with his retinue along the pilgrim roads in France, visiting the monasteries of Toulouse, Moissac and possibly Conques, as well as spending time at the abbey of Cluny where he was able to meet the now-aged Abbot Hugh, his spiritual mentor and for so long a primary sponsor of the pilgrimage movement.

Not long after sealing his relationship with Cluny, Gelmírez lost the man who had first promoted him by making him his secretary and church administrator. Raymond of Burgundy, Count of Galicia, died in 1107. Two years later King Alfonso and Abbot Hugh also died. Within a short time three men who had done more than any others to further the cause of the Santiago pilgrimage were dead. Furthermore Gelmírez now found himself dealing with a new ruler in the form of Alfonso's tempestuous daughter Queen Urraca, who was also Raymond's widow.

Despite civil unrest and the insurrections that broke out in Santiago during Urraca's troubled reign, soon the stars began to shine brightly on Gelmírez and the fortunes of his city. In 1119 the late Count Raymond's brother, Guy of Burgundy, was elected pope as Calixtus II, the ceremony taking place at Cluny where the previous pope had died. Calixtus, a Burgundian aristocrat with strong links to Cluny, was the very pope who is credited with the authorship (or co-authorship) of several chapters of *The Pilgrim's Guide*, as well as being 'one of the names of those who restored the pilgrim road'.

Gelmírez himself became a leading beneficiary of these recent events. A year after the new pope was elected at Cluny, Santiago was elevated to the status of an archbishopric. And in the following year Pope Calixtus appointed Gelmírez as the city's first archbishop. In the same year, 1120, as if in celebration of this great moment, the nave of Santiago's cathedral was completed. Meanwhile, in Rome Pope Calixtus chose this time to canonise the late Abbot Hugh, the progenitor – together with his predecessor Odilo – of the Santiago pilgrimage movement.

There followed golden days. Elevation to the status of an archbishopric led to unheard-of prosperity for the city. Added to the flood of humble pilgrims arriving on foot Santiago was now attracting ever-growing numbers of wealthy benefactors keen to be associated with what Archbishop Gelmírez was happy to promote as 'the new Rome'. To facilitate matters further the network of Cluniac abbeys and priories along the *camino* made it possible for quantities of bullion to be transported to the city to pay for lavish new building works around the cathedral, monasteries being 'safe houses' in more senses than one.

These years of triumph arrived too late to be recorded in *The Pilgrim's Guide*. Gelmírez lived on until the middle of the century, by which time the Romanesque cathedral he had supervised for forty years was complete in every detail except for the huge west portal. This remained in its partly restored state for at least twenty years after the archbishop's death, finally being replaced during the second half of the twelfth century by the present Pórtico da Gloria, set within the narthex of this most noble of cathedral entrances. The massive carved Pórtico is the most elaborate and probably the most celebrated of all the church portals along the pilgrim roads in France and Spain, matched only by that of Vézelay, to which in purely formal terms it bears some similarity. It is a stupendous achievement by a sculptor and master mason known simply as Maestro Mateo, or in his native France as Maître Mathieu, and about whom we know tantalisingly little beyond the fact that he and his team worked on this great portal for at least two decades.

In this late and magnificent flowering of Romanesque sculpture St James is appropriately centre-stage, high up on his commanding central pier, a figure at once modest and majestic. In his hand a scroll bears the Latin text *Misit me Dominus* – the Lord sent me. The apostle wears an expression of inscrutable serenity as he seems to be surveying the vast cathedral square below him where pilgrims from all over the world have been gathering in his honour for almost a thousand years.[41]

In 1974 I described the Pórticio da Gloria in *The Pilgrimage to Santiago*:

41. See Plate 30.

It is composed of three giant arches, each of them carved above, between and to the side. Dividing the central arch, which ids the main entrance to the cathedral itself, is the traditional central pillar, except that in the position normally occupied by the Madonna sits St James himself perched above an elaborately carved Tree of Jesse. By tradition, the pilgrim to Santiago completed his journey by placing his fingers between the twisted stems of the tree, and this is a custom still observed: I have watched many a toddler lifted by his father after Sunday Mass so that he might squeeze rubbery fingers into the folds of Mateo's stone, now worn smooth by generations of hands.

On the inside of this central column, and partly obscured by the gloom of the nave, squats another carved figure. He is the stone image of Maestro Mateo himself, humble enough in appearance, though one feels he can scarcely have been that in life, and this figure has been another object of respect and reverence among pilgrims. On leaving the cathedral they would lower their heads and touch the brow of the master-builder and sculptor, in order, so it is said, that they might acquire some of the wisdom of the great man. The statue accordingly received the nickname of *O Santo dos Croques*, meaning the Saint of Skull-rappings...

Then on either side of Christ are the figures of St John on his eagle, St Luke on his bull, St Mark on a lion and St Matthew on his knees. And on the right-hand arch is a final reminder of that theme which had accompanied pilgrims all the way from Paris and Vézelay, Arles and Le Puy: the Torments of the Damned—and never have they looked more damned than here—with, nearby, other figures, who are enjoying the bliss of finding themselves on the other side of that barbed-wire fence, being conducted as if in a dream towards the Almighty by a squad of beautiful angels.

For travellers of all persuasions and interests, coming to the end of this long journey in which four roads finally merged into one, Santiago's Pórtico da Gloria, with its vision of heaven, presents itself to us as the final jewel in the crown. Now, as then, it is journey's end. It has been a journey inspired by a legend with its roots in the circle of Christ's closest companions. This legend has been so powerful over the course of many centuries that it gave rise to a network of pilgrim roads right across the continent of Europe. Accompanying these roads some of the finest architecture and works of art of Christian civilisation have been created for the welfare of pilgrims, which make any journey along those 'roads to heaven' an unforgettable experience for these who travel in even greater numbers today than in the Middle Ages. There are those, like Robert Louis Stevenson, who enjoy 'travel for travel's sake. The great plan is to move.' Others, as they wearily complete their journey in Santiago, may feel more in the spirit of St Augustine: 'The world is a book, and those who do not travel read only one page of it.' For them *The Pilgrim's Guide* may stand as the first book of the world.

Selected Further Reading

This is a personal selection of books that have aided me in writing *The Four Roads to Heaven*. There are a great many others relating to the great pilgrimage of the Middle Ages, including numerous guide books to both the French pilgrim roads and to the Spanish *camino*. There are also many DVDs available, and these too can be found at many of the principal sites along the pilgrim roads, or in local bookshops.

Astbury, A., *Pilgrimage* (London: 2010)

Barraclough, G., *The Crucible of Europe* (London: 1975)

Bentley, J., *Restless Bones: The Story of Relics* (London: 1985)

Brooke, C.N.L., *Europe in the Central Middle Ages* (London: 1964)

The Structure of Mediaeval Society (London: 1974)

The Age of the Cloister: The Story of Monastic Life in the Middle Ages (New York: 2001)

Brooke, R. and C., *Popular Religion in the Middle Ages* (London: 1984)

Brown, P., *The Cult of the Saints: Its Rise and Function in Latin Christianity* (London: 1981)

Chaucer, G., *The Canterbury Tales* (London: 1997)

Conant, K.J., *Carolingian and Romanesque Architecture, 800-1200* (London: 1959)

Cowdrey, H.E.J., *The Cluniacs and Gregorian Reform* (Oxford: 1970)

Dunn, M. and Davidson. L.K., (eds), *The Pilgrimage to Compostela in the Middle Ages* (New York and London: 2000)

Evans, J., *Life in Mediaeval France* (London: 1969)
Art in Mediaeval France (Oxford, 1969)
(ed.), *The Flowering of the Middle Ages* (London: 1966)
Fletcher, R.A., *Saint James's Catapult: The Life and Times of Diego Gelmirez of Santiago* (Oxford: 1984)
Geary, P., *Furta Sacra: Thefts of Relics in the Central Middle Ages* (New York: 1978)
Living with the Dead in the Middle Ages (New York: 1994)
Gittlitz, D.M., *The Pilgrimage Road to Santiago: The Complete Cultural Handbook* (New York: 2000)
Haskins, S., *Mary Magdalene: Myth and Metaphor* (London: 1993)
Huizinga, J., *The Waning of the Middle Ages* (London: 1967)
Jacobs, M., *The Road to Santiago de Compostela* (London: 1991)
Kendrick, T., *Saint James in Spain* (London: 1960)
Mâle, E., *Religious Art from the 12th Century in France* (London: 1949)
Mullins, E., *The Pilgrimage to Santiago* (Oxford: 2001)
In Search of Cluny: God's Lost Empire (Oxford: 2006)
Pirenne, H., *Mohammed and Charlemagne* (London: 1939)
Porter, A.K., *The Romanesque Sculpture of the Pilgrimage Roads* (New York: 1966)
Southern, R.W., *The Making of the Middle Ages* (Oxford: 1953)
Sumption, J., *The Age of Pilgrimage* (New York: 2003)
Trevor-Roper, H., *The Rise of Christian Europe* (London: 1966)
Ure, J., *Pilgrimage: The Great Adventure of the Middle Ages* (London: 2006)
Vieillard, J., *Le Guide du Pélerin de Saint-Jacques en Compostelle* (translation from the twelfth-century Latin) (Mâcon: 1938)
Zarnecki, G., (with Grivot, D.), *Gislebertus, Sculptor of Autun* (London: 1961)
The Monastic Achievement (London: 1972)

Recommended websites

THE CONFRATERNITY OF ST JAMES

www.csj.org.uk

Everything you need to know about the pilgrimage: an invaluable resource, with practical advice and detailed route guides.

CAMINO ADVENTURES

www.caminoadventures.com

Useful information on the pilgrim routes and how to plan a walking expedition.

AMERICAN PILGRIMS ON THE CAMINO

www.americanpilgrims.org

A good mix of history and practicalities aimed at a membership organisation.

Index